Single Parents Are People, Too!

Single Parents Are People, Too!

How to Achieve a Positive Self-Image and Personal Satisfaction

Carol Vejvoda Murdock

Butterick Publishing NY, NY 1980

Contents

Design by Joyce Schnaufer

Library of Congress Cataloging in Publication Data

Murdock, Carol Vejvoda.
  Single parents are people, too!

  Bibliography: p.
  1. Single parents—United States. I. Title.
HQ755.8.M87   306.8'7   80-12444
ISBN 0-88421-070-7

I'd like to hear your reactions to the book and any ideas you have on problems, solutions, situations, etc., that weren't covered and that you'd like to know more about. You can reach me at the address below.

Carol Vejvoda Murdock
Bridgehampton, NY 11932

1/The One and Only You

"Hello inside. Is there anybody there?" When Barbara asks herself this question, her self answers: "I'm here. And I'm brilliant. I'm beautiful, I'm Barbara."

The message could have come back: "Oh, I'm here all right. Just me. Divorced for six years. My kids only see their father once a year. And I have to nag the kids into helping around the house and I'm living on less than $10,000 a year and I just lost out on a full-time library job that I really wanted." Those are the facts of Barbara's life that I extracted from a questionnaire she and hundreds of other single parents filled out for me as part of the research for this book. The answers to the questionnaires were honest, practical, warmhearted and filled with courage. You'll meet many of these single parents and share their experiences as you read along. And I think you'll be as impressed with them as I am. But I'm introducing Barbara first because she's been able to achieve so completely what we all must if we're to live as self-fulfilling adults and successful parents. She has learned to love herself.

Barbara's problems are familiar ones to many of us: grandparents and relatives unsympathetic to the divorce; trouble with child support payments. And because she missed out on that library job, she's had to take a summer school position that will create sitter problems with her 7-year-old daughter. Still, she's optimistic and positive. When a dinner meeting she'd agreed to host was suddenly canceled, she invited two single friends and their daughters in for dinner instead and "we had a great meal." Summer sitter problems? This summer will be "the great experiment. Day camp, campouts, unsupervised mornings. It will be interesting." As for trouble with relatives, "They are going to stay the way they are; I'm going to be what I am. Therefore, I don't like to see them too often." She doesn't minimize her problems, but she doesn't clutch up about them either. Her ability to accept herself and like herself creates the self-confidence that gets her through.

For me, that kind of self-acceptance and confidence takes work. Long ago, I discovered that I had plenty of self-esteem as long as it wasn't challenged. Like money in the bank: it only becomes a problem when you're overdrawn. So it goes with my self-image—robust and plenty of muscle when I don't need it, a little flabby when I do.

Part of this, of course, is due to my own personality, but part of it is caused by the fact that our society makes it damned hard for us single parents to keep self-esteem at full mast. I've been divorced for 12 years. My son, CH Murdock, has suddenly reached the age of 20. The years that transformed my round-nosed 8-year-old into this booted, bearded man have been spent mainly in staying alive. Thanks to some writing ability, a healthy constitution, luck, a thread of common sense inherited from my immigrant grandmother and plenty of help from others—we've made it. Along the way, I've picked up my share of the usual comments: "Can't understand why you did it . . . I suppose you regret it by now . . . You'll have to expect problems; divorce is tough on children." Well, looking back in time, I have no regrets. And CH doesn't seem to be too bent out of shape. But I've also met myself in the dark hours and gone to my knees under the weight of my own fear and self-doubt. So for those of you who share my problem, here's some information about that elusive quality known as self-love or self-esteem.

Who Am I?

You can't love yourself until you find yourself. It all starts by knowing that you exist as a complete and unique individual. And because you're you and no one else, you don't have to measure up to anyone else's standards or live by anyone else's code. You do have a responsibility to fulfill your own capacities and to meet your own needs and goals. But they must be your own! That's the first rule of survival as a single parent. Find yourself and love yourself!

People's Basics

Each of us has a unique set of personality needs that shape us as individuals. And since individuals differ in many complex ways, there is no single combination of personality needs that can be called ideal. It's important to realize that recognizing and coming to terms with your own unique set of personality needs is the first step toward knowing yourself better. Why not try the short self-test on the next page? Called "People's Basics," it was developed by the Center for Organization Development, Inc., in Rochester, New York, and was presented as part of a workshop they gave at the 1979 Parents Without Partners (PWP) convention in Atlanta.

The test lists thirteen basic personality needs, each with a brief description. Rate yourself from 1 to 10 for each (with 1 indicating a low level of need and 10 a high level). These basic needs help show us what kinds of people we are, what kinds of situations we handle best, what kinds of people we're most comfortable with. Remember, there's nothing "right" or "wrong" about these needs. They simply exist.

P *Physiological Awareness*
A body-need...intense aware-ness of food, exercise, rest, sex (any and all forms of physical activity).
Rating _____

E *Excel*
A need to win, to be the best in anything you do.
Rating _____

O *Own*
A need to own physical things...often expressed in compulsive saving.
Rating _____

P *Power*
A need to get things done, to have things stop and start.
Rating _____

L *Learn*
A need to pick up new knowl-edge...an enjoyment of learn-ing for its own sake.
Rating _____

E *Exactness*
A need to be organized, to get things "just right."
Rating _____

S *Security*
A need to have a close, secure, outlined future...a need for definite job outlines...a dislike for risk-taking.
Rating _____

B *Belong*
A need to belong to people and/or organizations...you like to define interpersonal relation-ships.
Rating _____

A *Achieve*
A need to set your own goals, to compete with yourself...you look for things to do, challenges to meet.
Rating _____

S *Status*
A need for recognition of your-self, your accomplishments...you enjoy the outward signs of success.
Rating _____

I *Inspire*
A need for liking and respect from others.
Rating _____

C *Create*
A need to look for the unique, the different...you like change...you look for some-thing basically new, not just an activity. (Cleaning house can fulfill an achievement need but not a creative need.)
Rating _____

S *Serve*
A need to serve others, some-times at the expense of your own time or money...you are often drawn to the serving professions (doctor, nurse, teacher, etc.).
Rating _____

Finding "You"

Here's another little test you can try right now. Touch this page with your fingertip. Now rub that fingertip across the back of your hand. What do you feel? First, something outside yourself, the page. Then you get a two-way experience: you're touching something else and you're being touched, both at the same time. So there are things out there, like the book page, and there's a you.

We need to know how to be here better.

When you were an infant, touch experiences like these helped you discover yourself. And once you learned that you existed separately, apart from your physical surroundings and from other human beings around you, you loved this self you'd just discovered. And you kept on loving you until people started telling you not to! This kind of self-love, whether it is conscious or not, keeps us buoyant in childhood and throughout our adult years. It protects us from the kinds of emotional and psychological catastrophe that could devastate our well-being. As single parents, we all know something about crippling or seemingly life-ending experiences. But we're still here, battered self-esteem and all. What we need to find out is how to be here better—for our own sakes and for the sake of our children.

How Can the "You" Get Lost?

You were smart enough to discover yourself and love yourself at the age of about 8 months. What can make you, as an adult, love yourself less and even lose your sense of identity? Dr. Harold W. Haddle, psychotherapist and advisor to Parents Without Partners in Atlanta, Georgia, listed the following as some of the reasons that can cause self-esteem to drop:

- Not accepting our own limitations. Most of us will concede that our parents were not all that we wanted them to be. It's important to realize that we, in turn, won't be all our children wish us to be. (We can't return them to the womb, for instance.) Parents fail so that children can grow. If you understand this, you can stop beating your breast and bruising your self-esteem because "I've failed them and it's my fault." As one mother puts it: "I once thought I had to 'make up' to my children for their father's absence. Now I know it's better for all of us if I 'just' handle being me."

- Not getting over the fact that our marriages ended. This is another big hurdle for our self-esteem to clear. Realistically, was there anything we could have done about it at the time? I've finally come to believe that marriage is a two-person arrangement. If one carries the whole load—makes all the adjustments and all the excuses—that's not a marriage, it's a power trip.

- Living in a completely controlled structure set up by parents or a mate. Here we have no personal identity or freedom at all because we live within the framework of what they want us to be. We're afraid to develop or find our own identities because if we did, maybe they wouldn't love us anymore. You can overcome this problem by arriving at the concept of "finite freedom," which allows you enough room to exercise your identity while letting you accept the fact that you do have limitations.

In his book *Marital Separation,* sociologist Robert S. Weiss makes two points about the loss of personal identity that can occur *in marriage:*

> Some (people) . . . feel they have meaning and worth only as they are linked to the spouse. When their marriages end they feel that they have lost more than just a part of themselves; they feel they have lost themselves entirely. . . .
>
> Among the issues decided fairly early in every marriage is the kind of person each spouse believes the other to be: reliable or unpredictable, stodgy or exciting, someone to lean on or someone to guide . . . because of the marriage the individual is in constant contact with someone who almost requires the individual to maintain a particular self-image.

"With separation," Dr. Weiss continues, "there is no further need for pretending: it is possible to be one's self. But what self that is may now have become uncertain."

"When I think of the way I punished myself during those years—what I laid on myself," one mother-of-six and grandmother-of-seven exclaimed during an interview at a PWP conference near New York City, "I feel as though I'd been in the closet for 30 years." Now she's not only out of the closet of her marriage, but this bouncy lady has also solved her identity crisis satisfactorily. "I'm having the time of my life . . . going to college, studying hotel management."

Separation Distress

We all know this distress exists because we've all been through it. And it does a lot of damage to our self-esteem. Though both sides feel it, there's a difference in the *kind* of distress felt by the "leavers" and the "left." Dr. Weiss describes the differences this way:

> [The leavers] tend to feel guilty, even anguished, at the damage their departure inflicted on those they were pledged to cherish. They may anticipate the condemnation of others and feel such condemnation to be partially deserved. They may also question their capacity to meet emotional obligations. . . .
>
> [The left] may feel aggrieved, misused not only by one man or woman who ended the marriage to them but by the entire human race. They may feel that friends and neighbors . . . may have lost respect for them. And they may have lost respect for themselves; they may question their capacity to hold the love of anyone. They may accept their spouses' accusations . . . and decide that they are utterly without value.

You'll find more information about guilt, anger and other post-separation trips on page 145. I just want to make the point here that as a singled parent, you can live through a double dose of misery. You can smother yourself in marriage and then lambast the substitute self you created with recurring bouts of separation sickness.

Society's Attitude That "Divorce" Is a Dirty Word

This commonly held opinion doesn't help your self-esteem, either. Clinical social workers Susan Gettelman and Janet Markowitz describe the position very strongly in *The Courage to Divorce:*

> The decision to divorce need not be a destructive one, but it often is . . . [because of] cultural taboos and erroneous beliefs and customs fostered by . . . American

Don't let distress pull down your self-esteem.

society—the schools, the media, the mental health professions and the courts. In varying degrees these forces all support the notion that divorce destroys family relationships, inhibits individual growth and encourages social chaos.

I think we've all had encounters with school personnel, neighbors, members of our own families that clearly showed what they thought of divorce: "You're being selfish. You're a failure because you couldn't keep the marriage together. If there were no divorce, you'd have to stick it out." If there were no aspirin, would pain disappear?

Divorce can fill your life with enriching new experience.

Many single parents I interviewed also mentioned discrimination in housing, nosy neighbors who "spy on everyone who visits me," and, most hurtfully, discrimination against their children. "My daughter's best friend is allowed to play at our house during the day, but she's never allowed to sleep over."

Being divorced can make recoupling difficult, too. "About a year ago I was really in love with a guy," Nancy Simpson explained during our interview. She's a 26-year-old divorced mother who is working full time as a waitress to support her 9- and 10-year-old sons. "But because I was divorced, his mother had a fit. I'm not a bad person. What did I do that was so bad? I got married, I had two kids and after my husband split, I got a divorce."

Contrary to society's prejudices, the breakup of a marriage can be the springboard for enriching new experience. "Divorce does not have to result in emotionally crippled, hostile men and women," write Gettelman and Markowitz, "or in embarrassed, maladjusted children . . . Nor does divorce merely undo a marriage . . . Rather, it restructures family relationships and often results in new kinship groupings whose positive dimensions have never seriously been gauged." And finally, they point out that "divorce potentially opens doors to new kinds of emotional fulfillment, unavailable to people whose energies are sapped by continuous marital conflict in the hothouse of the nuclear marriage."

Divorce Can Actually Help Your "Self"

We've already mentioned that divorce can leave you free to be yourself—a self you may have distorted in order to please a mate. But divorce can boost the "self" by defining new responsibilities and providing a new framework of standards for decision-making. Nancy, the young mother with the potential mother-in-law problems, put it this way: "It's been a growth thing for me. Definitely. I'm smarter now. I think more before I do something." Jill, a young social worker for a children and youth council, says of her own divorce: "I feel sorry for women who feel they have to live a lie. I feel like I've been reborn. If I make a wrong decision, I live with it. I don't have to answer to anybody. It's my own responsibility."

New responsibilities mean a new sense of self.

Fathers who are taking an active role in their children's lives or who have full custody feel the same sense of growth. "Look, a woman can hire a plumber to fix a leak. But a man can't call someone in to cook in an emergency. We ate a lot of fast-food dinners at first. But now it's routine. It's good to know I can deal with it." That's one father with two kids who visit him three weekends a month, spend one day a week and six weeks of the summer with him. Another father says: "To tell you the truth, I was scared when Johnny first came to live with me. But now it's no big deal. We both feel good about being able to work it out—the house, the food, the cleaning. I never did any before, but it's working OK."

Other fathers I met were proud of their ability to furnish and decorate a home for themselves and their children and of being able to "keep things going in general." Howard Cain, whom you'll meet again in Chapter 9, believes that "people tell a man he can't raise children. I believed that at first, after Peg died. But then I said to myself 'I'm already doing it. So I'll keep on until something shows me I can't.'" That was 10 years ago and Howard's daughter is now 17, a National Honor Society student, editor of her school paper and planning to enter college in the fall of '81. She's also open and fun to talk to, and all 5'0'' of her exudes the same enthusiasm and self-confidence that Howard projects.

How Do You Repair a Battered Self?

Working from the theory that we need all the help we can get, I've rounded up suggestions for restoring our self-image from several experts, each of whom represent an individual area of expertise.

Mel Krantzler, who has an M.S. degree in rehabilitation counseling, was awarded the James H. Woods Fellowship in Philosophy at Harvard, has worked as a career and rehabilitation counselor and, in 1972, established New Horizons, a counseling service for the divorced. He suggests, in his best seller *Creative Divorce*, that you send yourself positive messages. Get in the habit of complimenting yourself on a job well done. As an example: "If you wash the kitchen floor and it looks good . . . your message to yourself should be 'I washed the floor and it looks good,' not 'I washed the floor but the rest of the house is still dirty and anyway all I'm good for is washing floors.'" This is the technique that Barbara, whom you met at the beginning of this chapter, put to work for herself. On her questionnaire, she wrote: "Prior to an operation last year, I didn't love me." Then she learned to send herself those "brilliant, beautiful, me" messages. But she's honest enough to admit that "sometimes it's hard."

Send yourself positive messages.

Krantzler also advises learning to accept compliments from others as "an honest expression of how at least one outsider views you." He suggests six additional guidelines for coping with the new, post-separation realities:

> *Separate your real feelings and needs* from what you think society is requiring of you as male and female role players.
>
> *Take tiny risks,* and give yourself permission to make mistakes. An error-free life is a dead giveaway for zero personal growth.
>
> *Set realistic goals for yourself,* and don't wait until the job is over before assessing your progress. Knowing how much you have accomplished will give you the boost you need to finish the task.
>
> *Consider the present as a series of choices,* not inevitabilities. If circumstances force you temporarily into an unpleasant situation . . . learn what you can from it and begin to make plans to move ahead, rather than resigning yourself to permanent unhappiness and despair.
>
> *Don't underestimate* the capacity for even the smallest act of self-assertion to enhance your own opinion of yourself as an independent single person.
>
> *Seek help when you need it*—from family, friends, or from professionals. Life is not a test, and you aren't cheating when you request assistance from others.

Caseworker Mary G. O'Connell, M.S.W., who heads up the South Fork Chapter of the Family Service League and whose career as a medical social worker includes establishing the first social work unit in the Suffolk County (New York) Department of Health, has two suggestions:

First, don't be too nice. You have to have a little mental hardness [to stay mentally healthy.] Learn the happy medium—be able to help people but not to the point where you'll resent it and hate them.

Also, be realistic about what you're coping with. In today's world to work at the job of being a human being, to raise kids, hold down a job, and relate to a mate (married or not) is almost overwhelming.

George and Sally Finger, who together direct the Family Forum of Staten Island, worked with a group of Parents Without Partners at a workshop on self-esteem held at the Sheraton Inn outside of New York City, and also ran a special single parents' workshop at Great Kills Park on Staten Island, New York, especially for this book. The following points about dealing with self-image grew out of these workshops:

- *Remember, you can't be too selfish.* Otherwise you're not being honest.
- *Remember that your happiness depends on yourself.* The ideal emotional relationship puts together two people who don't need each other and decide to live together.
- *Remember that you own your own emotions.* Don't let anyone else own them. When someone else can make you angry, he or she is controlling that emotion of yours.

I discovered some final pieces of advice in the October 1978 issue of the journal *Social Casework* in an article titled "The Process of Separation and Divorce: A New Approach." Here, Samuel P. Chiancola, who is coordinator of clinical services for the Valley Adult Counseling Center, South Grafton Clinic, in South Grafton, Massachusetts, advises other therapists to help their separating clients shake some damaging myths out of their lives. In other words, let's *stop* telling ourselves:

- "Divorce creates broken homes." Rather, the breakage occurs while the marriage is going on, before the separation and divorce take place.
- "Divorce happens to those who dislike marriage." This is untrue; if anything, most people who seek a divorce have a high regard for a rich relationship and for intimacy in a marriage and are striving toward those goals.
- "Children are scarred for life by divorce." There is no valid proof of this belief. What can be said is that, like other major crises in a person's life, this one will affect them as they mature. (Or, as someone else said: "Marriage doesn't protect children. People do.")
- "Children are hurt the most." This is a natural projection that adults constantly use so that they will not have to accept and deal with their own pain, loss and guilt.

Marriage doesn't protect children. People do.

- "Someone is at fault." This is followed by the idea that someone must be punished. Who punishes whom? Everyone, including those who are divorcing, punishes a divorced person. First, to end a marriage, fault must be found, hurt feelings must receive satisfaction. The punishment is continued in court, again by expressing fault. Then, in the minds of many, the divorce itself labels these people failures and assigns to them a status that is less than respectable.

The following pages show you how to put self-esteem and self-love into practice. And you'll hear how some other single parents work to keep theirs healthy.

Feeling Good About Yourself

Yes—or you walk with your head to the ground. I included the question "Do you think it's important to feel good about yourself" in the questionnaire I sent to hundreds of single parents. The resounding sentiment is summed up in the words above. Answers were phrased in many different ways and lifestyles and situations differed widely; together they make up a roll call of men and women willing to stand up and be counted as individuals. I don't know their names, but their "self" comes up off the pages of the questionnaires so strongly, I feel I know each one personally. They have a right to be heard in their own words.

Feeling good about yourself:

- "Makes the difference between a happy, self-actualizing person and one who merely exists."
- "It affects all other areas of your life—job, parenting, friendships."
- "Your need to feel good is removed from the goodwill and approval of others. Therefore, you can run your own life."
- "I'm not saying that I do, but one very important thing I have found out—if you don't feel good about yourself no one else will either."

> **"If you don't feel good about yourself, no one else will, either."**

And in answer to the question "Do you think that how you feel about yourself affects the way you deal with your kids":

- "Of course! They're doing well because I am."
- "If I'm feeling good, my daughter knows immediately and reacts positively. We enjoy each other's company. I'm attentive, she's cooperative. I'm fair, consistent, 'all good things.' The reverse is true, needless to say."
- "Definitely. If I'm feeling sorry for myself I won't really listen to the kids."
- "Yes. You tend to vacillate a lot if you're not too fond of yourself because you don't trust your own judgment."

Following are answers to two other questions—"What one thing have you done in the past week that made you feel best/worst about yourself?" Feeling best about yourself was strongly connected with helping others which included loving others, and doing something for yourself:

- "I convinced a best friend who is going through the breakup of a marriage to get professional help. I've been there, too, and it helped me."
- "Bought groceries for, and spent time with, an 80-year-old friend."
- "My ability to relate my love to one other human being who is only a friend. I was given love in return."
- "Spent time with a lover. Made a sensational presentation at work. Without the one I mightn't have done the other."

Doing something for oneself included:

- "Researched a paper for Freshman English that received an A grade."
- "Went to 'Opryland' in Tennessee and saw 16 shows while there (some three times)! I felt absolutely elated!"
- "Joined in a performance for children, performing the role of the graduate of an 'Art of Clowning' class."
- "Spent $11,900 on an organ to play—and even let the kids play on it."
- "Held my youngest son and told him I loved him."

Failing yourself or others can be a nasty bringdown.

Other answers showed that these single parents also got a good feeling from coping with crises, doing well on the job and trying new things.

Feeling worst about yourself involved failing to help others: "Did not stop car to aid fellow human when he dropped cases all over the road." It also involved failing self: "Overindulged in spirits" . . . "Realized I'd gained a few pounds by overeating" . . . "Let my ex-wife insult me unreasonably." Another concern: dealing with kids, such as "inability to cope with my 17-year-old daughter's deep depression over the sudden death of an old school friend" and "yelling at my son every morning for he is so slow."

Jobs were also cited as a problem. "Things have been very difficult at work lately, which causes a lot of tension within me." Illness is mentioned as something that saps self-regard: "In the past week I have been flat on my back, recovering from pneumonia." And there is a definite group who feel that they shoot off their mouths too much. One example: "Criticized the high school principal too severely for a mistake he made concerning graduation." It took a lot of guts to do it—and then to admit that it was a mistake!

Put your self-love into practice.

Now that You Know and Like Yourself— Make It Pay Off

It takes a while to get the hang of it. But once you know who you are and like who you are, you can put your self-love into practice and start living in more rewarding ways. At first, most of us edge up to that big pool of fulfillment in a pretty gingerly way—just sort of test it with one toe. But experts and other single parents are quick to tell us, "Come on in, the water's fine!"

Taking the First Steps

Leslie Harris is a counselor and caseworker for the East Hampton Counseling Center on Long Island, New York, part of a network of community services called the East End Project. She is also a single parent. Speaking both professionally and personally, she feels that singled people live through three stages on their way to recovery and renewal.

First comes the *crisis period*—the cut is so new that everything hurts. This lasts different lengths of time for different people. "It was months before I could do much more than get out the door," a friend of mine remembered. (You'll be meeting her and her husband in Chapter 10 as they discuss their gradual growth toward a secure and satisfying separate life.) This is the time when you can feel crushed by financial responsibility, if nothing else. "You feel the odds are stacked against you," Sandra Morse, whom you'll meet again in Chapter 2, recalls. "You're very frightened." This fear of having to be financially independent is particularly strong among women because our society still stamps the man as "Earner." But men feel it, too. "I thought, 'My God I'll never make it' when I first signed the lease on a studio apartment," one father told me. "I knew Phyllis could handle herself because she'd been working part-time right along. But the thought of the kids' getting older and needing more things scared the pants off me."

Fear, guilt and anger fight their way around inside during the crisis period. And if you're the custodial parent, your children are apt to react with a pretty violent backlash of their own. "Half the battle was trying to walk upright and not feel that Abby was being completely ruined." That's how Joan English, a young teacher whose picture-book marriage fell apart when her daughter was only 2, remembers her first separated days. And only those who've been there know how rough they can be.

The second phase is the *mourning period*, experienced by both widowed and divorced. The agony may gentle down to a dull ache that seems like relief. But "Don't prolong it," Leslie Harris warns. "Lick your wounds but remember there's a difference between mourning and melancholia. Get out and make a life for yourself."

This final *action period* is the reward point. How do you make it happen and keep it happening? "Join support groups, get a job, get involved," Harris advises. "Fill the time. Emptiness leaves room for negative thinking and feeling."

For some, it can start with a roasting pan. Mel Krantzler's *Creative Divorce* translates the whole business of coping with new realities into very human terms: "I bought a roasting pan," said a woman in her fifties who had left her husband and thirty years in the suburbs and moved to an apartment in the city . . . "For me that pan was a coming out symbol . . . I said to myself it's about time I stopped living like a mole . . . and I decided to have a party." She also got herself a job and was on her way to living.

Isolation is a deadly pitfall for any singled parent. Precautions you can take to guard against it include making a change in housing if you're not deeply rooted to your neighborhood, and devoting time and energy to an involving job or continuing education. Developing an interest or a new skill will go a long way as an escape from the seclusion trap, and so will long-term time investments such as becoming active in politics. (Almost all single-parent advisors cite this as the best way to start meeting people and working into a group.) And you should probably start dating, too.

The first steps that were the most helpful for Joan English were "when I first got a job, when I started going out with other men and when I slowly started making friends, including women friends." She began to realize that she "could lead a life, work, go out." One high point she remembers came "the first time I did something by myself. Filling out the car registration. I was floored. Then I sat down and figured it out." This struck a personal memory. I didn't even realize you had to fill them out every year until a policeman gave me that news the morning of January 1. Fortunately, he was so macho he was amused at "this idiot" and let me go with a warning.

Always be on guard against isolation.

Learning to Treat Yourself Gently

I asked Dr. Selma Miller, Past President of the New York Association for Marriage and Family Therapy, what advice she would give single parents. Dr. Miller, deeply humane and gentle herself, advises us to treat ourselves the same way. "I always worry about telling patients who can barely walk across the room that they ought to get out and get active," she says. Here are some self-supportive measures she feels we can all use:

• Remember—the feelings of abandonment, rejection, failure *do* go away.

• Don't let the world look as though it's all lovers. This is easy to do on beautiful spring or fall days. Statistically, just about half of those couples strolling by are headed right for the same singled situation you're in or have already been there!

• It helps to talk with others who've shared your experience, especially if they're within easy reach.

• Don't get into situations where you'll be lectured. "How could you do this to those beautiful kids" can be the theme song of a family party or holiday gathering. Avoid it; you're having a tough enough time as it is.

• Help smooth over the difficult times by thinking ahead to holidays and family parties. Be good to yourself. If you don't want to go to some function, make other plans well ahead of time so you avoid the double bind: "I don't want to go but I don't want to stay home either."

• *Always* remember that a separated home is better than an unhappy home left intact!

In line with Dr. Miller's advice is this woman's experience, shared with us via questionnaire. She's widowed twice with nine children, and says, "On bad days like my wedding anniversaries, husbands' birthdays, etc., I take myself to a shopping center and walk around a lot and take myself out to lunch. It beats sitting at home and listening to the phone not ring."

Dr. Roy Kern, Family Counselor and Professor of Counseling at Georgia State University, also offered sound advice in his workshop "Maintaining Sanity in a Single Parent Family," conducted at the 1979 International Convention of Parents Without Partners in Atlanta, Georgia. He calls this part of the workshop *"Stopgap Measures for Self"*

• Remember that you're in a stress-laden situation that takes a lot of physical energy. *So get on a physical program.* First try walking, then jogging, at least 25 minutes a day.

• Change your eating habits so that you cut down on your sugar intake. And do the same for your children. Sugar is an addictive substance and one that increases hyperactivity and agitation.

• Watch your alcoholic consumption. There's an established relationship between depression/agitation and alcohol taken the night before. (Because we're people under stress, we're prime candidates to become alcoholics.)

I'd just discovered the second basic rule of surviving as head of a single-parent family: Avoid the trap that says, "I can do it all—all by myself." You can't. And if you continue to try, life will become, as one single parent put it, "full-time nothing."

possible to do ourself, and OK.

Others phrase it even more directly. Sandra Morse, a talented young decorator and interior designer, divorced three years and busy raising two daughters now 3½ and 7½, hit it with the first words of our interview: "I guess the first thing I learned was that you can't do it all. You have to realize that's impossible and that it's OK for it to be impossible." Sandra is now working full-time at her profession, one that is emotionally rewarding and financially profitable enough for her to freight the charges of a live-in helper. In fact, that was one of the decisions Sandra made in facing the limitations of time and energy—to cut out other expenses in order to provide "someone in the household besides me."

Five years after her "perfect" marriage disintegrated, Joan English, who now feels that she'd been "hiding in that once-comfortable marriage," describes her evolution to identity this way: "At first I felt 'I can't do anything.' The second stage was 'I can do everything. I don't need any help.' Then I got over that." Right now, Joan is deciding whether she can handle being a parent and full-time career woman at the same time and if so, what that career should be. She "fell into teaching" because that's what her former husband did, but she now feels it's not for her. At the moment, she doesn't feel that she can do it all—parent 7-year-old Abby through her growing years and train into a new job field. So, she's settling for jack-of-all-trades—driving a bus, working as an adjunct at a local college, house painting—while she decides.

But this realization of one's limits is not confined to women. Hugh James, a full-time math teacher who has complete custody of his grade-school son and daughter, says, "At first, I wanted to keep everything the same. Then I realized it was better to change things. Now I've changed almost everything and the kids love it." Here, changing meant simplifying both furnishings and daily routines so that both became manageable for a one-parent family.

Different words and different lifestyles, but the same message from some who are coping with the time-tight, trial-and-error job of living as heads of single parent families. No, you can't do it all—all by yourself.

OK—so you decide that you're not Superman or Wonder Woman and something's got to give. But what? Anyone who's ever headed a household for even a few weeks understands the discomfort and discouragement that utter chaos generates. But if you try to do too much, setting unrealistic goals for yourself, you'll end up paralyzed. Or you'll start down a tunnel of compulsive routine that shuts out real living. The routine itself becomes a goal. It goes something like this:

Mary N. decides that dishes should be cleared right after dinner. No problem usually. But tonight she's hearing: "Ma, we'll miss 'Kiss.'" Or she realizes she'll miss the start of a one-time TV special. But on she goes, and those dishes get cleared! Terrific! Of course she could have waited and cleared later, used paper plates, changed the dinner hour or served the meal as a TV picnic. But then she wouldn't have had the satisfaction of chalking up one more time when she made that schedule! Mary's begun to get her kicks from the schedule itself, when the whole thing started as a way of making the evening pleasanter and more relaxed for her family.

And here's a special reminder to all single parents. It seems to me that many of us are particularly prone to compulsive housekeeping when we're under nerv

Giving Yourself a Treat

"Do you ever give yourself a special just-for-you treat? If so, what little ego-builder works best for you?"

These questions were also part of the survey I sent to single parents as background for this book. ("Treat" examples included morning coffee in bed, dance lessons, a bubble bath.) I find the answers stimulating, joyful, practical and thought-provoking. They prove to me that all of us can take the time to be gracious to ourselves, even when income is limited and there are heavy demands on our time. Once again, I'll let single parents speak for themselves. Their answers are grouped into several types of self-rewards, however, because I saw definite patterns emerging from the questionnaires.

Do something nice for yourself—and make it a habit.

Friends, lovers and food. These headed the list. About 20% of the answers mention one or two or all. Socializing includes: informal dropping in at friends', a night out dancing, a morning in bed with a lover, getting drunk. One man, newly divorced, mentions "meeting new friends" as his reward. Food pleasures include breakfast in bed, eating breakfast out, a morning cup of coffee sipped slowly and alone, taking oneself out to dinner, eating a Chinese or Japanese dinner out and "getting all dressed up, going out to dinner with friends and eating good seafood." One father with custody combines both rewards by having his daughter spend a night with friends so he can "give special attention to a lady friend—dinner at my place or hers."

Quiet times and mind times. Many of us, obviously, have learned the difference between "alone" and "loneliness." Nineteen percent of the answers listed quiet pursuits like reading, loafing, browsing, taking time to work the crossword puzzle and "walking on the beach to think about what's important to me." Others go for a drive to collect their thoughts, take a half hour to sit in the backyard or "do only what I want from 9:00 to 10:00 p.m.—my hour!" One takes "oddball courses my parents never geared me for." (Relax parents—it's Piano Tuning.) Two fathers either arrange "a day to do only what I want to do" (a man in Worcester, Massachusetts whose two sons visit once or twice a week) or "take a day off from work" (a father who has full custody of his school-age son and daughter).

Bingo games and buying things. Actually, only one single parent mentioned this particular combination but it sounds so great I couldn't resist including it. It's true that buying ranks third (14%) on the list of rewards. Most of it falls into the "little trinket or bottle of wine" class. What's important is that it be "something just for me—a lipstick, a dinner, a book, a show." Really, it can be anything, just as long as it's "buying myself a little something and not spending all the money on my kids."

Both men and women indulge. One father specifies "buying a luxury item" as a self-boost, and one recently divorced mother ruefully says, "Still, as before, I like shopping for clothes. Trite but true." Not so—if it satisfies you, that's all that's important.

If it satisfies you, that's all that's important.

Health, hot tubs and caring about how you look. About 13% of these single parents have discovered the most personal and least expensive way to reward themselves: they've developed body awareness. Some mention the pleasures of turning a daily bath into a celebration—a leisurely soak combined with a glass of wine, a good book, music or candlelight. Others in this percentage concentrate on hair care, manicures, pedicures and "tinting my hair. Then I don't feel as old as the sneaky gray wants to show." One sums it up: "To take care of others you have to take care of yourself first. Two weeks ago I got a permanent. Today I painted my nails." And one father mentions a monthly shampoo and hair styling as part of his body-treat. "Just plain exercise" rewards another, while dance lessons, a good game of tennis and running do it for others.

Singles groups and going places. Some who answered set aside time to attend single-parent functions or to work actively with single-parent groups: "I'm on the answering service for Parents Without Partners [in Rockford, Illinois] and I try to encourage frightened single parents to attend orientation. That makes me feel good inside." A few find travel and vacation both possible and rewarding. "Even overnight vacations are my best ego-booster." One mother has developed vacations in reverse "I have my son [13] spend a night with relatives or friends. To be able to leave the bathroom door open during a tub or shower is freedom." Another: "I problem-solve and take mini-vacations of the mind by going back to bed after the kids get off to school."

The no's. In addition to those who wrote "NO" or simply left the space provided blank, one woman wrote "ALL" for the sample ego-builders suggested on the questionnaire. One mother from Arizona who holds down two jobs in the sales field to support her 8-year-old daughter says "No" to self-treats and adds, "I try to please others. Doing for others gives me the most pleasure in life." Several who also indicated a negative for self-treats said in effect that the best they could hope for was a night without stress or free from work brought home from the office. And a father from New York City, divorced two years, wrote that "a treat is not an ego-builder for me." He felt that the whole concept of a treat "sounds distinctly feminine."

The single parent we should all take a lesson from says: "I'm over-ego'd, if anything. I look myself in the eye and say 'go get 'em'—and I do!"

2/I Can Do It All— All by Myself

I kissed my son CH goodnight, watched him roll and snuggle into sleep position and walked back into the living room in a haze of happiness. It had been a good evening for both of us. After dinner we'd horsed around together in an impromptu pillow fight, taking big, wild swipes at each other, missing as often as we hit. It was the first playtime we'd shared in days, so every connect brought on giggles.

But now, back in the living room which also served as my bedroom and work area, time took over. I'd been separated for a year, was a teaching assistant at a nursery school, working on a master's degree in early childhood education at New York University, and wrestling with the never-ending grit and unbending walls of a two-room ground-floor apartment that just wasn't big enough for an active 7-year-old and me. In my more dramatic moments I felt that I was living in a stand-up coffin, the rooms were so narrow and high-ceilinged.

Well, time for the mental checklist. Dishes? Done, thank God. I still had papers spread out on the work ledge that doubled as a dining table. I could catch up on those tomorrow if I set the alarm an hour earlier. The day's allotment of New York City dust sneered at me from the windowsills and tabletops and a couple of dust bunnies skittered around as I pulled the convertible couch out into nighttime position. To hell with grit, grime, dust bunnies or whatever—cleaning would have to wait till Saturday. I had made a firm resolve about that one night when I suddenly found myself in the middle of a crying bout so severe that I started to hiccup from the clenching sobs. It was the film of dust that had done it. In my mother's home, tabletops glowed from polishing and, of course, that was the way tabletops were supposed to be! But she wasn't holding down a job, going to school and trying to raise a kid on her own while she kept those tabletops gleaming. "You can't do it all," some nub of sanity inside me said. "Something's got to give. So face it and quit hassling."

Giving Yourself a Treat

"Do you ever give yourself a special just-for-you treat? If so, what little ego-builder works best for you?"

These questions were also part of the survey I sent to single parents as background for this book. ("Treat" examples included morning coffee in bed, dance lessons, a bubble bath.) I find the answers stimulating, joyful, practical and thought-provoking. They prove to me that all of us can take the time to be gracious to ourselves, even when income is limited and there are heavy demands on our time. Once again, I'll let single parents speak for themselves. Their answers are grouped into several types of self-rewards, however, because I saw definite patterns emerging from the questionnaires.

Friends, lovers and food. These headed the list. About 20% of the answers mention one or two or all. Socializing includes: informal dropping in at friends', a night out dancing, a morning in bed with a lover, getting drunk. One man, newly divorced, mentions "meeting *new* friends" as his reward. Food pleasures include breakfast in bed, eating breakfast out, a morning cup of coffee sipped slowly and alone, taking oneself out to dinner, eating a Chinese or Japanese dinner out and "getting all dressed up, going out to dinner with friends and eating good seafood." One father with custody combines both rewards by having his daughter spend a night with friends so he can "give special attention to a lady friend—dinner at my place or hers."

Quiet times and mind times. Many of us, obviously, have learned the difference between "alone" and "loneliness." Nineteen percent of the answers listed quiet pursuits like reading, loafing, browsing, taking time to work the crossword puzzle and "walking on the beach to think about what's important to *me*." Others go for a drive to collect their thoughts, take a half hour to sit in the backyard or "do only what I want from 9:00 to 10:00 p.m.—*my* hour!" One takes "oddball courses my parents never geared me for." (Relax parents—it's Piano Tuning.) Two fathers either arrange "a day to do only what I want to do" (a man in Worcester, Massachusetts whose two sons visit once or twice a week) or "take a day off from work" (a father who has full custody of his school-age son and daughter).

Bingo games and buying things. Actually, only one single parent mentioned this particular combination but it sounds so great I couldn't resist including it. It's true that buying ranks third (14%) on the list of rewards. Most of it falls into the "little trinket or bottle of wine" class. What's important is that it be "something just for me—a lipstick, a dinner, a book, a show." Really, it can be *anything*, just as long as it's "buying myself a little something and not spending all the money on my kids."

Both men and women indulge. One father specifies "buying a luxury item" as a self-boost, and one recently divorced mother ruefully says, "Still, as before, I like shopping for clothes. Trite but true." Not so—if it satifies *you*, that's all that's important.

Health, hot tubs and caring about how you look. About 13% of these single parents have discovered the most personal and least expensive way to reward themselves: they've developed body awareness. Some mention the pleasures of turning a daily bath into a celebration—a leisurely soak combined with a glass of wine, a good book, music or candlelight. Others in this percentage concentrate on

> Do something nice for yourself—and make it a habit.

> If it satisfies you, that's all that's important.

hair care, manicures, pedicures and "tinting my hair. Then I don't feel as old as the sneaky gray wants to show." One sums it up: "To take care of others you have to take care of yourself first. Two weeks ago I got a permanent. Today I painted my nails." And one father mentions a monthly shampoo and hair styling as part of his body-treat. "Just plain exercise" rewards another, while dance lessons, a good game of tennis and running do it for others.

Singles groups and going places. Some who answered set aside time to attend single-parent functions or to work actively with single-parent groups: "I'm on the answering service for Parents Without Partners [in Rockford, Illinois] and I try to encourage frightened single parents to attend orientation. That makes me feel good inside." A few find travel and vacation both possible and rewarding. "Even overnight vacations are my best ego-booster." One mother has developed vacations in reverse "I have my son [13] spend a night with relatives or friends. To be able to leave the bathroom door open during a tub or shower is freedom." Another: "I problem-solve and take mini-vacations of the mind by going back to bed after the kids get off to school."

The no's. In addition to those who wrote "NO" or simply left the space provided blank, one woman wrote "ALL" for the sample ego-builders suggested on the questionnaire. One mother from Arizona who holds down two jobs in the sales field to support her 8-year-old daughter says "No" to self-treats and adds, "I try to please others. Doing for others gives me the most pleasure in life." Several who also indicated a negative for self-treats said in effect that the best they could hope for was a night without stress or free from work brought home from the office. And a father from New York City, divorced two years, wrote that "a treat is not an ego-builder for me." He felt that the whole concept of a treat "sounds distinctly feminine."

The single parent we should all take a lesson from says: "I'm over-ego'd, if anything. I look myself in the eye and say 'go get 'em'—and I do!"

2/I Can Do It All – All by Myself

I kissed my son CH goodnight, watched him roll and snuggle into sleep position and walked back into the living room in a haze of happiness. It had been a good evening for both of us. After dinner we'd horsed around together in an impromptu pillow fight, taking big, wild swipes at each other, missing as often as we hit. It was the first playtime we'd shared in days, so every connect brought on giggles.

But now, back in the living room which also served as my bedroom and work area, time took over. I'd been separated for a year, was a teaching assistant at a nursery school, working on a master's degree in early childhood education at New York University, and wrestling with the never-ending grit and unbending walls of a two-room ground-floor apartment that just wasn't big enough for an active 7-year-old and me. In my more dramatic moments I felt that I was living in a stand-up coffin, the rooms were so narrow and high-ceilinged.

Well, time for the mental checklist. Dishes? Done, thank God. I still had papers spread out on the work ledge that doubled as a dining table. I could catch up on those tomorrow if I set the alarm an hour earlier. The day's allotment of New York City dust sneered at me from the windowsills and tabletops and a couple of dust bunnies skittered around as I pulled the convertible couch out into nighttime position. To hell with grit, grime, dust bunnies or whatever—cleaning would have to wait till Saturday. I had made a firm resolve about that one night when I suddenly found myself in the middle of a crying bout so severe that I started to hiccup from the clenching sobs. It was the film of dust that had done it. In my mother's home, tabletops glowed from polishing and, of course, that was the way tabletops were supposed to be! But she wasn't holding down a job, going to school and trying to raise a kid on her own while she kept those tabletops gleaming. "You can't do it all," some nub of sanity inside me said. "Something's got to give. So face it and quit hassling."

I'd just discovered the second basic rule of surviving as head of a single-parent family: Avoid the trap that says, "I can do it all—all by myself." You can't. And if you continue to try, life will become, as one single parent put it, "full-time nothing."

Others phrase it even more directly. Sandra Morse, a talented young decorator and interior designer, divorced three years and busy raising two daughters now 3½ and 7½, hit it with the first words of our interview: "I guess the first thing I learned was that you can't do it all. You have to realize that's impossible and that it's OK for it to be impossible." Sandra is now working full-time at her profession, one that is emotionally rewarding and financially profitable enough for her to freight the charges of a live-in helper. In fact, that was one of the decisions Sandra made in facing the limitations of time and energy—to cut out other expenses in order to provide "someone in the household besides me."

Five years after her "perfect" marriage disintegrated, Joan English, who now feels that she'd been "hiding in that once-comfortable marriage," describes her evolution to identity this way: "At first I felt 'I can't do anything.' The second stage was 'I can do everything. I don't need any help.' Then I got over that." Right now, Joan is deciding whether she can handle being a parent and full-time career woman at the same time and if so, what that career should be. She "fell into teaching" because that's what her former husband did, but she now feels it's not for her. At the moment, she *doesn't* feel that she can do it all—parent 7-year-old Abby through her growing years and train into a new job field. So, she's settling for jack-of-all-trades—driving a bus, working as an adjunct at a local college, house painting—while she decides.

But this realization of one's limits is not confined to women. Hugh James, a full-time math teacher who has complete custody of his grade-school son and daughter, says, "At first, I wanted to keep everything the same. Then I realized it was better to change things. Now I've changed almost everything and the kids love it." Here, changing meant simplifying both furnishings and daily routines so that both became manageable for a one-parent family.

Different words and different lifestyles, but the same message from some who are coping with the time-tight, trial-and-error job of living as heads of single parent families. No, you can't do it all—all by yourself.

OK—so you decide that you're not Superman or Wonder Woman and something's got to give. But what? Anyone who's ever headed a household for even a few weeks understands the discomfort and discouragement that utter chaos generates. But if you try to do too much, setting unrealistic goals for yourself, you'll end up paralyzed. Or you'll start down a tunnel of compulsive routine that shuts out real living. The routine itself becomes a goal. It goes something like this:

Mary N. decides that dishes should be cleared right after dinner. No problem usually. But tonight she's hearing: "Ma, we'll miss 'Kiss.'" Or she realizes she'll miss the start of a one-time TV special. But on she goes, and those dishes get cleared! Terrific! Of course she could have waited and cleared later, used paper plates, changed the dinner hour or served the meal as a TV picnic. But then she wouldn't have had the satisfaction of chalking up one more time when she made that schedule! Mary's begun to get her kicks from the schedule itself, when the whole thing started as a way of making the evening pleasanter and more relaxed for her family.

And here's a special reminder to all single parents. It seems to me that many of us are particularly prone to compulsive housekeeping when we're under nervous

It's impossible to do it all yourself, and that's OK.

The trouble arises from the fact that I'm drawing an irrational belief (irresponsible, negligent homemaker) out of the rational (provable) fact that my mother cleaned thoroughly *every* Friday. Because *she* did does not mean that I'm irresponsible or negligent when I don't. Maybe my house doesn't get as dirty! More realistically, I don't have as much flexible time as my mother, I don't do any formal entertaining, *and I simply do not like to clean.* I'll trade less gleam on tabletops for more time to read, run, talk to CH and other friends and—sometimes—cook.

You can play the ABC game for making up the beds the traditional way versus with sleeping bags; serving a full dinner to school-age kids who are already eating one as part of their school lunch program; using china plates instead of paper when restaurant cost accountants consistently find that paper is cheaper than china if you add in what it costs to heat water, buy detergent, run a washer and pay salaries to kitchen help. And so on, down the list of everyday chores and activities.

When I played the game I was amazed at how often I came up with the answer "my mother did." She was a delightful and practical lady who ran a taut ship as a first-grade teacher (pre-marriage), marched in early feminist parades and firmly believed in college and careers for women. But she did polish those tabletops while the only claim I can make for my own housekeeping is "Look, Ma, no hands."

There's no right or wrong way to cut corners.

I'm not putting you down if you derive deep satisfaction and pride from opening your front door and walking into a well-groomed home. If you do, the work is worth it and you can cut corners (and hours) some other way. Others prefer to skimp on housework. There's no right or wrong.

The following excerpts from a questionnaire sent countrywide to single parents represent a range of values and ways of coping with limited time.

- From New York City, a mother of two states: "I have earned a lot of money (as a magazine editor) so that I have considerable freedom from child care and household chores."

- A teacher/student from Indiana with a 7-year-old son says: "What is considered a shortcut for others is the way it's always been with me. I'm a full-time teacher and have also been a student since 1968."

- A registered nurse from Connecticut, who has four daughters, says: "I don't participate in Girl Scouts as I used to."

- Another mother from Louisville, Kentucky, with two sons feels she has "more time than money, so I shop at two or three stores a week."

- Another mother from Nassau County in New York, with three daughters aged 17, 14, and 7, feels that she has now learned "to be more of a mother—not wanting to get out of the house as much."

- From Staten Island, New York, a secretary with children 7 and 9 finds that "I'm limiting my own outside activities so that I have enough time for my responsibilities, work, social ties (family and friends)."

Don't forget the energy factor when you start to unclutter your life. Some people *do* possess more physical energy than others. A higher metabolism is one element; emotions and personality are important, too. Here are a few facts about physical energy from the Gilbreth/Thomas/Clymer book, *Management in the Home*:

- "The best stimulant to energy is happiness. Not only does it increase energy but anger and *unhappiness* use up so much energy that an unhappy person has really only a small part of his/her strength to devote to the job." (So if your ABC, discussed on page 34, shows any job you really don't care about, find a way to cut down on it. You'll be "working angry" and thus inefficiently.)

Decide if you're a morning or a night person.

- "Some people are so fond of activity . . . they must always be doing something. Others resent jobs like dusting, cooking and washing dishes which have to be done over and over again." (If you're the latter type, try to get rid of as many routine chores as you can or do them as seldom as possible.)
- "Try to remove causes of pressure or tension. Some people think they like pressure. They let the work pile up . . . like to do it at top speed. But usually tension is not a good taskmaster." (The panic approach is OK if you want to work this way but it makes it tough to get help from others. Kids, in particular, get balky if they feel pressured.)
- "Some people like to work in the morning. They want to get up early and get everything done fast. Others do best at night." (Try to decide whether you're a morning or night person and adjust your schedule correspondingly. A job that starts at 9:00 or 10:00 a.m. gives a morning type the time to get housework done before work. Evening types can learn to live happily with a schedule that sends them crashing out of the house mornings with nothing done, but includes pickup time when they get home.

There's one other important point about energy and its opposite: you may feel fatigued all the time when really you're bored. This can be a vicious trap because the less you do the more bored you become and the more fatigue you feel. Two questionnaire respondents clearly describe this boredom fatigue. One Minneapolis mother with a 9-year-old son finds that planning for and scheduling a good evening out (including finding a babysitter) "is more bother than it's worth. So I usually stay home." Another mother of two, from Michigan, says that she rarely plans activities for herself on weekends "although I know I should begin doing so. While working I find I'm just plain tired . . . Weekends are spent preparing for the week. Sundays I just like to stay home."

I suspect that this syndrome is one reason Dr. Roy Kern so strongly urges us to get out of the house even if we don't feel like going. And it's certainly the best possible reason for making sure that some part of each weekend is set aside for fun—for both you and the kids.

No one can work all the time without paying a price for it. I learned that several summers ago when I doubled up a six-day-a-week job at a local summer theater while also working as a housekeeper four mornings a week. On double days, I worked from 8:00 a.m. to noon in the town of Southampton, then raced 16 miles to East Hampton town to be at the theater by 1:00. Often I didn't leave until midnight. Weekends I researched and wrote articles for a local magazine (which was supposed to be my "fun"). It was like banging your head against a cement wall because it feels so good when you stop. I came out of it a robot. It took two days of bed rest and loafing before I was humanized enough to recognize that I'd done this to myself—by overestimating my limits. While it was going on I was too tired to quit!

Even if you're a naturally revved-up type, you have limits. One young mother at a seminar on time management admitted she knows "I'm cramming in too much. There isn't anything I want to cut out, however." Well—there are ways to learn how and how to benefit from doing so.

Learning to Let Go: It's Simpler Than You Think

One mother from Erie, Pennsylvania with sons 3 and 6, sums up the whole process for us: "I have *had* to learn that things have priorities. Sometimes reading is more important than finishing the dishes. Actually, letting go of household duties for time with the kids, extra rest and recreation has been the hardest to learn but it's worth it." The technique is really based on developing these two abilities:

- Learn how to set priorities.
- Learn how to say "no".

Setting Priorities

I mentioned Alan Lakein's book *How to Get Control of Your Time and Your Life* earlier, in regard to deciding how much sleep you really need. He also gives some valuable tips on setting priorities. Start by making a list of what you want to do, he suggests. Then label each item with an A, B or C in order of importance. It's the A's you want to concentrate on. The list of B's and C's can go into a drawer to do "whenever." Some may never get done, which means they really weren't that important to *you* anyway. This kind of listing forces you to find the highs (A) and the lows (B and C) in your activities instead of just running along a never-ending plateau of chores. How do you decide what's an A? One rule of thumb is to ask yourself, "What will it do for *me*?" Will it make me healthier, happier, wealthier or wiser? If the answer is "no"—scrap it!

Keep a To Do list and cross off as you go along.

Lakein also suggests keeping a To Do list for each day and crossing off as you go along. Very satisfying! Other time-conscious experts suggest that you write down your To Do list and then number each item in order of importance. Start with #1 first, and go through the list as far as you can. You may not get everything done, but you will have accomplished the most important items.

Personally, I divide planning into This Week and Today. I start with This Week, list everything I want to or have to do, and decide which are A's. Then I develop a daily To Do list from that. The weekly list keeps me from getting bogged down in spur-of-the-moment daily To Do's.

Saying "No"

Learning how to say "no" is obviously part of assigning priorities. Hopefully, you've already decided there are limits to your time and energy. So whenever you choose to do one thing you are making a parallel decision *not to do* something else. Dr. L.W. Osher suggests that often we don't say "no" because we believe that we will feel badly about doing so. "It's easier to change what you *do* than what you *feel*" he explains. He has a formula to help you say "no" based on Empathy (letting the other person know that you understand their feelings), Conflict (letting the other person know how *you* feel) and Action (saying "no"). Suppose your kids want you to drive them to the movies and you want to sit at home and finish a book. Here's Osher's formula in action:

Empathy	Conflict	Action
I understand that it would be fun for you if I drive you to the movies.	But I really want to stay home and finish reading my book.	So I'm going to say "no, I won't drive you to the movies."

You've shown them that you understand their point of view but that you have a different way of looking at it, and so the answer is "no." Understand, you haven't knocked out the possibility of the movies. They're free to go if they can find some other way of getting there.

Dr. Osher also makes another point. When you consistently put other people's needs ahead of your own, you're simply training them to take advantage of you. Every time you say "yes" to a request, you're making it easier for them to ask again. And pretty soon asking passes from request to expectation. Sure—you'll always drive the kids to the movies, or you'll always stay overtime on the job, or you'll always sell chances for the school fair. If you really want to say "yes" each time, do so by all means. Otherwise, say "no." And if it's something you *never* want to do, keep saying "no." Eventually, people get the picture and quit asking.

Housework Simplifiers

Realistically, the most difficult demands on your time, energy, economics and emotions are home-grown. Even if you dislike your job, that regular paycheck makes up for a lot. It's the routine of meals, marketing, cleaning, running errands and meshing your kids' activities with your own—the basic stuff of which days are made—that hurts. So it pays to learn how to operate as efficiently as possible. The keys are to *simplify* and *share the work*.

I'm a great believer in asking those who've been there. In the questionnaires that I mailed out to 500 single parents, I asked how they handled marketing, meals, laundry and housecleaning. And the suggestions were great. I'll pass them on, along with some additional hints from home economists, for anyone who's looking for help in this area (and who isn't).

Marketing—the less the better. Most respondents said they did their food buying once a week or even less. (If they handle this the same way I do, they go to the supermarket once a week, and possibly make a mid-week quickie trip to fill in on milk, juice, bread. If you have a decent-sized freezer area in your refrigerator, you can even get by without the fill-in trip.) Some who answered the questionnaire said they were able to market every two weeks, and a few, including one father from Connecticut who has custody of his two daughters, were able to get by with marketing once a month. Most also suggested written shopping lists and menus. "Do 1 BIG shopping list for about 3 or 4 weeks and just fill in on milk, bread, etc." You'll save marketing and meal-making time, too, because you "always know what to cook ahead of time."

One mother from Kentucky, whose five children range from a 16-year-old son to a boy 7, also advises using a small hand calculator as you shop so you can make sure to stay within your budget. There are $1 versions of these available in stationery stores and I have found that they're useful, particularly if you're doing a lot of shopping all at once. Even with a list, you can get carried away.

One New Jersey mother regularly shops at 6:00 p.m. when other people are eating dinner. And one mother with young children makes sure she has a supply of "storables" (canned and packaged foods) to cover times "when the kids are sick or the weather's bad."

One of the most interesting suggestions came from Florida, from a university staff assistant who wrote that she supplemented grocery shopping by being a member of a cooperative garden. A lot of single parents are too busy to take on

Simplify your tasks and share the work.

gardening chores but if you *can* team up with someone else (maybe swap seed and supply money for work), you'll be putting garden vegetables on your table!

Cook-ahead: the favorite mealtime shortcut. A lot of single parents have discovered the efficiency of cooking ahead. But their systems vary. Suggestions include:

- Cook double batches and freeze half.
- Cook a week's worth of main dishes at one time and reheat to serve.
- Make oven dinners (roasts with vegetables or meat-and-vegetable casseroles). With some extra planning you can cook two or three of these meals in the oven together and then reheat.

One single parent who manages an optical studio in Kansas and runs her own dressmaking business on the side, takes one evening a week to prepare main dishes, and the whole family pitches in. "My sons [ages 12 and 14] seem to enjoy this evening together." Many other parents indicated that they cook ahead on weekends. Slow cookers and microwave ovens were also frequently mentioned as work and timesavers. And some parents have really cut the cooking down to a minimum by using "instants" or frozen foods, by eating out frequently with the children or by "picking up something on the way home."

Learn to cook ahead: it can be a great timesaver.

Food and freezer hints from the experts. Check over the following suggestions from home economists for additional ways to cut marketing and food-preparation time.

- Type up a general shopping list covering all the items you normally buy. Include brand names and sizes wherever they apply. Then run off a batch of photocopies. When it's time to make your week's shopping list, just check off the items you need. Use another copy each week to jot down items you're low on or have run out of.
- Keep a list of what's in your freezer and keep it up to date. Plan a couple of "from the freezer" meals every few months to use up items that have been in there awhile.
- If plans change and you don't cook fresh meats or vegetables the night you'd intended to, freeze them instead. You can always defrost them later, but once spoiled they're irretrievable.
- Learn to package dinners by grouping foods you're going to serve together in one plastic bag before freezing. You'll save on "here's the chicken but where are the green peas" hunts through the freezer.
- Apply this same logic to party meals. Develop one or two favorite menus and group-freeze the makings (in quantities for four or six). You're sure to have what you need when cooking time arrives.

Experts recommend kitchen work centers. Lillian Gilbreth and her co-authors of *Management in the Home* suggest adapting an "efficiency expert" technique to your kitchen. Try to develop these three work centers in your kitchen: a sink center, a stove center and a mix center. The method? Group together the utensils and the foods used in specific operations.

- *For the sink center:* The idea is to group together all the materials that involve water. Try to store some cooking pots, strainers, paring knives, measuring cups and dishwashing materials near your sink. Store vegetables like potatoes and onions, dried beans and peas (all have to be washed) and canned soups that need to be diluted at the same center. Also, keep a garbage pail or bag nearby.

- *For the stove center:* Here you'll need frying pans, griddles, lids, stirring spoons and several pots. Cereals, pasta, canned vegetables and other foods you pour directly into pots could be stored nearby, plus spices and shakers of salt, sugar and flour. (Store coffee and coffeepot at either the sink or stove center, depending on your coffee making method.)

- *For the mix center:* Ideally, this should include a clutter-free counter top. Meat loaves, pies and cakes, salads, etc. are put together here, so you need measuring cups and spoons, stirring spoons, bowls and electrical appliances like blenders and mixers. Also store flour, sugar, salt, baking powder, prepared mixes, oil, vinegar and salad seasonings here.

If your stove and mix center are side by side, one set of shelves and/or pegboard hooks can serve both. Gilbreth suggests duplicates of measuring cups, measuring spoons and other small utensils if they're used in more than one place. One housewife clocked off five miles a day on a pedometer in a poorly arranged kitchen!

Tips on buying kitchen equipment. If you're just setting up on your own, here are some more *Management in the Home* tips to help you choose pots, pans and other equipment wisely. Invest in:

- Pans and lids with heat-resistant handles
- Lids that fit pans
- Tongs and a long-handled fork (to avoid burned fingers)
- Casserole dishes you can cook, serve and store in
- A utility tray for carrying a lot of little things in one trip

Always check pots and pans to see if the cup or quart capacity is marked on them. Many recipes suggest a specific size pot and if you're a beginner cook it doesn't pay to guess.

Laundry: once a week or every night, but ironing never! One mother of four sums this matter up about as well as it can be: "Discard all items not wash-and-wear and throw out ironing board." I couldn't agree more. Hugh James, the full-custody father who found his kids loved the simplified furnishings and routines he worked out, states it just as succinctly: "I never iron!" Both quotes sum up the general attitude of the single parents who answered my questionnaire.

When it came to laundry, however, schedules differed. Some do it once a week, others every day, still others as the need arises. Size of family has something to do with it. One practical mother who's on the once-a-week routine adds that this schedule does mean more clothes for each member of the family.

Four interesting solutions to doing laundry at home were these:

- One mother with a 2-year-old son does laundry on weekends when her son is "visiting his dad."

Buy only wash-and-wear clothes. And get rid of the ironing board.

- A mother from Mastic, Long Island, says, "throw clothes into the washer at night, transfer them to the dryer the next morning and fold when I get home from work."
- A mother of teenagers, from Baton Rouge, says that each member of the family "must wash our *own* clothes plus other clothing if there's room in the machine. My boys have the most laundry but less than if I did it for them."
- One mother of three says that "Instead of gathering up all the laundry around the house, I announce that I will be washing and if anyone has anything they want washed they must bring it downstairs. Don't worry if everything doesn't get washed."

Several parents—both men and women—stated that they used launderettes regularly. One mother with a large family mentioned that although she owns her own washer and dryer, she switched to the launderette when she went back to work. "I could do the whole load at once, using several machines at the same time, rather than separate loads at home." Another parent also made the point that using a launderette kept her from doing a lot of little loads. With utility bills soaring, we might all think over the number of wash loads we do. And we should also think about cutting down on dryer time, which is the real bill booster.

Laundry tips from the experts. A book called *Betty Crocker's Starting Out* offers the following helpful laundry advice:

If you own your own washer/dryer:

- Use your washing machine for drip-dry items instead of washing them by hand. Just run them through the washer the normal way but stop the cycle before the final spin. Use a plastic pail or dishpan to carry these laundry items from the washer to a spot where you can hang them up dripping wet. The shower rod above your bathtub is a good drying spot.
- For heavy-duty laundry (clothing or other items that are badly stained), follow this procedure: turn on your washer and let it fill with water. Add detergent and bleach and let the machine run for a few seconds until soap and bleach are thoroughly mixed through the water. Add the soiled items and let them swish around for a few seconds. Then stop the cycle and let those items soak according to the directions on the bleach package. Then restart the machine and let it run through a normal cycle. You can do this in lieu of a soak cycle, which may not be long enough to remove really stubborn stains.
- Hang up permanent-press clothing as soon as it comes out of the dryer. This is easier to do if you keep a batch of hangers near your dryer. You can sort and hang clothes right out of the dryer.
- With sturdy paper shopping bags, one for each member of the family near the dryer, you can sort and fold small items like socks, underwear and sweaters and drop them straight into the bags. Provide an extra bag for towels, washcloths, sheets and pillow cases. Your kids can live right out of their paper bags or stick the stuff in bureau drawers. Draw straws to see who unloads the sheets and towels. (My advice: cheat a little.)

If you use a launderette:

- Buy a small-size shopping cart and liner. It's the best way to truck laundry around on foot.

- If you travel to the laundry by car, invest in one or more plastic laundry baskets. They fit neatly onto auto seats, and laundered clothing can be folded into them at the launderette.

- Make the most of the folding counters, and bring hangers for shirts and dresses—the more you bring, the fewer wrinkles you'll have!

- Use the same paper-shopping-bag routine (mentioned above for at-home machines) to sort small items like socks and underwear straight from the dryer, without folding.

Housecleaning: Swiss cheese it.

Housecleaning advice from other single parents. Some single parents express themselves very strongly on this topic. Answers on the questionnaire included: "Ignore it as long as possible" from a mother in Wisconsin; "Let the dust gather but go to discussions and meetings with singles" from another in Staten Island, New York; "People are more important than vacuuming, *any day!*" from Kenai, Alaska; and a father who's had custody of his daughter for nine years summed up the whole routine as "Work your ass off!" Another father from Colorado, who has an "open" visiting arrangement for his 8-year-old son, wrote, "Just don't procrastinate." As a dedicated procrastinator, I agree. I've learned that no matter how much or how little housework you do, get at it, learn to live with it and don't agonize.

Many who answered the questionnaire had obviously worked out an approach that Alan Lakein calls "swiss cheesing it." They take a big job and nibble small holes in it. Some, like one mother from Warren, Ohio, set up special days for things. She does "laundry on Wednesdays, waxing floors every 3rd or 4th Saturday." Another, from Kings Point, New York, tries to "get one special job (like cleaning the oven or bathroom) done every day." Another, from Largo, Florida, cleans "part of the house every weekend—not the whole house." Many find that a series of little pickups and wipe-ups will take the place of heavy cleaning, or at least reduce it to an occasional job. One or two, however, take the blitz approach and use a Saturday to clean thoroughly.

Some parents have made the decision to use hired help. And they feel that any dollar sacrifice is worth it. "The *best* thing I ever did was hiring a cleaning person for half a day per week. What a load off my mind." Another mentions that she had used a cleaning service before her divorce and by dint of scrimping everywhere "kept that cleaning service!" But even with cleaning help, one Maryland mother finds that "Clutter rules. So—who cares. When the children no longer live here I'll have neatness." The most creative solution to the whole problem comes from a New Jersey mother of three who suggests: "When the house gets really dirty, leave the vacuum out. If someone drops by they may think you were at least planning to clean and maybe one of the kids will do it."

Cleaning hints from the experts. Since everyone's attitude toward cleaning is so personal and since, judging from the questionnaires, most single parents have come to terms with it, I'll just pass on a few time- and energy-saving tips:

- Make a couple of dusting mitts from old toweling and leave one in each room where dusting will be done. They really are easier to manipulate than dustcloths.

- Put your vacuum to work for you. This means vacuuming kitchen and bathroom floors before you wash up. In fact, you usually don't have to wash up at all once you've sucked up dust, crumbs and hair.

- Park a dump basket in the living room, family room or wherever clutter tends to accumulate. Throw everything into it that doesn't belong in that room when you have to do a fast emergency cleanup. You can always sort out later. Some things will never get out of the basket, which means nobody needs them very much anyway.

- If you have young children, provide a smaller carrying basket so they can remove some of their clutter themselves. I made up a jingle for this—"a tisket a tasket, pop it in the basket"— which can get to be so much fun that your 3-year-old may trot back and forth tisketing and tasketing for a good hour at a time.

- In every household, there's usually one surface somewhere near the front door that acts as a catchall for mail, car keys and the like. Stick a couple of small baskets on top of it (one for mail, one for miscellaneous), and at least you'll know where to look for the stuff.

Children's rooms. The only real answer is to have them marry and move out. While you're waiting, here are a few suggestions:

- Forget closets. No child has ever been known to use one, except for the closet floor. Put up a row of large hooks on one wall for clothes, plus some low, open shelves for underwear, socks, etc.

- Provide more low, open shelves for toys and games. The more shelves, the better.

- For some reason, children of all ages love to bring food into their rooms. So either lay down a flat rule "no" and stick to it, or be prepared by setting up one corner of the room as an "eating area." Put a large square of cheap linoleum on the floor to define the area; if you can, provide a child-sized table and chairs and a small portable TV. It will help somewhat.

- Ask your local liquor store to save you some corrugated boxes. Turn them on one side so the top acts as a flapped door and announce that these are garages for toy trucks and cars, houses for dolls and stuffed animals. If you really get into it, you can draw a funny face on one and explain that that's the Junk Eater.

Teenage rooms. Suddenly, marriage doesn't seem like the answer. I'm not sure there really is one. I've tried introducing a 30-gallon size garbage pail with a 3-mil plastic-bag liner. But I've discovered that mine stashes the filled bag in the closet. He also uses it as a laundry receptable although I've also provided one of those. Dirty socks and empty beer bottles make a combination you soon become aware of. I've probably raised him all wrong, but then maybe I'm working on the guilt trip (see page 150).

Other Simplifiers

The combination of divided income plus inflation can make a lot of choices *for* single parents. For some of us, it means cutting down on personal pleasures like eating out or buying clothes. It can also mean overhauling the household-running budget in very basic ways. One mother from Charlotte, North Carolina, sums up these changes this way: "I no longer eat out (except on dates). I look for the best bargain in clothes—budget basement stuff. I don't use the air conditioner and don't keep the house as warm in winter. I only purchase what is necessary." A secretary from Largo, Florida, says that "inflation is my worst enemy." One mother who has three children and is a cost analyst in New York State says that she has simplified in "every way, from shopping to use of electrical appliances, food, clothing and how I pay my bills. I'm constantly shuffling things around to make ends meet."

Divorced fathers also feel the pinch. One real estate and mortgage broker from Toronto, Canada, mentions "not being able to save any money" as well as "not being able to replace the same quality of furniture and not being able to drive a better car." A general manager for a building materials distributor mentions having to give up his garage workshop, as well as having to curtail business and social activities to care for his apartment and four sons. Another father, a construction worker who has custody of his daughter, mentions the problem of not being able to take out-of-town jobs.

> **"The only demands on us are those we impose on ourselves."**

Sometimes, simplifying results from physical plus financial limitations. Many women who become heads of households find yard work and house maintenance a problem. Some solve the problem by moving—into condominiums, townhouses or mobile homes. Others do the work themselves or share it with older children. Many of my questionnaires mention arrangements like "my son mows the backyard, I mow the front." Or "the older kids do the outside work and take out the garbage." One widow with grown children mentions that her daughter visits frequently but her son rarely does because "he's afraid I'll have chores for him to do." One mother that I talked to at a Parents Without Partners conference mentioned that she had decided against moving into a condominium because the overhead included $137 per month for outside upkeep. She figured it would be better to put that same amount of money into yardwork for the house she owned. "But, I don't," she added; other expenses have a way of eating into maintenance money.

Singlehood sometimes simplifies emotional drains. One Colorado mother thinks that "Our life has been simplified in that ... there are no demands on us other than those we impose on ourselves. There is no one person who thinks that our life should evolve around him/her. There is no one to DEMAND." Another mother from upstate New York, who splits custody of her children with her remarried husband, says: "I used to worry about things I had no control over. Now I take care of today. My children and I spend more time together now, since my income is so limited." And, finally: "I don't live in fear anymore (I was a battered wife). I don't *have* to cook a big meal every night, and I can come and go whenever I want."

Simplifying Should Involve the Kids

Most of the simplifying I've mentioned above happens to us, the parents. There are also simplifications of lifestyle that happen because we make rational choices, that involve the kids. Decisions to "make meals more informal," to "dress more casually"—even decisions to "spend less time with my children"—are all practical solutions that many single parents have evolved as a way of dealing with the fixed versus flexible time seesaw. But sometimes we're better at simplifying our own schedules than those of our children.

We and our children, together, must recognize the necessary changes in lifestyle that result from the pressures on our time, economics and emotions. And this applies to the parent who does not have the day-in, day-out care of the children as well as the one who does. Both are readjusting to households where there is no one else to take over when there's a down day or actual illness. Often, both share the trauma of "visitation," although from opposite sides of the fence. For many men, coping with everyday housekeeping means learning new skills they have been conditioned to think of as "unnatural" for them. And for many women it means entering or returning to the full-time job market. Few single parents want to cut their children out of activities that are valuable or meaningful. But sometimes it is impossible to maintain the previous after-school and weekend schedule that your children have been used to. Here, honesty is the best policy.

Eleanore Berman, who authored the book *The Cooperating Family—How Your Children Can Help Manage the Household*, deals with this very specifically. When she was first divorced she was "determined that divorce would change day-to-day life as little as possible for the children. If anything, I planned now to spend more time with them and take even better care of them, since I would be their only full-time parent." Among other changes that occurred when she became a full-time working mother, "the children took a hard look at what they were doing with their time after school to decide what was important to them ... Some of the things they turned out to care least about were things they were doing at my urging. We found a way to manage things that really mattered."

Here are some of the solutions that Eleanore Berman found for that unending round of activities that can occupy our kids' and our own time:

- The school located a new clarinet teacher for her son, one who was willing to come to her home to give lessons. (Substitute any other special lessons for "clarinet.")
- For school plays and team practice sessions, she offered to do the driving to evening activities if other mothers would cover days. "It worked."
- She cut out the kids' after-school visits to friends who lived miles away unless the other mother wanted to do the driving.
- She gave her teenage son use of the car for specified hours if he would do the Saturday marketing and some of the other Saturday chore driving.

Her children didn't resent the changes. In fact, "I learned that my children were capable of far more responsibility than I had ever thought of giving them ... they seemed to feel good about it. We all seem to like each other more now."

Habit, guilt, a desire to outdo the other parent or sheer panic over "what to do with them when they come visiting" can turn life into a three-ring circus for our kids. In his book *Creative Divorce*, Mel Krantzler describes one father who "turned off the Disneyland Daddy ... and found the alternative much more satisfying." Krantzler quotes this father as saying "... after six months of movies, ball games and restaurants I could see that they were cranky and bored all the time ... So the next weekend we just cooled it." Separated parents or the loss of one parent isn't exactly fun for any kid. Both mean a lot of emotional upheaval and often a complete change in routine for children. What they really need (and so do the parents) is a chance to settle down and find out that life can and will go on. And the only way anybody finds that out is through a lot of bread-and-butter living, not through a constant diet of cake.

Share the work?
You bet.

Ask almost any single parent "Do you think kids should share the work at home?" and you'll get a resounding "Yes." But putting that into practice is something else again. We're anxious to keep our children as untouched as possible by death or divorce. And we have a way of translating this into an eternal play situation for them. Single Mom or Single Dad staggers through the living room with a load of laundry big enough to buckle the strongest knees—and three kids' eyes never leave the television screen. Or a single parent who works eight hours a day and handles the cooking and laundry at night takes precious weekend hours to clean up after youngsters who flow through the house like high tide, leaving their debris behind. Why do some adults put up with this? Because they've brainwashed themselves into believing that somehow their work will make up to the kids for the other "failure." They're wearing a hair shirt down to their knees and what kid is crazy enough to share the penance?

I'm exaggerating, of course, but not by much. In their book *The Courage to Divorce*, Susan Gettleman and Janet Markowitz, both practicing clinical social workers, state that "as much as the realities of divorce create a greater need for all family members to pitch in with household tasks, some custodial parents shrink from imposing these on their children." They back up their statement with a case history from their own files:

> Emily, aged twelve ... After her parents announced their intention to divorce, her mother immediately took over Emily's chores, which at the time included making her own bed and helping with the supper dishes. When Emily's mother went back to work she found herself resenting her daughter, who by this time did not participate in any household chores.

At the 1979 Parents Without Partners convention in Atlanta, L.W. Osher laid it on the line just as clearly. He told members of his time management workshop that survival lay in *setting priorities* and in *eliciting help from the kids*. He also stressed that in setting priorities, our first obligations are to ourselves and our children. But within the parent-child relationship a balance is needed. As he put it, "not the kids all the time and not you all the time." And that, as far as he's concerned, means that even young children should have responsibilities within the home.

Setting priorities +
getting help from
the kids = survival.

I asked Regina Rector, Extension Associate in the Department of Design and Environmental Analysis at the New York State College of Human Ecology at Cornell University, for her suggestions about involving children in managing a single-parent household. Her advice on *attitudes* toward work-sharing are important. She makes these two points:

> Even young children can perform simple tasks. It makes them feel important. Let each person know that you *depend* on him/her to care for his or her own

possessions and to put them away when play or project is completed. Show appreciation for what is done.

Don't complain about or show distaste for household duties because children will reflect your attitude. Cleaning will be satisfying if you stand back and admire the results.

And, finally, here's some hardheaded advice from Eleanore Berman, a divorced mother with a full-time and demanding job. She created a completely cooperative family arrangement and believes that "however much children may complain about duties at home, in the long run the child who learns to give as well as take feels better about himself and, eventually, about his parents." Her oldest son Tom, now 18, seems to agree. When asked to write up his opinion of the cooperative experiment, he came up with: "If a child is to learn to make his own decisions, gain responsibility, and respect himself, his parents must treat him like an adult—within reason, of course. That means expecting him to have obligations at home . . ." And for a clincher, Eleanore Berman quotes family expert Eda Leshan, author of *Natural Parenthood*: "Young people need opportunities to feel that they are helping and giving to others. When they have none of these experiences, they cannot discover their own strengths and durability . . . they cannot have the self-respect that comes with knowing you are a good person helping others."

Woman's work was never done—and it still isn't. Dr. Kathryn Walker's studies have done much to point up the awesome load carried by whoever earns a living while functioning as "the houseperson." In her studies this slavey was always a woman, but of course single-parent situations are changing. The work hours aren't, though. Cast an eye over these "time bombs" culled from her article in the October 1973 *Journal of Home Economics* (adapted from a paper she read at the American Home Economics Association's Annual 1973 Meeting):

- The technology of the seventies has not given us more leisure time.
- Fifty years ago the length of a woman's work week was found to be between 42 and 49 hours long.
- Today, employed women work a 66 to 75 hour week at combined job and household duties. This includes care of family members.
- Today's employed woman averages four to eight hours daily on household work (again including family care).

"Where," Dr. Walker asks, "is the leisure society we are brainwashed to believe we have?" She concludes, in an article written for *Human Ecology Forum* (Autumn 1970): "Since many women [we might substitute "housepersons"] work to provide for the needs and desires of their families, it seems regrettable that the family members for whom mothers [housepersons] work do not recognize the length of their . . . work day and share more actively the family's work load."

How much help can children give? "Much more than you might expect" is the experts' answer. Dr. Osher lists the following "possibles" for young children:

Children can provide more help than you might expect.

- Get themselves up via their own alarm clock. (Let them hate the clock, not you!)
- Dress themselves.
- Make their own school lunches (the night before).

Furthermore, he suggests that when a child does not cooperate, you let the punishment fit the crime. Example: if Ellen doesn't fix her school lunch, Ellen goes off without it. If Andy doesn't set the table when that's his job, he doesn't eat at the table—there's just no place for him, right? The child is learning the logical consequences of actions. If you constantly shield your kids from consequences (by making sandwiches for them when they won't), they'll never learn.

Eleanore Berman found that her sons Tom and Eric, ages 15 and 13, and her 10-year-old daughter Terry could handle all the weekday cooking for the family, plan out the menus, help with the marketing, make their own school lunches and look after themselves without benefit of baby sitter while she was at work. Certainly her experiences help create an alternative to Dr. Walker's question in the February 1975 issue of the *American Vocational Journal:* "Why do parents often assign to children the most menial and uninteresting tasks?" It's obvious that some children, anyway, can acquire "adult" talents, like cooking, at quite an early age.

Here are some Berman Basics of Success for setting up a cooperative family:

- Make it clear that this is the way it's going to be and why.
- Let the kids choose, swap and share jobs.
- Make them completely responsible for whatever they take on. Don't "sidewalk superintend."
- Praise and be appreciative. Don't get guilty or fearful.
- Stay flexible.

How do we stack up as cooperative families? Since we, as single parents, have the greatest need to develop workable cooperative arrangements with our children, I've discussed this question via conversation, questionnaire and interview with literally hundreds of other single parents. Many feel they've worked out very good arrangements: "They [three daughters aged 17, 14 and 7] are just as capable as I am." Some frankly state that their kids don't cooperate: "I try but they fight me every step of the way," one mother of two sons, 14 and 17, wrote in. Others feel it's so-so. Many more feel it's a good situation than feel it's a bad one, however.

How do these answers stack up against expert studies? Recent Cornell studies give us an interesting look at how much time some kids in the U.S. are putting in at home, and how they're spending that time. The figures, for all types of housework plus maintenance of home, yard, car and pets, break out this way:

| | TIME SPENT PER DAY | |
Age	Girls	Boys
6 to 8	48 minutes	42 minutes
9 to 11	1 hour	54 minutes
12 to 14	1 hour: 54 minutes	1 hour:20 minutes
15 to 17	1 hour: 18 minutes	1 hour:20 minutes

The study also showed that, in general, jobs were not sex-stereotyped. Both boys and girls put in about the same amount of time in food preparation, shopping and housecleaning—except that, from ages 9 to 17, girls put in more time dishwashing while boys did almost none at all. So, except for those dishes, we're making progress!

Single parents share some ways-and-means ideas. The questionnaire I sent out brought in very interesting descriptions of how some single parents are sharing the work load with their children. As a single parent myself, I appreciate the time and trouble they took to answer the questions in detail—just wait till my own kid walks in that door!

Two mothers of young children are obviously headed in the right direction. One with boys aged 6 and 3 writes that "The kids are so young their ability is limited, but the 6-year-old helps out when he is able. His one chore is to make his bed. Even the 3-year-old knows he must pick up toys, put dirty clothes in the hamper." The other mother, who has a son 5 and a 10-month-old daughter says: "It's my son's responsibility to pick up his toys, make sure his clothes are in the hamper, his shoes in the right place. We make a game of chores. He brings the wastebaskets together at garbage time. He also helps keep the baby busy when I'm housecleaning."

Parents with older children explained various ways they're working it. Here's sampling that sums up a variety of approaches:

Your *can* have some time for yourself each day.

- *Two sons 14 and 16:* "Each has 2 chores a day. If not done I don't deliver *them* anywhere 'til finished. Next two chores added to next day. Eventually they need a ride."

- *A son 13 and daughters 11 and 9:* "I don't 'owe' my kids a clean house. All have assigned chores with lots of flexibility. If all but one agree on a simple supper, the one who wants a big meal cooks for all. All three kids know how to cook."

- *Three sons ages 18, 16 and 14:* "They live here, they pitch in. I think it's easier if you play it by ear. If routine works, fine. If rules need to be broken, also fine. Flexibility is the key. My guys are better and more supportive than many I've seen."

- *Two daughters 20 and 25:* "When I was young I was continually on call to do chores. It's much more fair to divide them. I always let my kids choose what they preferred to do and then set a deadline. But there is no reason you can't be flexible. The drawback to this method is that they never developed the habit of pitching in in an emergency."

- *Five children, ages 7 through 16:* "Have a list posted on wall. Each child knows what his jobs are and when they are done special favors are granted. Doesn't always work, but helps remind each one they have a share in keeping the work done."

- *Two sons 12 and 14:* "One evening set aside for domestic chores. Everyone helps and we don't stop until completed. Each individual has own assignment each time. Assignments change each time."

- *Nine children from 11 to 21:* "We have always had certain jobs in the house that each of the kids was responsible for. As they get older or master the job they get moved to something more responsible. But as the kids get older they work outside of the home. So the younger ones are carrying most of the load."

From those who feel it's not working:

- *Two sons 12 and 9:* "They help me if it's requested. No—I don't feel they're doing their share of the work but that's because I have not developed and enforced a system."
- *Four children 17 through 31:* "No—but I guess I never required it of them."
- *Three children 24 through 28:* "Some of the fault was mine. I couldn't always wait for them to get around to doing it."

Being a single parent puts a lot of "musts" into each day. But if you learn to budget your time, sort out the real musts from the not-so-real and recognize the fact that you have a right to ask for help and cooperation from your kids, you can still end up with some time for yourself each day. Start right now by sitting down and telling yourself firmly, "I *can't* do it all—all by myself. But I *can* get on top of what I really have to do and want to do!"

3/Making Money Easier

Money! Mention the word and everybody sounds off—former wives and husbands (divorced and widowed), lawyers who represent divorcing clients, women's lib, men's lib and financial experts. But sounding off leads to constructive suggestions about how we can handle money more rewardingly.

Obviously, a lot of the emotion single parents feel stems from which side of the fence they were born on. The traditional male attitude toward divorce sees husbands bled white by parasitic wives, scheming lawyers and unsympathetic judges who have joined in a plot to make marriage a never-ending meal ticket for women. One recently divorced father of four answered "Too much!" to the question "Do you feel your payments are large enough in terms of today's living costs?" and then added, "Why should a husband have to pay anything if it's the wife's choice to separate?" Women, on the other hand, are supposed to feel that they are at the mercy of male judges who allow former husbands to shirk obligations, leaving the wife to bring up children on support payments that are pittances, if paid at all. "He made a commitment to me and, by fathering the children, to them. After 3½ years he ran for no apparent reason and left me with two babies. I have had the entire responsibility for 7½ years and I'd like to see him pay it all till the youngest is 16.

Society also has its viewpoint: all single-parent homes are financially distressed, requiring help from social services—a drain on the economy.

All three viewpoints have validity. Certainly there are situations where a man forks over a ruinously large proportion of his income to a wife who refuses to share any financial responsibilities. There are also cases of upper-income men who will not make any support payments at all, even when court ordered. A report called "Nonsupport of Legitimate Children by Affluent Fathers" (co-authored by Marian Winston of the Rand Corporation, and Trude Forsher) is quoted in *Money* magazine (December 1974) as saying that "a surprising number of divorced physicians and attorneys have children on welfare. The fathers are financially capable but unwilling to pay court-ordered support." And there *are* single-parent families that cannot make it without help from the outside. The largest single group of people on welfare in 1971 were the 10.6 million women and children on Aid to Families with Dependent Children (AFDC).

These viewpoints represent extremes, however. In many, many instances both sides of single-parent families are doing their best for their children. Fathers make regular support payments and mothers work to augment those payments. And the welfare figures, remember, include many individuals who were financially dependent (due to illness, lack of education and/or marketable skills) before they became single parents. This may stand as an indictment of our society but it can hardly be taken as criticism of single-parent households in general.

It's true that two households cost more than one to support. It's also true that women, on the average, earn just about half what men do. Nevertheless, the majority of single-parent families *are* making it financially, even where mothers are their sole support.

Connie Manfreda, President of Parents Without Partners, is one divorced mother who feels very strongly about the stereotype of financially dependent single-parent families. When I first spoke to her over the telephone about this book, she made the point that "Many of us have good incomes and are bringing up our kids in comfortable and stable homes." You'll hear more of her views about the real problems we face, the legislation we need, in a later chapter of this book.

Widowed families, as opposed to those in divorce situations, face very particular problems. Two obvious ones are the cost of replacing homemaker services when a wife dies, and the fact that our social security system can be very unfair to widows, particularly those with young children. Payments are really not large enough to support widowed families, yet, as one mother put it, "Over $3400, I have to give social security $1 for every $2 I earn." If child-care costs and other job expenses are added in, these women must decide if it actually pays to work!

Why Is Money Such an Emotional Issue?

The mother who's working her butt off to support three children is angry—with good reason. She's holding down two jobs that total up to 70 hours a week and earn her $10,000 a year. But a mother who's earning $16,000 a year and receiving support payments of $750 a month, with one college-age son, is just as angry. Why? Psychologists Herb Goldberg and Robert T. Lewis propose some answers in their book *Money Madness—The Psychology of Saving, Spending, Loving and Hating Money.* They believe that "success, money, and esteem are often interchangeable as values in our society," so "the need for power and respect then becomes a need for money." This helps explain why $10 a week given or taken in alimony or support payments can become a fight-to-the-death issue between two former mates. If either side sees that $10 as the difference between adequate food and clothing versus real lack, of course you battle. But it can also become a symbol for winning or losing, for feeling stronger or weaker than the other person, for feeling *worthier of respect* from others. "That Joan, she's not going to let anyone get the best of her!" Or, "Good old Harry, when he makes up his mind, you can't budge him!" The fact that Joan and Harry are wasting a lot of time and effort behaving like saber-toothed tigers escapes everyone, including themselves. How does it end? Joan gets into a depression (she's an oral type who substitutes money "for the breast or the bottle") and Harry gets constipated (he's anal and withholding money is his way of lashing back at traumatic toilet training). And both still see that $10 as the real issue!

The Real Issues

"The biggest block to a workable financial settlement is the inability of the splitting partners to realize that they cannot continue to live as they were." That's John Rome, a partner in the Boston law firm of Hutchins & Wheeler, speaking in an article entitled "Divorce: Make Sense, Not War" in the February 1973 issue of *Money* magazine. In December 1974, the First National City Bank of New York estimated that maintaining separate households drives up living costs by as much as 35% (again from an article in *Money* magazine). Given today's rate of inflation, that would be a very conservative estimate.

Freedom costs. That's the first reality single-parent budgets must deal with. When divorce is involved, the real issues then become: who pays what and how much, and how can both sides stretch those dollars as far as possible. The most important factors involved in these issues are the amount of money really available *and* the attitudes of both parties. One expert divorce lawyer I interviewed, Jack Zulack of the New York firm of Flemming, Zulack & Williamson, puts it this way: "There are only two insoluble problems in arriving at money agreements—when there's just not enough money to begin with and when one or both parties enjoy litigation."

> Learn to separate the real from the emotional issues.

How much money is enough? U.S. Department of Commerce (Bureau of the Census) statistics for 1977 peg the poverty line at $4,833 per year for a non-farm family of three persons, up to $10,216 per year for a non-farm family of seven or more. Obviously, any sharing of this level of income (unless it's supplemented by additional earnings and/or welfare payments) is going to leave both sides financially helpless. If you take away 35% to 50% (which some experts figure as the norm for settlements made to mothers with young children) from a $10,000-a-year salary, you're leaving one side well below the poverty line (at 35%) and both sides perilously close to it (at 50%). Furthermore, Bureau of the Census figures show that there are over 22 million working wives in the United States. While some may work for self-satisfaction alone, many more obviously feel the family budget needs help, which their earnings supply. All this adds up to the fact that unless a father is in the upper-third financial bracket, a singled mother of a household is going to have to supplement support payments with a salary of her own.

Money-Related Facts—From Both Sides

Some of these relate to the man's position, some to the woman's. It's a case of putting yourself in the other person's shoes and realizing how the situation looks standing "over there."

Single fathers must face these facts:

- Men's incomes generally rise in the years after the separation; women's usually don't. In our society, women tend to get stuck in dead-end jobs. They are also stuck with the rising rate of inflation, which takes the biggest bite out of smaller salaries.

- Children become more expensive to support as they become school age and grow into their teens. They eat more, their clothes cost more, they become involved in activities and social occasions that cost money. Some of this added expense they can earn themselves. But not all of it.

- Housewives are not paid for the work they do within the home. One cold, hard result of this is the fact that full-time housewives don't pay into social security; so when they do start earning a salary, they're way behind in accrued benefits. And except in community-property states, where everything earned by either partner in a marriage is owned jointly by both, the work they have contributed toward enlarging the dollar value of family assets (for example, decorating the house, or running the household on a budget that leaves money free for savings or investment) is not legally recognized. It should be!

- If a marriage has lasted for a number of years and both partners have reached late forties or early fifties, the woman may be completely unprepared to earn a living outside the home. She needs time and training to become job equipped.

- Even if the woman has terminated the marriage (and this is the hardest to accept), the father still has an obligation to help support the children. Marriages dissolve because of mismatched needs. You may disagree with hers but it's madness to argue that she doesn't have them. (See the Needs Game in Chapter 1. It tells you something about your own needs, but it also indicates that others have theirs as well.)

Both sides should understand each other's needs and realities.

Single mothers must face these facts:

- Former husbands can't live on air. They pay for housing, food, clothes and incidentals just as you do. And initially, anyway, their lack of experience as housekeepers can make day-to-day living expensive.

- Quite practically, smaller support payments that are made regularly are more useful than larger amounts that go unpaid.

- Sharing family financial responsibilities isn't the end of the world. It can be an important step in the process of becoming a free and adult human being.

- Even if the man has terminated the marriage (and this is the hardest to accept), support payments aren't "punishment money." Marriages dissolve because of mismatched needs. You may disagree with his but it's madness to argue that he doesn't have them. (The Needs Game in Chapter 1 can tell you something about your own needs; it also indicates that others have theirs as well.)

If both sides can understand something about each other's needs and realities, both have a better chance of dealing more rewardingly with the money that *is* there.

New Trends: Problems and Solutions

Our society is changing rapidly, and the traditional ways of thinking about and handling money in single-parent situations is also changing. Included here are some thoughts and suggested solutions that represent these new trends.

Non-Payment of Support

Deeply concerned by statistics and reports that indicate that many women are forced onto the welfare rolls because support payments are being widely ignored by even those fathers able to pay them, MOMMA, *The Sourcebook for Single*

Mothers, quotes the same Winston-Forsher Study on non-support by affluent fathers mentioned earlier. MOMMA also cites census figures and reports dealing with this problem. Some women's groups have suggested that husbands be required to put a portion of their income in an escrow account to guarantee support payments if a divorce occurs. (See the last chapter of this book, which covers general new trends in single living, for even more specific forms of divorce insurance that have been suggested by women's rights groups.)

Many of the men's rights groups are equally concerned about fathers' non-payment of support. They make the point, however, that much of this can be explained by the traditional custody situation, which tends to give women the major responsibility for raising children and grants rather limited visitation rights to fathers. This causes some fathers to gradually lose interest and "fade away," as one psychologist puts it. Many men also feel that child support should be recognized as a shared responsibility right across the board. If a father has custody (and this is becoming increasingly common), the mother should contribute support if she is financially able to do so.

Money Compromises

Judges' attitudes are changing, too. There is an increasing tendency to award "maintenance money" instead of alimony. Maintenance money takes the form of payments given to wives for a specific, limited period of time, to tide her over while she equips herself to earn her own living.

Family counselors (and divorce lawyers, too) are beginning to suggest direct mediation between separating partners and between those who have already separated but are still warring over money arrangements. Here, both sides voluntarily sit down with a counselor or other trained mediator, and hack out compromise agreements. The Family Dispute division of the American Arbitration Association helps hundreds of individuals negotiate settlements each year. Bob Meade, the Association's New York Regional Director, points out that this process is usually much cheaper than a court battle. Also, both sides are more likely to honor these agreements because they're not imposed on them from the outside. The end result is that "nobody wins, but nobody loses, either."

How single parents feel about their money arrangements. Answers to the money questions in my questionnaire show that many single parents *are* aware of the difficulties involved for both sides. About 90% of the women answered "No" to the question "Do you feel your ex-partner *could* pay more?" When asked "Do you feel he should pay the entire amount needed to support you and the kids, if he could," most declared a very firm "No" and went on to explain that they felt willing and able to support themselves. They wanted fathers to share in the children's expenses only. Here's a cross-section of answers from women who live in many different parts of the country and who have widely differing incomes:

- *Kentucky, a factory worker with two boys. Income: $12,000-$25,000.*
  "Not for my support, but he should give all the support for the boys. I give all the moral and emotional support."

- *Florida, a receptionist with three children. Income: Under $10,000.*
  "Should support kids entirely. I don't earn enough. I don't expect him to support me."

- *Florida, a dental receptionist, one daughter. Income: Under $10,000.*
  "No. I feel that it is both our responsibilities to take care of our child. I wouldn't want my ex to support me because then I would be obligated to him."
- *New York City, editor for a magazine, two daughters. Income: over $25,000.*
  "No—I have no problem about contributing to their support. I have the lion's share of both time and financial burdens with them but I've grown up a lot as a result."
- *Ohio, full-time homemaker, a 2-year-old daughter. Income: Under $10,000.*
  "No. I feel it's important as a single parent not to have to depend on anyone and to be able to make it on my own."
- *Illinois, factory worker currently on disability, one daughter. Income: under $6,000.*
  "No, I can support myself! I've become very independent and stubborn! My *daughter* is partly *his* responsibility."
- And one mother from Minnesota, a bank bookkeeper with two *teenage* children and an income of under $10,000, has a very direct approach:
  "The kids—yes. Me—no." When asked "If a friendly genie presented you with Aladdin's lamp, would one of your wishes include money for extra child care and/or alimony payments?" she answered very directly again: "If a friendly genie appeared, I'd take him!"

While a few of the men felt both their payments were large enough—even too large—many others showed a very real sympathy for the money bind that separation can cause. Here's a cross-country selection of answers to the questions "Do you feel your payments are large enough in terms of today's living costs?" and "Do you feel they are too large?"

- *Queens New York, a judge with two sons. Income: over $25,000.*
  "Yes. Wife should work."
- *Canada, a real estate broker with three children. Income: $15,000–$20,000.*
  "No." This father doesn't feel his payments are large enough or too large. And he would use Aladdin's lamp to wish for extra money to pay larger amounts of support and alimony.
- *Colorado, director of a student union, one son. Income: $20,000–$25,000.*
  This father feels that his payments are large enough, but not *too* large. He states: "I don't want my ex-wife and child to suffer and scrimp."
- *California, a construction worker with one daughter. Income: $20,000–. $25,000.*
  This father's answer indicates the new trend in custody and support payments. He states that during the seven years he had custody of his child, "my ex-wife didn't pay a dime. I definitely feel she could and should have." He would use Aladdin's lamp, however, to wish for "the patience and ability to be a more understanding parent with the ability to take my share of time for *me*."
- *Long Island New York, a painter with three boys. Income: $12,000–$15,000.*
  There's no better way to sum up the problems we all face than this father's simple statement: "Before I got custody of my kids, I was paying $300 per month. Now,

it costs me $400 a month just to feed them. I'm not complaining. I wouldn't give them up."

Four practical ways to take the emotional punch out of support payments. Both sides benefit when they make the transfer of support payments as painless as possible. Most importantly, parents should try to keep their children out of these money deals. When I asked one legal expert, herself the product of a single-parent home, for advice on this topic, she came up with the following hardheaded suggestions:

Make the transfer of support payments as painless as possible.

- Always mail support checks. Never use the children as messengers. This simply involves them in a grown-up process that is neither their responsibility nor their concern.

- Think of your support payments as part of your "withholding." Ask your employer to deduct them from your paycheck and mail them out to your former wife/husband so that you are spared this emotional trauma.

- Or make your bank the "transfer agent." Some ex-parents arrange to maintain separate accounts with the same bank so that monthly support payments can be shifted from one account to the other without the emotional strain of writing and mailing checks.

- If welfare is adding a monthly allotment to your support payments to bring them up to subsistence level, sign your support checks over to them. Welfare will then send you a monthly check for the entire amount due. If your ex defaults, welfare still makes the total payment, but it's their responsibility to try and track down the defaulting partner to collect what's owed.

How to Win Out Over the IRS: Some Practical Strategies

This isn't intended to be a course in divorce law, nor will it replace the services of an expert divorce lawyer. But the advice and facts given below *will* help to show how important a realistic attitude toward settlement dollars can be.

Before I get into the finer points, however, I would like to remind you that first, if there *are* no dollars available you can obviously forget the whole thing. The Child Support Enforcement Program became effective in 1975. It provides a Parent Locator Service which can be used to trace parents who are in default of court-ordered payments and who have moved to other states. If you need to find an absent parent, contact your State's Child Support Enforcement Unit, part of the Department of Social Services. If you apply for AFDC, you will *have to* try to locate your missing spouse through this service (there is no charge). If you are not part of the AFDC program, there is a charge for use of this service.

Secondly, separation agreements aren't carved in stone. You and your former spouse can always decide, mutually, to renegotiate them on the basis of some of the information below, for instance.

A word from the wise: the divorce lawyers. Since lawyers often bill by the hour, you might think they would encourage lengthy court battles. Oddly enough, many don't. In discussing a study done on divorce lawyers (by Hubert J. O'Gorman in 1963), Robert S. Weiss' book *Marital Separation* describes some lawyers as "understandably exasperated with their clients" who not only "did not know much about the law but they also didn't know much about their own minds." The latter can be fatal most experts agree. If you don't know what you want, how can anyone else? (And here, I want to make a public apology to my own divorce lawyer, who exhibited the patience of Job. From the vantage point of 12 years later, all I can say is, "Larry, I'm sorry.")

Jack Zulack, the divorce expert I interviewed for this book, listed "a tax plan as vitally important" when couples are separating. He also stressed that "agreements are almost always better than court decrees because both sides get a chance to tailor the agreement to their particular situation."

He tries to help his clients define their emotional and economic objectives with this question: "What do you see your 'dream life' being like three years from now?" You might use this question yourself to size up your present arrangements with your ex. Dollar-wise and emotionally, are you getting what you want? If not, could the arrangements be changed? Zulack cites one case history from his files. His client, the wife, wanted to maintain her pre-divorce style of living as closely as possible, but she also wanted to have her husband continue in an active fathering role to their three children. The couple finally worked out an arrangement that suspended support payments when the children were with their father. This might not work in many cases, since a wife is usually stuck with housing costs (rent or upkeep) even when the children are away visiting. In this case it was possible and helped achieve the desired result.

In all-out financial war, only the tax man wins.

Another thing most expert agree on: in all-out war between separated individuals, only the tax man wins. As beginning reading in this area, Jack Zulack sent me a copy of Publication 504 of the Internal Revenue Service Tax Information for Divorced or Separated Individuals, with a note to "tell your readers to obtain the current version of this publication." As a help in dealing with it (although it is written fairly clearly), I've extracted some general pointers on the most important single-parent issues.

Alimony vs. child-support payments. Almost all of us know that alimony is tax deductible by the persons paying it and taxable to those receiving it, while child support is not tax deductible at the paying end and is tax-free at the receiving end. However, in the heat of battle, some overlook the fact that, to quote the February 1973 issue of *Money* magazine, "there is often a definite tax advantage in increasing an ex-wife's alimony, even if it means decreasing child-support payments." Why? If the tax deduction lowers the father's tax bite, he has more dollars available for his ex (that would otherwise go to the tax man). The rule of thumb is: When the gap in tax brackets is large (the husband's being much larger than the wife's), both benefit by putting as much of the payments as possible in the form of alimony. As the gap narrows, however, it may be in the wife's best interests to increase the percentage of support versus alimony. You might want to think over your present arrangements in light of this information. I would also suggest looking up the article "Dealing the Tax Man Out of a Divorce" in the June 1977 issue of *Money* magazine.

Who declares the children as "dependents" and do I qualify as "head of household"? The rules that determine this are very complicated and depend upon factors such as whether you are married or divorced; if married, whether you have a written separation agreement or court decree; and how much you or your spouse contribute to your child's support, as well as a few other factors. So, for starters, pinpoint exactly what your status is, then check Publication 504 of the Internal Revenue Service: "Tax Information for Divorced or Separated Individuals." After that, if the publication doesn't answer your questions, you might call your local Internal Revenue office. If you still aren't satisfied, you might consult a knowledgeable attorney or accountant.

You can now get a tax credit of 20% (up to $400 for one child and $800 for two or more) of your child-care costs. Remember, a tax *credit* is deducted in full from your net taxable income (what's left after you've subtracted all your deductions), so it's much more valuable than a deduction. And you don't have to claim the child as a dependent to get it (although you must have custody).

Property transfers can be "taxable events." One recently divorced father I interviewed was outraged to discover that he was going to be socked a capital gains tax on the house he had just given to his ex-wife as part of their separation agreement. Because the house had gone up in value since he had bought it (which they usually do) and because the house was in his name, he owed the whole capital gains due on that increase in value. *The solution:* Give your ex possession of the house, but not title. Or, if you're really *planning* this separation, change the title to a *joint* ownership before the separation, and you'll be liable for a capital gains on only *half* the increased value when you sign over full ownership.

For other property transfers (stocks, jewelry or other valuables) you can lessen the tax bite by transferring ownership over a period of several years. If you live in a community property state, where each of you is regarded as owning half of the total assets, you probably wouldn't get taxed on property-sharing unless one side came out owning much more than the other.

Other Considerations Besides Taxes

Here are a few other monetary facts to keep in mind, for both divorced and widowed:

- Wives (or husbands) don't pay social security on money they receive as alimony or child support. However, this means they also don't build up credits on that money.

- A divorced wife whose husband dies can claim his old-age social security benefits only if they were married for 10 years.

- With these points in mind, it might pay an ex-wife to take out an insurance policy on her husband and pay the premiums herself (although she needs his permission to do this). Or she can pay the premiums with money he provides her. Or she might decide to insure her own life if her earnings are essential to the support of the children.

- Widows with jobs should also think about taking out life insurance if *their* earnings are essential for the children's economic survival.

- One step in the right direction is that widowers can now collect their wife's social security credits, which can do a lot to help defray "replacement homemaker" costs.

Picking a Lawyer

Look for compassion and a sense of equality in a divorce lawyer.

If you're negotiating or renegotiating, agreements, how do you pick a lawyer? Here again, Jack Zulack has some practical advice. He suggests asking any lawyer you're considering some test questions. But make them questions to which you already know the answers.

Sample Test questions:

1. If, in the separation agreement, my spouse gives me money for my children and me that is not specified as either alimony or child support, who pays taxes on the money? *Answer:* Unspecified payments are classed as alimony and, if you accept them, you'll pay the tax on them.

2. My spouse wants to give me his interest in our house, which we jointly own. The house has appreciated substantially in value since we bought it. Are any capital gains taxes to be paid because of the transfer and, if so, who pays them? *Answer:* Yes, in almost all states, your spouse's transfer of his/her interest in the house is considered to be the same as a *sale* to a third party, and your spouse must pay capital gains taxes on the appreciation.

Any experienced matrimonial lawyer should know the answers to these questions. Jack also suggests that "compassion and a sense of equality" are important qualities to look for in a divorce lawyer. (In a second mate, too, I might add.)

One Starting Point for Renegotiation

Check page 62 for a copy of the form that the Family Disputes division of the American Arbitration Society gives both sides to figure their Average Monthly Expense for Maintaining Household. If you and your former mate manage to fill it out honestly, and acknowledge each other's real expenses, you're halfway to a decision.

Are Single Parents "Spending Prone"?

Yes—some of us can be! Many single parents have such good, hard money sense that nothing disturbs it. In fact, some make out better without former mates, even on reduced incomes. Several men and women who answered the questionnaire indicated they were gradually getting on top of their former mate's debts. And at least one mentioned that although her income was now smaller, it was her own salary and she could budget efficiently because she was dealing with a known quantity. But separation is a stressful situation. We get depressed. And spending money is one way to relieve depression. It creates a quick high, a sense of accomplishing something, a feeling of filling up the empty spaces with "things."

Friend or Enemy: Credit Is What You Make It

Credit cards make spending so easy! Just sign your name, no cash needed. If you're really stuck, you can take out cash loans on those same credit cards and debt gradually builds until it becomes overwhelming.

We can also use money for revenge. We hear that our former partner has bought a new car. We go out and charge up a suit, a TV, a super deluxe bike for one of the kids—anything as long as it makes us feel "even" with the other side. But we're stuck with the bills. And when they come in, again it's so easy to hit the plastic money box—the cash loan or the credit card! I know what you're saying. "It's not so easy to get a credit card for a single person." And that's true if you're applying for one as a single person. (See the information on credit discrimination on page 64.) But if you already have one that was issued through a bank where you had your own checking or savings account, there's certainly no need to tell them you're now a single. Just keep the card—and use it. I'm *not* knocking sensible uses of credit, just pointing out that it makes "credaholics" possible.

The other great trap is the consolidation loan. It's a perfectly legitimate financial move, as Fred Tonney of the Atlanta Consumer Credit Counseling Service pointed out in a workshop on "Single Parents & Money" he conducted for the 1979 Parents Without Partners convention. You borrow enough money to pay off all your debts, so you're just dealing with one loan. The problem is we may not have the self-discipline to avoid borrowing again (and charging is a form of borrowing) before we have that loan paid off. Single parents aren't the only ones who get into trouble via a consolidation loan. But again, if you're feeling hassled and depressed by separation blues, you're apt to see it as more appealing than it really is.

Some us become such compulsive spenders that we'll even part with cash—any amount we have on us. We'll blow it on one big item or dribble it away on a batch of little impulse buys. I can get rid of $20 while walking two or three blocks. And the tighter up I am for money, the surer it is I'll buy the Lucite pencil holder (I've been using a china mug for years) and the double-socket plug we've really needed (but why now!). This is also the time I buy the 15-pound economy-size box of laundry detergent. A wise buy, but not when you're scratching for frankfurter money.

The answer to all of this is: empty your pockets before you leave the house. Stash the credit cards in with the pile of unpaid bills (that should give you pause when next you grab for them) and just carry enough cash to get you "there and back"—at least until you're over the crisis.

How credit works. Sign a lease on an apartment, take a mortgage on a house or buy a car on a payment plan. These are all forms of credit. In each case, you've made yourself liable for a total amount of money that you (and the other half of the arrangement) agree you can pay off in a series of planned payments. The creditors are banking on the fact that you'll make the payments. And since in a sense you're using their money until the final amount is paid off, they charge you for that use.

There's absolutely nothing wrong with all this. No business can exist without credit. And very few individuals can, either. Nor would it make sense to do so. For one thing, it's almost the only weapon you have as a consumer that can force a merchant or manufacturer to stand behind the goods or services he sells you. If the product doesn't live up to its claims, and you haven't paid for all of it, you are in a much stronger position than you would be if the total bill were paid.

Credit can be especially useful to single parents. Setting up a new household, tiding yourself over until alimony and/or support payments are agreed upon, changing household furnishings to suit revised visitation or custody arrangements, or freighting yourself when a support payment is missed may all call for sane and

> Don't overspend: Empty your pockets before leaving the house.

Average Monthly Expense for Maintaining Household

Name: _____ Date: _____

**Resident, Rent or Mortgage Payment,
  Taxes and Insurance** $ _____

Utilities
     Heat—Fuel   _____
     Water   _____
     Electricity   _____
     Gas   _____
     Telephone   _____
     Refuse Disposal   _____ $ _____

Laundry/Cleaning/Maintenance:
     Cleaning help   _____
     Yard   _____
     Repair and decorating   _____ $ _____

Food: _____ $ _____

Automobile
     Gas and oil, repairs   _____
     License and Insurance   _____ $ _____

Personal
     Clothing   _____
     Grooming   _____
     Medical: Doctor   _____
           Dentist   _____
           Drugs   _____
     Insurance—life, hospital   _____ $ _____
     Miscellaneous: Clubs   _____
           Social obligations   _____
           Gifts   _____
           Donations   _____
           Newspapers/Magazines _____
           Vacation   _____ $ _____

Children: Number _____

    Clothing _____

    Grooming _____

    Education: Books, tuition,

             school activities _____

          Transportation _____

          Lunch _____

    Medical: Doctor _____

        Dentist _____

        Drugs _____

    Insurance _____

    Personal allowance _____

    Gifts, donations _____

    Books, magazines, theater _____

    Clubs _____

    Summer camp _____ $ _____

        Total $ _____

Source: American Arbitration Society

sensible uses of credit. The problems arise when individuals begin to get credit-happy. They get into situations where the interest payments alone are more than they can squeeze out of their discretionary spending money. And as was mentioned earlier in this section, single parents can be particularly susceptible to irrational, emotional spending and use of credit. In fact, the New York City Consumer Credit Counseling Services, an affiliate of the National Foundation for Consumer Credit, which provides a national network for non-profit financial counseling to their communities once defined their average clients:

- They are heads of households 35 to 36 years old.
- Fifty percent are divorced with two children.
- Gross family income is $11,000 (this figure is probably higher by now).
- They owe $7,800 to 8.8 creditors.
- They are spending $397 a month more than they make.

In Atlanta, according to Fred Tonney, they owe $7,000 to 12 creditors (harder-nosed shopkeepers in Atlanta, I gather).

If you're in trouble with credit debts or if you just want to learn how to manage money better, you'll benefit from contacting your nearest Consumer Credit Counseling office, listed in your local phone directory. If there isn't a branch in your particular city, contact the Washington headquarters for the name of the service nearest you:

> *National Foundation for Consumer Credit, Inc.*
> *Federal Bar Building West*
> *1819 H Street, N.W.*
> *Washington, DC 20006*
> *Tel.: (202)223-2040*

In Canada, contact:
> *Credit Counselling Service of Metropolitan Toronto*
> *Suite 618, 74 Victoria Street*
> *Toronto, Ontario M5C 2P2*
> *Tel.: (416) 366-5251*

For other Canadian counselling locations, contact:
> *The Ontario Association of Credit Counselling Services*
> *200 Queens Avenue, Suite 306*
> *London, Ontario N6A 1J3*
> *Tel.: (519) 433-0159*

Credit discrimination against single parents. Two attitudes (both disgusting) cause unreasonable difficulty in getting credit as a single parent: out and out discrimination against singled people and/or the particular problem that many formerly married women face—they simply don't exist as far as the credit world is concerned.

Banks, department stores, credit card companies and other credit institutions piously maintain that "There is no discrimination against singled people." Hogwash. Discrimination happens to be illegal, so, of course, they're not anxious to own up to it. But it does exist, for men as well as women. Certainly there's an Equal Credit Opportunity Act. Its purpose, as defined in a national magazine in 1977, is to "reconcile the ideal of equal access to credit with the creditor's need to judge an applicant's credit worthiness." But, the article continues, "The law does not prohibit a creditor from knowing your marital status; in some cases he has to know it to protect his rights as a creditor. ... Federal Reserve Board regulations prohibit creditor rules and practices that: exclude alimony and child support payments in evaluations of credit worthiness." Prohibit away! But who pays any attention? I know of one divorcee who receives $36,000 a year in support payments and alimony. When she tried to raise a first mortgage on a house she owned outright (part of the divorce settlement), she was refused because the bank wanted to know what she would make the mortgage payments with. They would not accept alimony/support payments as income, even with the house as collateral. And when I called to change my name from Mrs. T.K. Murdock to Carol V. Murdock on a department store charge card, I was told flatly that I wasn't even supposed to have the card "since you're divorced." (That was the last time I made that mistake. Since then I've changed the address only and kept my mouth shut about any other little lifestyle adjustments.)

In their book *Dealing with Divorce*, Robert K. Moffett and Jack F. Scherer have this to say about credit ratings:

> The single man who hasn't married faces no difficulties, but the divorced male is another matter. The banking business has an instinctive aversion to anyone who has retreated financially. Also, to a credit officer with visions of alimony in his head, the ex-husband is by definition a bad risk.

And about women:

> For the ex-wife, the credit problem is again a matter of being unmarried and female.... While the Federal Home Loan Bank Board issued a policy statement, in 1974, saying that savings and loan institutions may not discriminate against women in considering applications, it granted that this was not specifically forbidden in the 1968 Civil Rights Act.

And you can bet that any discrimination that's not "specifically forbidden" is still in practice!

For women only: how to develop a credit rating of your own. If you were a full-time homemaker while married, or if all bank and charge accounts were in your husband's name you may be a non-person as far as the credit world is concerned. You'll have to work at establishing a "credit identity."

First, check with your local credit-reporting agency to find out whether or not you *are* listed under your own name. Find this agency in the Yellow Pages under "Credit" or "Credit Rating and Reporting Agencies." You may have to pay a small fee for checking your file. If you have a separate (under your own name) credit history, and it's a good one, you'll have no problems unless you've just changed jobs or have recently moved. If you've moved, be sure to tell banks and/or stores at which you want credit about your credit listing in your previous town. If you've taken a new job, proceed as outlined below.

You're starting from scratch if the credit history is under your former husband's name. (This applies to widows as well as divorced women.) But these little steps will start to put you in the credit picture.

Creditors are required to tell you why they've turned you down.

- Open savings and checking accounts in your own name. Be sure to keep the checking account in good shape—not overdrawn.

- Then apply for a "ready check" or "overdraft" account with your bank. If you're accepted, that fact goes into your credit file even if you never use the overdraft feature.

- Apply to a local department store for a charge account. If you're turned down at first, ask if they have a layaway plan. If so, start "laying away." Or try to arrange a purchase on the store's installment plan. And make your payments promptly. After you've made regular payments, reapply for a charge account. They may then be willing to grant it. And that first credit account makes others much easier!

- Apply for a gasoline credit card with a major oil company. Use it and pay up promptly.

- After you've had a store account and/or a gasoline charge card for several months apply for a multipurpose credit card (American Express, Master Charge, Visa or Carte Blanche). After the first few months, you can charge up larger bills and spread the payments out over several months. But *always* pay the minimum balance due each month—and pay it promptly. Late payments harm your credit rating.

- Some experts suggest taking out a small bank loan (passbook loans are cheapest) just to develop bank credit. But if you've been able to get the types of credit mentioned above, this "see what a good girl I am" type of loan may not be necessary. If you do decide to take a loan, stick the money into a savings account. The interest coming in will help cover the interest you'll be paying out.

- With these credit credentials racked up in your name, you should be OK. If you're turned down on any future credit applications—ask why! Start politely but build to a good college yell if you don't get answers. The Equal Credit Opportunity Act requires creditors to tell you exactly why they've turned you down. The Fair Credit Reporting Act forces them to tell you if you've been turned down because of information received from a credit reporting agency. If you're not getting anywhere with the employee or officer you're dealing with, demand to see a superior and point out that violations of the two laws I've mentioned are very serious offenses indeed. Those in charge are usually bright enough to realize that you're not going to do the decent thing and just fade away. They'll mentally curse women's lib but they'll also begin to deal with you realistically. For stubborn problems, contact the local chapter of NOW or the Legal Aid Society for further advice.

General credit guidelines. Federal Reserve Board regulations prohibit creditor rules and practices that:

- Make married persons more credit worthy than unmarried or separated persons.

- Disallow, for reasons of sex or marital status, any portion of an applicant's income (singled mothers— that means alimony and/or child support).

- Require an applicant to reveal information about childbearing plans or the use of birth control devices.

- Terminate your credit account or automatically impose new conditions on it when your name or marital status has changed.

- Delay acceptance of, or reject, your credit application because of your sex or marital status.

- These are taken from a March 1977 article in *McCall's* magazine, and this section of the article ends: "There are stiff civil penalties for creditors who violate this law." Who has time or money to sue? But, understand that you can threaten to do so. This should get results!

How much credit can you afford? "As much as you can get" is one answer. But the National Foundation for Consumer Credit advises otherwise. Their pamphlet "Measuring and Using Our Credit Capacity" sets up some guidelines.

First, they strongly advise setting up a budget as the initial step. You can then figure out how much money you have available for specific kinds of purchases. Say that you're budgeting $25 a month for furniture. They suggest leaving $3 a month unspent to cover little, impulse home-furnishing buys. So if you can lay out a $50 down payment you can safely commit to a purchase of $314 on a 12-month contract, $380 on 15 months of installments, or $446 on an 18-month contract.

> The larger your down payments, the smaller your credit service charge.

About down payments. The larger they are, the smaller the credit service charges will be. However, don't make them so large that you blow the budget and make it difficult to keep up the monthly payments. Missed payments harm your hard-won credit rating.

If you've bought something on an installment plan and have it about two-thirds paid off, you may want to purchase additional items on an add-on basis. Under this arrangement, your $22/month payment is prorated so that part of it continues to pay off the original debt and part is applied to the add-on debt. Eventually, all of each month's payment is applied to the additional purchase. Although you're extending the length of time it takes to pay up, you're not increasing the amount per month you pay.

Their final piece of advice: Don't buy items on credit that won't last at least as long as the payments do. Otherwise, you're paying for something you no longer have!

Additional Financial Planning Advice

Elizabeth Wiegand, a professor in the Department of Consumer Economics and Housing at New York State College of Human Ecology, Cornell University, talks about the importance of goals in financial planning:

- Financial management is the wise use of money and other assets to reach a goal.

- Goals are the specific objects or general images that we feel it is important to do and/or have.

- Identifying one or more goals is essential in order to direct resources toward their achievement. Without goals a person isn't managing; he or she is acting impulsively or letting someone else manage for him or her.

- It's normal to have some of our values and goals in conflict with one another.

- When you act as a financial manager, a whole bundle of activities are occurring. There seem to be three or four key activities, each having several parts:

  1. *obtaining income*
     earning (i.e., wages, salaries, commissions); receiving (i.e., dividends, interest, gifts, allowances, tips, loans, pensions, subsidies)
  2. *protecting assets*
     insuring personal and real property through insurance policies, safe deposit box, smoke detectors
  3. *spending (using) money and property*
     comparing income and outgo, selecting products and services, maintaining and repairing products and real property
  4. *transferring assets to others*
     (e.g., gifts, will, trusts, joint tenancy, tenancy by the entirety, named beneficiaries for life insurance, pensions and/or U.S. savings bonds)

- The whole time you're acting as a financial manager, goals are continually jockeying with one another for a higher priority rating.

Use these tools to help you make and carry out financial decisions:

  1. *an inventory of the papers and other evidence of your ownership of personal and real property*
  2. *a net worth statement made at repeated intervals*
  3. *a plan for matching spending and saving with income*
  4. *a place or places for creating, keeping and using financial papers*

Single Parenting and Your Job

Living as a single parent, whether divorced or widowed, can cause you to do some rethinking about your job. Many of the following questions on jobs apply particularly to women, but not exclusively so; the financial and emotional responsibilities of single parenting raise job issues for men, too. I'll deal with the problems of the "displaced homemaker" separately, because they are so special and so acute.

Is This a Job or a Career?

I think this is the first question you should ask yourself when you begin sizing up your job in light of your new role as a single parent. And this one goes for men as well as women. Does the job offer you any chances for advancement? Will you be able to increase your earnings as you go along? Is it a growing field or one that's earmarked for gradual decline? The January 1978 issue of *Changing Times*, The Kiplinger Magazine, mentions contacting the local office of your state employment service for job counseling. They also mention contacting the Federal Job Information Center in your state. If you're thinking about new fields, I would also suggest contacting your local community college for information on training and requirements. This is particularly important for women who are stuck in "pink collar" jobs. You'll be surprised to discover the rate of hourly pay and the number of opportunities available in non-traditional job fields. Your chances are particularly good if it's an area that relies heavily on government contracts—they need women employees to prove that they're equal opportunity employers!

What Fringe Benefits Does the Job Offer?

Men are trained to consider this in sizing up a job. Many women are not. Only around 50% of women who answered the question about fringe benefits in my questionnaire indicated that this *was* a consideration in taking the job. One woman mentioned that the medical insurance program her company offered had cut her costs from $100/month to $30. Others mentioned that they took the job "because it was offered to them" or because they needed the money and grabbed whatever came up first. One woman, working as a salesperson, with no fringe benefits whatever (not even a paid vacation), wrote that she "hadn't even known that jobs like this exist." And obviously she hadn't thought to ask about it. I'm not blaming her, just pointing out that as women, we need to start looking at something besides that paycheck. David Watson, the tax expert I consulted for this book, has some good advice on this score: try to divert job income into benefits you would normally have to buy yourself. If you're given a choice between a $600 raise, for instance, and full medical coverage—take the medical coverage. Or if you're offered a $20/week raise vs. covering some of your car costs, take the car costs. Remember—you'll pay taxes on that $600 raise and you'll *also* be paying out for medical insurance. Ditto the $20 and the auto costs.

Watson also offers advice for when you're trying to size up two job offers:

Estimate the value of your fringe benefits.

- Estimate what the fringe benefits would cost you if you were paying for them yourself.

- Figure out what tax bracket the salary will put you into.

- If one job is offering fewer benefits but a larger salary, and the salary puts you just a few dollars over the line into a new tax bracket, you're probably better off with the other job.

- Don't be afraid to ask questions about benefits, either. Ask for a brochure that shows the kinds of coverage the company's medical insurance provides, for instance. Some plans may work better for you than others. If you have a kid with an allergy and one plan covers costs like this but another doesn't, take it into consideration when making a job decision. Sensible, thoughtful questions show a personnel officer that you're serious about the job and your future.

What Intangibles Does the Job Offer?

All of the women I've spoken to and 95% of the women who answered the questionnaire said that their jobs offered a mental and emotional lift as well as money. Jobs gave them "a chance to get out of the house," "a chance to meet and relate to other adults," "a feeling of personal worth." So think about that when you're looking. Are you going to be happy in a very small office? Or would you be better off in a larger organization where you have the chance to meet more people? Maybe the smaller setup will provide a more "personal" approach. One divorced mother who works for a doctor mentioned that he is a very sympathetic employer who always understands if she has to take a day off when one of her kids is sick.

They've worked out a flexible arrangement that's worth much more to her than increased salary in a larger firm.

Many women also mentioned that their jobs were "close to home." This can be a real advantage. When I first separated, I taught nursery school just a few blocks from the apartment I'd rented. I could walk to work, drop off CH at his school on the way and pick him up on the return trip. Working close to home also means that you can get home in a hurry if there's an emergency. Some mothers also mention "going home for lunch" as an advantage.

That brings up another point. Will a new job make it easy to "brown bag" lunch? Some offices just aren't set up for this. And they may not be located near a park or plaza that will give you a place to sit while you eat your picnic lunch either. Paying for lunch every day can be very expensive. On the other hand, an employee cafeteria can be a real boon to a single mother. If your kids are getting a hot lunch at school, you can sometimes eat your main meal at the cafeteria and settle for soup-and-sandwich suppers with the kids. Saves time and money!

Would You Prefer to Work at Home?

All single parents, including men with custody of their children, might think about this. And it can sound very appealing. But it has drawbacks, let me tell you. First of all, it's hard to do if your children are young. Secondly, you're working on your own, with no one else around for company. Also, spending most of each waking day at home may sound appealing when you're shaking out of bed after a late night and dashing through dressing, breakfasting, getting kids to school and traveling to work. But you can get awfully sick of looking at the same walls. Usually there's an idyllic picture of "spending more time with the kids." This can be a trap, too—you're *working* at home, remember? In her feature page "Money Facts," in the July 1979 issue of *Woman's Day* magazine, Jane Bryant Quinn suggests referring to the book *Working for Yourself,* published by Rodale Press, for a clear picture of some of the drawbacks of working on your own.

On the positive side: it's true that an awful lot of time is wasted in offices. You can get a great deal more done, in less time, on your own at home. And you can adjust your working hours to suit family schedules—sometimes. This means a lot of hours working at night, however,

Maybe what you want, if you can afford it, is a permanent part-time job. This is becoming a more usual situation. Just make sure that you don't end up doing a full-time job for part-time pay!

The Special Problems of Displaced Homemakers

This is one of the toughest situations anyone can face. Laurie Shields, national coordinator for the Alliance for Displaced Homemakers, is quoted in the January 1978 issue of *Changing Times*: "Today's middle-aged former full-time homemaker, lacking any record of recent paid work experience, is as vulnerable as the young person who hasn't lived long enough to acquire a work record." What are some of the things you can do to help yourself?

- Contact the Alliance for Displaced Homemakers, 3800 Harrison Street, Oakland, CA 94611, and enclose a 15-cent stamp. They may be able to tell you about a displaced homemaker center near you. Unfortunately, there aren't many of them, but you may luck in. You can also contact your local chapter of NOW, the YWCA, Parents Without Partners or your local United Way headquarters. All may be able to advise you.

- Make up for your lack of recent job experience by being as businesslike as possible when you apply for a job. Make sure you put together a typed résumé. Give your education, any work experience you do have, any office skills. *Also list any volunteer work you've done, or volunteer positions you've held*, and in one brief paragraph explain how or why you feel this will be valuable in the business world. You may have gained experience in dealing with people, administration, involved record-keeping, salesmanship (selling at fund-raising bazaars, selling raffle tickets, etc.) or making telephone contacts. If you've never seen a résumé, check with your local library and ask them to suggest a book on how to get a job. You'll find sample résumés in most of these.

- Consider a job that utilizes your homemaking skills. Check the Yellow Pages to see if your town has an employment agency for domestic help. Working as a cook/housekeeper can be a damned rewarding job. Also check with local hotels or motels to see what they have to offer.

- Post a notice on as many public bulletin boards as possible (in shops and supermarkets, for instance) offering your services as a full-day sitter—your home or theirs. Many working mothers are desperate for help with child care.

- Tell your doctor, dentist, lawyer that you're looking for work as a receptionist. Ask them to pass your name along if they hear of a colleague who's looking for one. Many professional offices prefer older women as receptionists.

- Check out your hobbies for job possibilities. For instance, if you like gardening, check the Yellow Pages for phone numbers of greenhouses, garden centers and plant shops, and make some calls. You may scare up a job as a salesperson or "girl Friday." The same goes for crafts shops, food shops, decorating shops.

- If you like fresh air and physical activity, you might check out some local gas stations. There's always big turnover in these jobs because, frankly, the pay and the working conditions stink. (I know because I spent five months working for one. I liked it, but I'm a nut for physical activity.) However, it's a start at a paid job. And again, they're looking for women because they want to look like equal opportunity employers. In fact, you're beginning to see quite a few women working in stations. Most of the major oil companies even have specially designed uniforms for their female employees.

Be as businesslike as possible when applying for a job.

Special note to everyone: If you want some help in sizing yourself up (your likes, dislikes, strong and weak points), take the Getting to Know Yourself quiz on page 72. This was developed by the Family Service Association of America as part of a series of workshops for a family life education program called "Career Planning for Women." It can be useful for men, too. And if you've never put together a résumé, it will give you some practice in rounding up the kind of information you should include.

Getting to Know Yourself

Interests

1. What kinds of activities do I find enjoyable and fulfilling? (List all the types of things you like to do, whether or not they are job-related.)
2. What kinds of activities do I dislike or find dull and uninteresting?
3. What kind of work do I *think* I would like to do if there were no limitations?

Aptitudes and Skills

1. What do I think I am good at doing? What could I do well?
2. Do I have any special skills? (List everything from cooking, sewing, driving a car to typing or any advanced training you may have.)
3. What is my greatest strength, talent or skill? What kinds of things do I do easily?
4. What do I do poorly? What types of things do I have trouble learning?

Education

1. Do I have a high school diploma? Do I have any college or special training? Specify.
2. What subjects did I excel in and why?
3. What subjects did I like least and why?

Work

1. What was my last job or volunteer position?
2. What did I like about it?
3. What did I dislike about it?
4. What part of the job did I do best and why?
5. What did I do least well? Why?
6. How well did I get along with my supervisors and co-workers?
7. If I did not get along with co-workers, why?
8. How long did I work on the last job, and why did I leave?
9. Do I have any physical limitations that would affect my job?
10. Do I have any time limitations that would affect my job?
11. Do I like to be in charge, or do I prefer to be told what to do?
12. Do I prefer to work alone or in an office where there are other people?

4/Making Your Dollars Work Better for You

We're all stuck with inflation. And many of us are stuck with divided paychecks to boot. So we're really hurting. I'm not sure there are any instant solutions, but there are some guidelines that can help. Magazine articles and money books are filled with suggestions on how to cut costs. I've tried to cull out those that deal most specifically with our single-parent problems. I've also included suggestions from other single parents who've taken the time and trouble to share their experiences with us.

Learn Your Budget Basics

If you've never operated on a written budget, now's the time to start! It's the only way to get on top of money. All you need is a sheet of paper and a little know-how. Even if you already have a budget, some of the new percentages the experts figure on may come as an eye-opener.

Here's a basic budget that the Consumer Credit Counseling Service of Greater Atlanta has worked out for its clients. It's for a family of three with a net monthly take-home pay of $1000. Amounts are given in percentages as well as dollars.

Fixed Expenses

Housing (Rental, includes what you can pay for utilities.)	33%–35%	$330
Food (Grocery bills, including non-food items.)	20%	$200

This also includes meals eaten out, except where you budget them as Entertainment. Brown-bagging school and office lunches is obviously necessary.

Clothing (This includes maintenance like clean- 10% $100
ing and laundry bills.)

**Fixed expenses
must be met first!**

Figuring housing, food and clothing as fixed expenses, you've already accounted for 63% to 65% of your monthly income. What could your flexible expenses (or discretionary income) look like?

Flexible Expenses

Credit Costs (This would include car-loan pay- 10% $100
ments.)

Opinions vary on how much credit you can afford. Some experts peg it at 25% of take-home pay; others say 20%; others 10% to 15%. Fred Tonney, of the Atlanta Credit Counseling Service, chose the lowest percentage for absolute safety.

Savings and Insurance (Includes life and 10% $100
health insurance policies.)

The national rate of saving is about 4%. So the Atlanta Consumer Credit Counsel suggests 10% of your net pay for savings and insurance combined.

You've now accounted for 83% to 85% of your total net monthly income. You've allocated $830, leaving $170 to spend on items like child care, car maintenance, medical expenses, entertainment and incidentals. That could take some squeezing!

Incidentally, this budget is set up a little differently from many you'll see. Here, food and clothing are listed as fixed expenses. Many other budgets list them as flexible. Since housing, food and clothing are all things you *have to have*, however, there does seem to be an advantage in figuring out the maximum amount you can lay out for them each month.

There's one vital fact to remember about fixed expenses: they're the costs that must be met first, and on a regular basis. So think very carefully before you add to them. Installment loans, charges on credit-card accounts, cash loans on a credit card or from a bank are flexibles in that you can decide whether or not to incur them. But the payments on these create fixed expenses. And they stay fixed until you've paid them off! Phone and utilities bills come under the same heading because by the time the bill comes in, you've used the services they supply, even though you don't have anything tangible to show for it (like charged merchandise) or extra cash (which a loan produces). I've included some tips on how to pare both costs in the next section on trimming expenses.

The figure in the Atlanta budget that really frightens me is that 33% to 35% for housing *must include utilities!* A single-parent family of three (one adult and two children) needs at least a two-bedroom house or apartment. If you deduct $1200 a year for heat and $360 a year for other utilities (which is bedrock at today's inflated costs for heating oil, gas and electricity) from a yearly rental of $3960 (the Atlanta housing figure), you're pegging your actual available rent money at $2400 a year, or $200 a month. This is sheer fantasy in my area. I live about 100 miles outside of New York City, a high-rent area compared with many other sections of the country. But even allowing for this, $200 a month for two-bedroom accommodations seems very low. For those who own their own homes or are considering buying, $200 a month represent the carrying costs on a mortgage of roughly $20,000 (figuring on a 20-year mortgage at 11%). Again, this is low as mortgages go these days. The food figure also seems bedrock to me. It calls for feeding three people for $50 a week. But I'm willing to admit that it can be done via some plain food and fancy figuring. Food stamps would help, too, and there are some thoughts about those in the section on trimming expenses.

The figure that seems high to me is $1200 a year for clothing. Even though it includes laundry and dry cleaning (and just try to figure out some way of estimating home laundry costs!), $400 per head for a family of three seems like a lot of clothes buying. I realize that neither CH nor I are exactly fashion plates. However, teen-size boots come in at a hefty $20 to $30 a pair (for heavy-duty models) even at discount stores, and I've never known him to make it through the year on one pair. But even allowing for teenage wear and tear on clothing, I figure $300 for each of us, tops. And that wouldn't be every year.

Writing Your Own Budget

To help you make up a budget of your own, I've included a copy of a Family Finances Sheet supplied by Mary Quinn, Services Director of the Consumer Credit Counseling Services division of the National Foundation for Consumer Credit in Washington, DC (see page 76). This finance sheet provides room for listing living expenses, all outstanding debts and a financial summary of your income (which I've adjusted slightly to specifically reflect single-parent situations).

Incidentally, one question that came up about income at Fred Tonney's workshop in Atlanta was about alimony and/or child support payments. How do you figure them into your budget?

- *If you're paying*, take them right off the top of your take-home pay and then figure what your net is, less these payments.

- *If you're receiving*, and they come in regularly, add them into your net income. At least that's what Fred Tonney suggests. Other budget experts suggest that you try to cover your fixed expenses out of your own earnings, and apply alimony/support money to flexibles. This can save you from taking a real pounding if those payments stop. (It may also be totally impossible to do, in many cases.)

Trim Down Rather Than Tense Up

Okay, we're getting down to the guts of single-parent budgeting. We're living on reduced income, or we've doubled our household expenses by creating two households (whichever way you prefer to look at it). And we're subject to the stresses of single parenting. Pile worry about financial problems on top of other stresses, and you end up a basket case.

The first thing you can do for yourself is to level with the kids. They can cope with a reduced lifestyle much better than they can with tension they don't understand. Many grown-ups shudder at the idea of discussing finances with children. That's why so many of today's teenagers have had sophisticated sex-education courses in school but are babies about basic money facts. Remember, it's no disgrace to tell your children frankly that there's less money than there used to be. You can even tell older children exactly what your income is and how much of it is going for rent, food, etc. If you're calm and matter of fact about it, they won't

Do yourself a favor: Level with the kids about money.

Family Finances Sheet

Living Expenses	Month	Pay Periods
Housing		
Utilities *(gas, electric, telephone, water)*		
Food		
Lunches		
Cigarettes		
Toiletries		
Allowances		
Barber/Beauty Shop		
Gas/Oil		
Car *(repairs, tires, tags)*		
Insurance *(car, life, medical)*		
Medical *(doctors, dentists, glasses, prescriptions)*		
Clothing		
Cleaning/Laundry		
Gifts *(birthday, Christmas)*		
Publications *(newspapers, magazines, books)*		
Vacations		
Entertainment *(movies, dinners out, sports, beverages)*		
Contributions		
Child Care		
Pet Expense		
Miscellaneous		
Total Living Expenses		

Creditors	Balance	Payments	Pay Periods
Total			

Financial Summary		Month	Pay Periods
Income:	Husband		
	Wife		
	Other		
1. Total Income			
2. Less Living Expenses			
3. Balance for Payments and Savings			
4. Less Payments			
5. For Savings, Emergencies, Future Purchases and Variable Expenses			

panic or feel guilty. And if you have to turn down a request for a bicycle, a TV or a special treat, or delay a purchase until everyone's helped save for it, they'll realize the reason for the refusal or delay.

When I interviewed Joan Russell, the founder and Executive Director of Single Parents On Campus, a non-social support network for single-parent families at the University of Colorado and throughout the Boulder area, she discussed this point at length. Her experience as a single parent and in dealing with other single parents and their children proves to her that:

> It's much better for parents to discuss the changes in their living arrangements very frankly with their children. I've been very open with my kids and it's worked out well. If you're using food stamps or if your kids are part of the free lunch program at school, explain that it 'helps out a lot with the food money at home.' The kids feel okay about it if the information comes from you. They'll see it as you see it. If you think of it as a positive idea, so will they.

Incidentally, you'll be reading more about Joan's organization in other chapters of this book.

Another mother from upstate New York tried a very specific approach she had read about in a budgeting book to explain money matters to her 8-year-old daughter. She turned her paycheck into single dollar bills, spread them all out on a tabletop and separated them into Rent, Food, etc. "And suddenly the children will begin to understand just where *all that money* goes. It worked, to a degree."

A Budget Breakdown

Well, where *does* all that money go? Let's break down the sum into its parts.

Housing

Housing takes the biggest budget bite, so let's start there. Many divorced mothers and widowed parents decide to stay in the same house they lived in while married. This maintains a familiar environment for children. But is it the wisest decision financially? Remember, you're harder pressed for both funds and time now. If the house ate up 33% to 35% of a pre-separation or pre-death budget, what's it doing to you now? If you own your own home, it may not make sense to sell it and have to pay capital gains tax on your profit. But it might pay to rent it and move into less expensive quarters. Your rent will probably cover the carrying costs on the house and may even produce a profit. Just make sure that you at least break even on the switch. Another possibility is to rent out a room or turn part of the house into a small apartment you rent out.

Consider swapping a room for live-in baby-sitting. I did this for about six years and it worked very well. Joan Russell, out in Boulder, also uses this arrangement and finds it satisfactory.

You should have a clear understanding about both sides of the swap in this system. Does it include food as well as quarters? How many hours of baby-sitting do you expect in return? What kind of business or study schedule does the baby sitter have? If your children are young, you want someone who will have some free evening time to play with your kids when you're out, in addition to just being there while they're asleep.

Be sure to ask for some references—from office, school or home town. And check those references! Also, check your phone bill carefully the first few months. If you find toll calls you can't account for, or if local calls rise substantially, crack down right away. Make it quite clear that this is *not* part of the deal and the first time it happens again all bets are off.

Some other aspects of housing to consider. How much yard work is involved? How far is it from your kids' schools, your job? How good is public transportation? If a move cuts commuting costs or means you can give up running a car altogether, those are added dollars in your pocket—and hours of time saved as well.

Cutting commuting costs means time and money saved.

If you move to new quarters, consider the same possibilities mentioned earlier—renting a room or swapping one for baby-sitting. It sometimes proves cheaper to pay a little more and get an extra room you can rent or swap than to pay less for smaller quarters.

Food

Food takes the second biggest bite out of the budget; how can you cut costs? First of all, to the single parents who mentioned in their questionnaires that they cut marketing trips down to once a week or less: Congratulations! You've discovered one of the best ways to control food dollars. Every trip into a food store increases your chances for the impulse buy. And this is expensive. So, for the rest of us: plan weekly menus, make out a marketing list and stick to it! In his money workshop, Fred Tonney mentioned the $5 quart of milk or loaf of bread. That's the one you buy in the local deli—along with a can of sardines, fancy crackers to go with them, a smidge of good cheese, a container of mushroom and artichoke salad . . . Stop— you're heading toward a $10 bill! Here are some other basic precautions touched on in the workshop:

Make out a marketing list and stick to it!

- Go into the store with a competitive attitude. It's you against the store and you intend to win!
- Don't shop at eye level. The better buys are usually stashed on the lower shelves.
- Buy store brands whenever possible. But check them out against the specials on national brands; I've found the latter are sometimes cheaper while the special is on.
- Plan your menus on Wednesdays when the stores advertise their specials and when food columns carry news of what's plentiful and cheap.

Tonney also includes a few don'ts: "Don't go to the store hungry; don't take kids; don't send teenagers." Here, I think it depends on the teenager. My own describes himself as "Mr. Cheapo" when it comes to marketing and I do stand in awe of the wonders he can accomplish. (Don't make it too much of a game, however, or they're apt to start shoplifting.)

I'm going to add a few hints of my own, some of which run counter to the accepted "expert" theories:

- Food is a very emotional experience. Anthropologists point out that man is the only animal who shares food willingly and that we cling to early food patterns more tenaciously than we do to language. So look at budget recipes with an eagle eye. Beans, chicken livers, canned tuna—is the basic ingredient something you really want to eat? If not, skip it. Preparing it is a waste of the food as well as the time and gas or electricity it took to cook it. There's nothing wrong with any of the above, incidentally. It's purely a matter of "acculturation." I adore the first two in any form and like the third cold, but can't stand it hot—either creamed or in casseroles. Some of my best friends turn green at the idea of chicken livers, however, while finding a tuna casserole very tasty.

- The more ingredients, the more expensive—that's a general rule of thumb to apply to casseroles, particularly if you have to buy some special ingredients like spices just for that dish. I find it's cheapest to concentrate on two or three "all in the pot" dishes we really like and keep alternating them. That way, I know they'll get eaten and I use up the spices I buy for them.

- Learn to mentally weigh bones. I just don't believe that it's cheaper to buy a whole chicken than parts, unless you're going to use the carcass in soup. (The same goes for bone-in vs. boneless beef cuts.) If you do buy any poultry whole, bear in mind that the basic bone structure weighs about the same for each type of fowl. In each case, the extra weight is meat. So head for the heaviest chicken, turkey or duck you can afford.

- Don't overkill on nutrition. If a dish features beans and any form of wheat, corn or rice, it forms a complete protein. So don't be "super feeder" and add meat or cheese. In fact, make your way through a basic book on nutrition—Butterick's *No-Nonsense Guide to Food and Nutrition* is one of the best I've found. Also try *Diet for a Small Planet*, by Frances Moore Lappé, which concentrates on meatless dishes. Personally, I'm a seasonal vegetarian. In summer, when vegetables are cheaper, I concentrate on those. In winter I head for beef, one of the cheapest meats at that time of year.

- For small families like mine (one adult, one youngster), I sometimes find it's cheaper to pick up a container of chili at a fast-food restaurant and stretch it with rice cooked at home. Ditto for Chinese food. As energy costs rise, we might all keep cooking costs (as opposed to food costs) in mind.

- Finally, try to work out a mini co-op or share-the-shopping arrangement with one or two friends. On an alternating basis, one does the shopping for all. This way, you can really take advantage of those "3 cans for $1" specials. You can sometimes work out case-price deals with the market, too. And, if nothing else, you save the time and gas you'd spend if you all marketed separately!

A special note about food stamps. Eligibility rules for these keep changing, but get them if you can! Depending on your income level, they'll increase—even double—your food dollars. This is a federally financed program administered through states and counties. So check your phone book under your county or state listing for social services or food stamp program. The food stamp application form runs to five pages, but a case worker will help you fill it out. Also, send $1 for the invaluable booklet *Guide to the Food Stamp Program* to: Food Research and Action Center, 2011 I Street N.W., Washington, DC 20006 (tel. 202-452-8250). This publication gives you the whole story on who's eligible, how to get emergency food stamps and how to get a hearing if you feel you've been unjustly barred from the program. And it's kept up to date.

Clothing

Planning and secondhands cut clothing costs. Unplanned buying at sales is rewarding but planning ahead for sales saves even more. This means end-of-seasons or out-of-season buying. There are two traps to watch out for: size and style.

Size applies mostly to growing children. For instance, you can nurse along last year's parka till after Christmas, buy a new one on sale and be fairly sure your kid'll get the rest of this winter out of it and probably part of the next.

However, it's difficult to buy kids' clothing a full season ahead because you can't guarantee they'll grow all in one direction. Usually, they get taller *or* fatter, broaden out through the chest or lengthen just in the waist. It's hard to outguess mother nature. The best rule of thumb is to try and buy on the half-year—winter clothing after Christmas, summer clothing after July 4th. And do a lot of patch-up in between.

If you have several children, hand down clothing. If your kids resist this, try swapping with a friend or using a clothing exchange. If your school doesn't have an exchange setup, try starting one.

Style is mainly your concern and that of older children. The most extreme clothing usually goes on sale first. One issue of a good fashion magazine can help you get a feeling for what's a one-season fad, as opposed to a look that's going to be around for a while. To use a fashion magazine wisely, check out the ads against the editorials—this goes for men as well as women. In fact, count how many ads featuring clothing that reflects any one editorial look. And pay particular attention to the more conservative manufacturers; it's a safe bet that whatever they're promoting most widely will be around for a season or two.

Separates are great money-savers, too. Skirts or pants that can be teamed with a variety of tops (blouses, shirts, sweaters, jackets) create more changes and span more seasons than one-piece dresses or matched suits. They're also easier to dress up with faddy but inexpensive accessories. And for God's sake, learn the trick of planning a wardrobe around one pair of shoes—brown or black, who cares. Settle on one and make sure that *every* major piece of clothing you buy is compatible.

The best buys of all. I've saved the best till last. Rummage sales, thrift shops, yard and/or attic sales and resale clothing shops are your best bets for cutting clothing costs. They're invaluable for kids who are sprouting like weeds. And they can produce skirts, shirts, pants, sweaters galore for you for about $1 or $2 apiece, sometimes less. But here's the trick: find one that's supplied by the wealthy. The clothes will be fresher, of better quality and more recent in design. If it's a thrift shop, haunt one that benefits a fashionable charity, one you see mentioned in the society columns. Head for rummage or yard sales in the wealthier parts of town. Many newspapers now carry regular weekly listings of these sales. They're also great places to pick up home furnishings. Remember, one man's rummage sale prize is another man's semi-antique!

Utilities

Cutting utilities and heating/cooling costs is a matter of survival! Because cutting fuel costs is really so vital for most of us, I'm going to pass on what tips I can in individual sections—no miracles, but perhaps some pointers you haven't already read about.

> Buy clothing during the traditional half-yearly sales.

> Close drapes at night to keep heat in.

Doors and windows are cheap, effective climate controllers. But they're so obvious most of us tend to sell them short. After spending winter weekends in a skimpily heated house in the northern Catskills (where temperatures drop to 12 below) and one entire winter in a delightful but totally non-airtight ark of a house on eastern Long Island during the coldest winter we've had in years, I'll pass along the door-window strategies I find most effective. First, heating:

- Put up curtains of tightly woven, non-porous material at each window. They must cover the glass area. Felt is an ideal material because it can be cut to length without hemming, and hung with grip rings. Or you can scrounge up pairs of heavy draperies in a secondhand shop and cut them up to fit your windows. Leave curtains open during the day to let in as much sun heat as possible, then *close them at night* to prevent heat loss. Heat moves toward cold, and hot air rises, so you lose a lot of heat through all uninsulated windows, most heat through upper-story windows.

- On windy, overcast days, leave the curtain closed to minimize heat loss. Actually, this gives a nice, cozy effect.

- Decide which door of a house you're going to use—front or back. Weather-strip all other doors as heavily as possible, then forget them. Be sure to seal off keyholes with a piece of insulating tape if they're the old-fashioned shank-key type. If doors have a glass section, curtain them (like windows) and leave the curtains closed. Cover up attic and cellar windows with a "pane" of thin styrofoam sheeting cut to fit and taped into place.

- If you live in a two-story house, hang a ceiling-to-floor drapery at the foot of the stairway to prevent heat from escaping to upper floors. Open it when you go to bed at night to allow heat to rise to bedrooms, and leave bedroom doors open to make the most of heated air rising from the downstairs level.

- Stand a three-panel screen just inside your main outside door. This prevents heat from escaping each time you open that door. If the door opens into a foyer, block off the foyer from the rest of the house with the same kind of screen.

- If you have outside cellar storm doors, fasten them securely and weatherstrip. The same goes for doors to the attic. Remember—expensively heated air will seep upward otherwise.

- If you don't have storm windows, make your own. Outfit each window (or at least those on the north side) with an inside panel of clear plastic staple-gunned to the window frame. For even better protection, seal the stapling with lengths of silver-colored insulating tape. (Don't use masking tape. Come summer, you'll never get it off.)

- Forget keeping the thermostat at 65°F. It's just not warm enough to be comfortable or function efficiently. So it's a total waste. You might just as well set it at 60°, which will keep the pipes from freezing and save another 5°—but plan to sew yourself into an insulated parka for the duration. I set mine at 68° and just forget the lectures from Washington; they're not living on eastern Long Island. And since I'm one-quarter Irish, one-quarter Welsh and one-half Czech, I'm practically a polar bear. As one lover put it while shivering his way to bed in the same delightful ark-house, "Those are all cold countries. But I'm Italian and I'm freezing."

- Develop a family room where you can huddle, particularly if you heat electrically. You can turn up the thermostat in this one room and keep the others at 60°. If you heat with gas or oil and have only one thermostat, body heat will compensate for a lowered thermostat until you make the mad dash toward bedrooms and electric blankets.

- Use higher-watt bulbs in rooms where you congregate. You'd be surprised how much heat they give off, and they're cheaper than turning up the thermostat.

- If you heat with oil, fill your tank during summer even if you have to take out a bank loan to do it. Better yet, try to make a deal with your oil man over the summer and early fall months to prorate the costs. You can always hint that you're going to deal with another supplier.

For cooling, you're putting a lot of these processes into reverse. The aim is to shut out sunlight during the day and let in cooler night air:

- Close curtains, particularly on the sunny side of the house, during the day, and open the curtains and windows at night.

- If you live in a hot, dry climate, introduce bowls of water into rooms to add moisture. They're particularly effective placed in front of open doors and windows or in front of fans, so that moving air has a chance to pick up the moisture. Some ideas: Put a few decorative pebbles in a flat glass container and fill it with water. Or float a flower in it, or a flat floating candle at night. Plants will also help balance the atmosphere, and they look cool.

Fans are cheaper to use than air conditioners.

- If your climate is humid, avoid anything that will add to the moisture already in the air. Install a window fan in the bathroom window to circulate air and evaporate moisture. Do as little home laundry (even in a washer and dryer) as possible. And do it during the cooler parts of the day or at night.

- Use fans, rather than air-conditioning, as much as you can. They're much cheaper, electrically. Hassock types are efficient because they circulate the cooler air at floor level.

- If you do use window air conditioners, try to concentrate as much living in one room as possible. Keep the door closed, turn the unit up full and make the most of it. If you've cooled the room overnight, try to seal it off from the invading daytime heat as much as possible. Make sure the window is curtained against sunlight, and always close the door as you leave. You might consider adding weatherstripping around the door if it doesn't fit tightly into its frame.

Cooking methods can cut utility bills, too. Here are a few small "savers" we often overlook. But they all add up.

- Measure water for coffee or tea before you heat it. Don't boil up a kettleful, then pour most of it away.

- Look for recipes that call for top-of-the-stove cooking rather than baking or roasting; using one burner is cheaper than heating up a whole oven. Stir-fry recipes are ideal.

- When you *do* use the oven, cook several dinners at once—a roast with vegetables around it, a baked ham to serve cold later, plus a casserole. Do the casserole in a dish that can be reheated on top of the stove.

- Cut vegetables into small pieces—they'll cook faster. And use a minimum of water and a French steamer-basket to preserve flavor and vitamin content and use less fuel.
- Make sure that pot lids fit tightly so steam doesn't escape. With one large cast-iron skillet, one Dutch oven and one medium-size saucepan, all with good lids, you can cook just about anything.
- Plan meals that combine "hots" and "colds"—a hot meat and a raw vegetable salad, for instance. Or a cold meat with a hot, one-pot mixed-vegetable dish.

Electric lights: why can't kids learn to turn them off! This is the constant cry of all parents, singled or otherwise. But when you're sweating to pay for rent and food, an extra-high electricity bill makes you want to kill. You can try removing all bulbs and living by candlelight for a night or two. Then gradually replace the bulbs, one by one. When you find a bulb left burning, it disappears for another night. Or confiscate the TV set, since that requires electricity, until there's noticeable improvement. A more positive approach was suggested to Joan Russell by one of the single-parent families who are part of her on-campus group at the University of Colorado. This single parent told her kids that "anything we save this month over last month's bill, we spend on a family treat." And it worked. Apart from disciplined kids, here are some other light-bill savers:

**Flourescent lights last six times longer than incandescents.**

- Buy an industrial clamp-on socket lamp with an aluminum shade, and move it around with you for high-intensity lighting when and where you need it—reading, writing, working in the kitchen, etc.
- Use those little night-light plug-ins to illuminate hallways, bathrooms, foyers and heads of stairs—anywhere you tend to turn on a full-wattage bulb (and leave it burning) just to find your way into the area.
- Substitute fluorescent lights for standard incandescents anywhere you can. They use about half the current and last about six times longer. They're worth the price (which is much higher than incandescent bulbs).
- Scrap decorative but inefficient traditional lamps whenever you can. Substitute art director's lamps (you can buy them in art supplies stores and some hardware stores). They focus light where you need it and have adjustable heads and stems.

How to control phone bills. Judging from the questionnaires, this is a particular problem for many single parents. In answer to the question "How do you deal with the feeling of aloneness," about 80% mentioned phone calls to friends. One California mother summed it up: "You should see my phone bills!" Since I'm a compulsive phone user, I've worked out a few gimmicks that help.

Basically, they involve developing a "phone center." Position your phone where you can keep phone directories and a pad and pencil right at hand (and where there's enough light to use both). Remember, you're charged for information calls now if your phone company bills by message units. Also:

- Select the highest phone bill you've had all year and tape it to the wall behind the phone or to the base of the phone itself.
- Provide a "timer." You can use one of those hourglass egg timers or a standard buzzer-type kitchen timer. In either case, three minutes are the limit.

- For real desperation calls, try to work out a mutual arrangement with one friend that allows both of you to call and conduct "phone therapy" after 11:00 p.m., when you're on minimum rates.

And the dirtiest little trick of all: if you need an out-of-town phone number, call information from a public phone booth (while you're out marketing or whatever). At the present writing, there's still no charge for information requests from public phones!

Extras

"What is the biggest extra expense you face as a single parent?" This was one of the money questions I included in my questionnaire. Many mentioned extra money spent on entertaining, higher food costs for "fast foods," more money spent on clothing because of job requirements. But the majority of answers, by a wide margin, mentioned child-care and auto-related expenses as the biggest extras. Child care was a concern to those parents who had younger children. Those with older kids mentioned the inflated costs of gasoline and car maintenence. Since these are such overriding concerns, I've rounded up as many ideas for cost cutting in these areas as I could find.

Child-Care Alternatives

This section is going to concentrate on child care primarily from the financial point of view. But I am going to include a brief recap of some of the research on the *effects* of working mother situations and outside child care on children. Most working mothers (whether singled or married) suffer guilt pangs about going out to work and leaving children with "surrogate parents." Our society does a lot to implement this guilt. "Oh, you're not worried about using a day-care center?" Or, "Of course you know best, but nobody sent a 3-year-old child to school when *I* was raising *my* children." Both of these remarks are typical of what working mothers have to put up with when the topic of child care comes up. But now, working mothers of the world (and fathers with custody)—take heart! Lift up your heads and thumb your noses at the armchair experts who've been predicting a life of crime and punishment for your deprived youngsters. The November 1978 issue of *Young Children*, the journal of the National Association of Young Children, carried a "Research in Review" article that summed up the findings of the major studies of "Working Mothers and Their Children." The conclusion is that:

> ... there is very little evidence of pervasive negative effects of maternal employment outside the home on the behavior and development of schoolage children. Although less is known about substitute care for very young children, it does seem to be the case that quality day care is not harmful to infants and toddlers. In the future, our own society will probably need to accept more alternative modes of child care than we have in the past.

You'll get more details on this article and on other aspects of child development, in Chapter 7. But I did want to share at least the gist of the good news right away.

Now that we know it doesn't spell disaster for a child—what are the most usual child-care arrangements available and how are they being used?

Parents and relatives: now tax deductible. Parents and relatives are still the most-used child care around. A report on "Children of Working Mothers" prepared by the U.S. Department of Labor, Bureau of Labor Statistics in March 1976, reports that 54% of older children (aged 7 to 13) and 41% of children 3 to 6, with mothers who were employed full-time, were cared for by a parent when they were not in school. Where this kind of care wasn't possible, another 17% were cared for in their own homes by someone else. As of 1979, changes in the tax law make it possible to claim a tax credit for sitter fees paid to relatives as long as you are not claiming that relative as a dependent.

Family day care is another popular option. This can be a licensed arrangement or "underground." In the latter case a woman, usually a mother with a child of her own, agrees to care for several other children for the day. If they are licensed, they can be set up either as a Registered Family Home, which enables them to care for one to six children, or as a Group Care Home, which is allowed to accommodate seven to 12 children. In an August 7, 1979, article for *Woman's Day* magazine, author Mike McGrady reports that while "an estimated two million youngsters are receiving day care in this country, only one in ten go to licensed day-care homes. The great majority are in "underground" or "outlaw" day-care homes. He estimates that rates for full-time child care vary from $25 to $40 per week. Part-time children are usually charged by the hour— approximately $1/hour. In some instances, licensed child care will be paid for by the welfare department, and the sitter-mothers may themselves be augmenting welfare income by providing day care.

Hired sitters. You can hire someone to function as a full-time live-in housekeeper for about $125 per week—which is pie in the sky for most working mothers. Baby sitters hired by the hour run anywhere from 50¢ to $3 an hour, depending on their age and the going rate in your area. Cost-cutter: team up with another parent and share sitter costs. Even if the sitter charges a little more than for "single family" sitting, it will still be cheaper than each parent paying his or her own.

Cooperative nursery groups or playgroups. These are becoming increasingly popular. They can be set up in one of several ways:

- All mothers and/or fathers take turns "on duty" with the group. For safety's sake, it's usually best to figure on having two parents, at least, on duty. Properly organized, this can mean that each parent does one day's baby-sitting and has four days off. This kind of group usually meets for only a few hours each morning, in the on-duty parent's home, and the size of the group remains small.

- Several mothers and/or fathers are assigned to regular stints on duty and the group meets in quarters rented for this purpose. The stints on duty are rotated. With this type of arrangement, more elaborate equipment can be provided, more children (and parents) can be included and, usually, the playgroup hours can be longer. The participating parents share equally in the costs of the rental and any equipment bought.

- Some playgroups are quite sophisticated and hire a professional preschool teacher, with parents rotating as assistants. These too usually meet in rented quarters and a small fee or contribution is part of the agreement.

Nursery schools. At the present time, there are still no public nursery schools in this country although educators and social workers as well as parents have been agitating for them for a long time. Private nursery schools are extremely expensive (up to $2500 per year). Many meet only half a day and they hold to a regular school vacation period. So working parents have to augment them with another group or sitter.

Child-care centers. These are the least-used child-care situations. In her book *Getting Yours—How to Make the System Work for the Working Woman,* Letty Cottin Pogrebin quotes these statistics: "While over five million preschool children have working mothers, there are day care centers for only 640,000 of them." She also points out that "The latest Revenue Act allows a business to deduct over five years, the expenses of acquiring, constructing or rehabilitating property for use as a child care facility for employees' children." However, the tax advantage to a parent for out-of-home care is limited to $200 per month for one child, $300 for two and $400 for three or more (as opposed to up to $400 for in-home sitter care of one child and up to $800 for two or more). Pogrebin feels this indicates a lack of interest and sympathy for working mothers on the part of the IRS.

> Work out a cooperative arrangement with another parent.

Some additional cost-cutting ideas. Since the whole child-care picture is rather grim from the cost point of view, you might consider these alternatives.

- Try to work out a cooperative arrangement with another parent who works part-time. You have to find someone whose hours mesh with yours. Pay them as much as you can deduct from your income tax for child care. Make up any additional amount on a swap basis, that is, you take care of their children a few hours a day or have them sleep over nights during the week in lieu of pay.
- I've already mentioned the possibility of swapping a room and board for free baby-sitting. An additonal wrinkle on this is to try and get another single parent who'll swap free baby-sitting for room and board for parent and child. Or the parent might function as a full-time housekeeper for a small additional amount.
- Try to interest your co-workers and your employer in starting an employee's child-care center. If it's run as a cooperative with parents chipping in to cover the running fees and the firm acquiring and furnishing it (under their tax-deductible allowance), it's really quite feasible. But it does take a lot of convincing.
- Another thought: contact a local college that offers courses in preschool education. You might be able to interest them in supplying students to staff a cooperative playgroup on a rotating basis. Or they might be able to get a "model" day-care facility on campus, partially funded by the college or by a foundation. Participating parents could share in the cost.
- If possible, replace a car with an automatic transmission with one with a manual shift. Automatics use a lot more gas.
- Switch to radial tires if you can possibly afford them. They increase gas mileage up to one mile per gallon. And keep tires inflated to the recommended pressure—this increases gas mileage, too.

School vacations: how other single parents have coped. I asked single parents to describe how they handled the problem of school vacations, particularly that long summertime break. Many mention sending children to visit grandparents or their ex. Day camp is a favorite for younger children, full boarding camps for older children. Some parents with older children mention that they worked part-time when the children were younger just because of this summer vacation problem. One mother from Indiana mentions that her children "are capable of taking care of themselves. I go home to have lunch with them daily and they can phone me at work if problems arise." Another mother says, "My daughter is in a private home after school and for the summer. The home was highly recommended by the school." Another mentions that her preschool daughter is in a nursery full-time now. "As she starts school she will be part-time at the nursery and full-time for vacations."

One mother from Minneapolis mentions a problem that I had to deal with. Her son is currently in an in-home baby sitter's house after school. However, she feels she will have a problem when "he feels he is too old to go to a baby sitter, and I feel he is too young to take care of himself. We do have several day-care camps for children 6-12 in this area which is very helpful." I used a day camp like this for two summers. My worst problem was every day after school, when CH felt it was babyish to be with a sitter. I finally made an arrangement with two other mothers (one of whom had three sons that were all close in age) and we jointly hired a young man who was training to teach phys-ed. He took all five boys to the park after school, dropped the others off a little after 5 p.m. and stayed with my son at my apartment until I got home from work. Somehow, CH didn't think of this as "baby-sitting."

Several parents with teen-age children mentioned that although the kids were old enough to take care of themselves during vacation times, they worried about the trouble they might get into through boredom. All were hoping their kids could find summer jobs. In a tightening economy, this is a very real problem for working parents with teenagers. If you're in this category, be sure to check with your state employment service about special teen-oriented job programs.

Another mother with pre-teen sons has come up with an interesting solution. Three days a week she drops the boys off at a local golf course before she goes to work and they're able to hitch back home. A public swimming pool also makes a handy "sitter" for pre-teen kids.

One mother solves the summer problem for pre-teen children by planning a summer project that needs doing around the house, then pays her kids to do it.

Cutting Auto Costs: Walk or Bicycle!

The annual cost of maintaining a car is around $2500.

Those of us who are being chewed up by the soaring prices of gasoline and oil should seriously consider these two alternatives whenever possible. At least consider the possibility of life without a car. Most experts now put the annual cost of running one at $2500 a year. That will buy a lot of taxi rides. If you live in an area where a car is a must, here are some gas-savers you can try:

• Work out car pools whenever you can—to get to work, to do household shopping and errands, even for social engagements.

- Plan your trips carefully so that you accomplish as much as possible with each one. Try to find stores that are close to each other so you don't find yourself driving all over town just to get a couple of errands done.
- Buy your motor oil at a discount store and put it in yourself. You'll save 30 to 40 cents a quart over what it costs at a filling station.
- Start paying for gas in cash if you've been charging it. You'll be more aware of what it's costing and you'll save interest charges on late payments.
- Think ahead so that you can fill up at stations where gas is cheapest. And if there's a station with a self-service pump near you, use it. You'll save a couple of cents a gallon this way.
- Try to fill up during the middle of the week. Stations have a tendency to raise prices on the weekends when demand is heaviest.

To cut maintenance costs, become a do-it-yourselfer. Many of the women who answered the money questions in my questionnaire mentioned that their former husbands did maintenance work on the family car that the women now have to pay for. I'm not suggesting that we all become expert mechanics, but there are simple maintenance steps almost anyone can do.

- You can learn to put in your own antifreeze. You'll save on the cost of the liquid itself, and also save yourself a $10 to $14 labor charge.
- Have someone show you how to take out old spark plugs and points and replace them with new ones. You needn't do the timing yourself; you can have a garage do that. But you'll cut the cost of replacing these parts by one half to two thirds.
- You can learn to do your own oil changes, too. It's messy, but a lot cheaper than using a service garage.
- Get in the habit of checking the fluid level in both your battery and radiator from time to time, and replacing fluid if it's low. This can save damaged batteries and overheated engines.
- Check with the community college and/or continuing education facility in your community. Many of them are starting to offer courses in basic car maintenance for amateurs. Some singles groups (Parents Without Partners for one) also sometimes offer Practical Skills workshops and/or courses.
- If you have a teenager who's interested in cars and who wants to do minor servicing jobs—let him/her. They're surprisingly knowledgeable.
- Check your local library. There are several good, clear books out, written in layman's language, that show you how to handle the maintenance jobs I've mentioned.
- If no adult education courses in auto mechanics are being given in your area, you might be able to put one together on your own. One friend of mine in Westchester County, New York, got together six other housewives and paid a local mechanic to give them classes in auto maintenance. With Audrey and the others hanging on his every word, he completely overlooked the fact that he was cutting his own throat.

All of these gas-savers and maintenance tips are stopgap measures. The only real way to save on auto costs is to become a non-car owner. Remember, if it's getting to work that necessitates that car, you can look for a job that's accessible by public transportation, bicycle, moped or on foot. You can even take a cut in pay and still come out ahead because of the savings on auto costs!

5/Living in Context: Your Life – Support System

The worst thing that can happen to you as a single parent is to fall out of the social web that supports us all. We're humans, highly social beings, so we arrive in the world already knit into an intricate pattern of relationships. First, there's family—parents, brothers and sisters, other relatives. As we grow up we extend the pattern to include friends, neighbors, the community we live in. As adults, we add to the pattern by creating families of our own. We adults also have to deal with social institutions—schools, churches, community organizations, the business world. And all of this taken together forms a life-support system that keeps us in contact with other human beings and maintains us as members of the human race. It worked before we were couples and while we were couples. Now, as a singled parent, you're a dropped stitch in this warm, comforting shawl of humanity. One of the linking threads is broken. And you can slowly ravel right out of the pattern unless you make a conscious effort to knit yourself back in.

You know that you're the same person you always were. In fact, you may feel you're *more* of a person than you were before the separation. But you have to prove that to society. It's unfair, even cruel sometimes. Why should society desert you now, when you most need the emotional support of others? Don't waste time or energy brooding about this. There are 8½ million single-parent families in the United States alone. Over 7½ million children live with separated or divorced parents. In Canada, one out of 10 families is headed by a single parent, and 850,000 children live in single-parent homes (according to Benjamin Schlesinger of the Faculty of Social Work at the University of Toronto). But our society is still not really ready to deal with us. We're an uncomfortable statistic and we're personally threatening to many individuals. Just recognize these attitudes as facts you must deal with and start repairing your lifeline as rapidly as possible. Your emotional well-being—and your children's—depend on it.

Maintaining Your Lifeline

Almost all of the experts who deal with the survivors of death or divorce agree on the importance of maintaining this lifeline. They see two important issues involved.

Your Children Can't Fill the Void

During the first "shock weeks" after a separation, there's a tendency to draw your children in around you and hole up—a wounded animal hiding in a cave with your cubs. If it had been possible, I think I would have stuffed CH into a pouch like a kangaroo, closed the front door and just "lived" through this time. Fortunately, my anatomy is normal-human (no pouch) and there were little matters to deal with like getting him to school each day and scouting out a job for me. Also, fortunately, he didn't feel that spending all his time cooped up with Mummy was such a great idea—what seemed cozy to me was lonely for him.

Kathleen Everly, Executive Director of the Institute for Family Research and Education in Syracuse, New York, puts it this way: "Obviously, one of the characteristics differentiating the marital [situation] from the single parent is that the single parent must reach outside the home for emotional support from other adults.... Emotional nurturance is not a child's responsibility." (Quoted from an article called "New Directions in Divorce Research" in the Summer 1977 issue of the *Journal of Clinical Child Psychology*.) No, it's not their responsibility and it wouldn't work for you even if it were. You're an adult and you need other adults to interrelate with. While I was attending the Atlanta convention of Parents Without Partners, one Wisconsin member told me this "horror story," as he put it. His chapter received a phone call from a widow who had lived almost totally isolated from the community for two years, ever since her husband's death. She never saw friends, no neighbors came calling, she almost never got out of the house or away from her children. By the time she read about PWP and made the phone call she was practically babbling. In fact, she was so shaken they had to send someone to escort her to the first meeting.

Most of us don't get quite this badly cut off, but I do remember talking to a friend of mine who had relocated in the Midwest shortly after her divorce. Apart from departmental meetings with other faculty members at the college where she taught, she had almost no other adult contacts. Even though she's an unusually self-sufficient person, she described it as "great for the girls. They're making friends in school. But I'm very lonely and depressed." After her call, I began to count up how many adults apart from family I'd seen in the previous weeks, and was appalled at the tally. I also realized that I had quite literally started talking to myself as I schmoozed around the apartment each night after CH was in bed.

I took the hint, sat down with my personal phone book and an old Christmas list from the ad agency I'd worked for a few years before, and managed to scrape up 10 names—people I'd always liked but hadn't seen much of while married because they were "singles." I invited all ten in for drinks—my first party as a single hostess. We were a little mismatched, but we all survived and three of the guests became fairly close friends of mine.

Children Need This Support System, Too

When children experience parental loss through death or separation, the reactions of the human network around them influence their views of themselves. If children are shunned or ignored, they may come to see themselves as worthless, deserving to be abandoned. If they're accepted and maintained within the web, they understand that they're still worthwhile, a source of pleasure to themselves and others.

The book *Children of Parting Parents,* by Lora Heims Tessman, is based on material from therapy or counseling sessions with 50 children and their parents. In her chapter about the human relationship network, the author says that:

> Children seemed best able to cope with the distress about parental death or separation when other meaningful relationships could remain undisrupted. For young children, this meant that it was usually worthwhile to keep the same baby sitters, nursery school, or day-care arrangements, contacts with extended family or neighbors as before.

Even if some changes have to be made, it's obviously better for our children to be able to remain in contact with grandparents, other relatives and family friends than to suddenly find themselves living in a void.

Remember, children keep in contact with this support system through you. If you let yourself get cut out, they're cut off too. Sometimes it's unavoidable—for instance, there are parents-in-law who are so completely tied in to their own child that, particularly in divorce, they literally "throw the baby out with the bathwater." In lashing back at you, they exclude your children—their own grandchildren—from their lives. I'm not implying any criticism if this has happened to you. I'm just saying that for all of us, it's worth making extra efforts to keep in touch with as much of our social web as we can.

If we become aware and angry enough, we can effect changes.

"Living in Context"

"All right. What did you have in mind?" Many of us are legitimately bitter about being dropped from the social pattern once we are singled. Also, quite frankly, I find that while most experts agree on the importance of "living in context," they're a little short on advice about how to accomplish this. The most helpful information I can share with you comes from single parents themselves. In formal interviews, in single-parent gatherings and in answering the questionnaires I sent out, they described a variety of situations they had themselves experienced and dealt with. Not all of the answers are positive. But they do show where the most common problems occur. And in many instances they show ways of maintaining or repairing these vital relationships.

Some of this reading will make you very angry. At least I hope it does, because it proves how badly some of our institutions fail us and our children. But if we become aware enough and angry enough, we can start to effect changes. Some of the reading is also very hopeful, I feel. It shows that we're not helpless. Our choices may be limited but we're not completely acted upon. We can take some constructive steps. And each successful step frees us further and opens the choices wider.

Communication and Cooperation

These seem to be the key words. The situations I asked about include a wide range of relationships and social institutions. But whether they are dealing with their own families, with friends, communities, schools, churches or the therapy establishment itself, the most successful single parents mention being able to "talk frankly," "open up" to the situation, "ask for help." They also mention becoming involved with and cooperative with the individuals or groups they are trying to reach. And as I read through the answers, I realized that these were the approaches that had always worked best for me, too. The worst times I've had were those instances where I failed to speak up or waited until the situation had deteriorated badly. But you'll see what I mean as you read the answers for yourselves.

Parents/Grandparents: Mostly Supportive, Sometimes Too Much So!

About two thirds of the single parents who commented on their relationships with parents/grandparents felt that the situation was good. Some, like my friend who relocated in the Midwest, mentioned that mothers had been very supportive. Mag specified that hers was great "before the divorce when I was a basket case emotionally" and after the move. "She actually came out and kept house for me for a while after I got my new job and was writing my thesis." Another mother, a credit manager in New York State with three teen-age children, mentions that the grandparents were "supportive and financially helpful." The mother of an 11-year-old, a factory worker from Illinois, says that "Grandpa is my backbone and my daughter listens to him!" Many of the men agreed with the Canadian father of two who wrote in that grandparents (as well as relatives and friends) were "all very cooperative and understanding."

Some have not had such an easy time, however. One father from Staten Island, New York, writes that his father-in-law requested that he stop corresponding because this in-law is "unable to deal with his feelings toward our separation." Another mother, an accountant with four kids 17 to 29, states that "My husband's mother wrote off her grandchildren as a result of our divorce." More specific problems include a "generation gap between my parents and my children" and parents/grandparents who maintain old-fashioned ideas about divorce. Several mention grandparents who spoil children by smothering them with love, by constantly buying treats and letting them do whatever they want to do; some grandparents make remarks about the absent parent in the kids' hearing.

Several singled mothers also mentioned conflicts over the question of their working instead of staying home with the children. And one mother writes that her own mother is very unsupportive because "I think she is jealous of my freedom."

How do you deal with problems like these? One very constructive solution comes from a teacher in Alaska who has two sons 7 and 9. She describes her family as "very supportive. I risked letting them know there was a problem at the beginning. Their answer was 'you are loved as you are.' " Wisely, I think, this woman went even further in frankly discussing her problems with her family. "I shared with them, through tapes, my pain in becoming an unmarried woman. Their answer, which came from my 90-year-old grandmother, my brother and my dad and step-mom was that when one door shuts another opens." Another single parent stresses the fact that you have to let parents know how you are feeling and when you need or want emotional bolstering. As she points out, "There are no mind readers."

Another Connecticut mother with four daughters found that while her own family had been wonderful, "my ex's were bitter at first. But since they have seen that I have no intention of stopping my kids from seeing them, they have been very helpful." A lot of in-law hostility springs from this fear that they will be cut off from their grandchildren. And to save *themselves* hurt, they begin to retreat or "fade away," as one father put it. Many times, too, it's easier for the live-with parent to keep up closer grandparent/grandchildren relationships with their own parents than with their ex-in-laws. Taking the time and trouble to reassure grandparents that you want to maintain these ties can be helpful. And if your kids *are* seeing more of one set of grandparents than the other, be sure to explain that it's a practical problem (if that's what it is) and not an expression of hostility on your part. Here are parent/grandparent problems and practical steps you can take to ease them:

- *Spoiling or smothering the kids*—start with a positive. Explain how much you appreciate their support and loving gestures. But *also* explain that it's best for children to face consistent attitudes about treats and about what they may and may not do. Be specific about the house rules you've laid down for your kids, and ask grandparents to try to hold the same regulations. Remember, they may not know what your rules are— they're not mind-readers!

- *The "poor you" approach toward you*—this can devastate your attempts to establish yourself as a capable, self-loving and separate individual. Thank them for caring but explain that you need their encouragement to stand alone and their respect for the progress you've already made. They may think that an overabundance of sympathy is what you want and need.

- *If distance is a problem* (and it sometimes is with grandparents)—realize that you're living in the twentieth century. Send pictures and taped messages from the kids. And encourage grandparents to keep in touch via tapes, too. It's a lot easier for many people to talk into a tape recorder than to sit down and write a letter. Photos and tapes can also ease the generation gap. Children generally look and sound adorable at a comfortable distance—who's to know that Johnny spilled his soda on the table while taping? It comes through as a gale of giggles (adorable!) and the mess is splattered over your table, not grandma's.

- *Discussing taboo topics in front of the kids*—let parents/grandparents know what you consider to be "no-no's," like derogatory remarks about the absent parent, sad-voiced discussions on the evils of divorce, conversations that classify your kids as Little Orphan Annies because one parent has died. If these conversations keep coming up, first try a relatively mild protest—change the subject. If they still don't get the point, get firmer. Announce that you (or they) will have to leave if the topic continues. If this doesn't work, start cutting the visits short. When they know you're only going to be there for an hour or two, they'll usually stick to important topics like how much the kids have grown, how are they doing in school, they've gotten fatter, thinner, etc. It takes time to work into the other stuff. Remember—most grandparents really don't want to harm their grandchildren. It's more a lack of understanding than it is malice. If the situation gets really bad, you'll have to cut down contact to a minimum. That's what brilliant, beautiful

Send pictures and taped messages from the kids.

and self-protecting Barbara from Chapter 1 did. But really, try everything else first—you may be overreacting a bit too, you know.

If I'm making this sound as though you need the patience of Job—you sometimes do. But at their best, your parents have a lot to offer you now that you're singled. They're your track back into your own past—proof that you existed as an individual before you coupled. Often, they have more time than you do, so they can give your kids the extra fun that you have to cut short on. And they can sometimes provide overnight baby-sitting at their home, which allows you some much-needed privacy in yours.

Remember that it's a two-way street, though. Don't be afraid to ask for help and understanding when you need it; but make it clear that you don't intend to impose. If they've agreed to baby-sit for you or take the kids overnight, don't change arrangements at the last minute. And if your kids are eating there frequently, try to pick up the expense in some way. Tell them frankly that you'd like to share in the cost of the food. Or say that the dinner's on you and arrive with pizza or Chinese food or a picnic meal everyone can share. Even if grandparents prefer not to have you do this, they'll appreciate your offer. It shows that you care about *them,* too.

Other Relatives

When they are good they are very, very good—when they are bad they are awful!

I'd like to make a strong case for trying to build up close relationships with relatives of your own generation—brothers, sisters, cousins, younger aunts and uncles. These family members are an investment in the future because their children will form a family network for your own kids as they all grow up. If you're divorced, these relatives are apt to be more tolerant of your situation, too. In fact, some may be divorced themselves. Joan English, whom you met in Chapter 2, mentioned that her divorced sister has been particularly supportive because she knows about readjustment difficulties first-hand. The woman mentioned earlier who feels that her own mother is unsympathetic because she is jealous of the freedom single parenthood confers says that her younger brother has been "very supportive all along." In cases where you're having difficulties with your parents, brothers and/or sisters can be the link that keeps you in contact with your family.

CH and I were really blessed when it came to relatives of all ages, both my own and my ex-husband's. In fact, I'd like to give a public thank-you to my Murdock in-laws and their kids (the cousins, as we call them) for the warmth and support they gave us during and after the separation. For CH, visiting back and forth with the cousins helped ease the strangeness of living in a new apartment and neighborhood, separated from his father. It meant that "the family," as he knew it, continued unshaken. I don't think I would have gotten through that first day without my sister-in-law who drove down from Greenwich, Connecticut, to be with me, and who brought the best possible "first day separation" gifts I can imagine—a picnic lunch, geraniums for the backyard and a bottle of gin for me!

As CH and I continued to live and develop as a single-parent family, our relationship with my own brother and his family was vitally important. When I took on a full-time editorial job, which often kept me working until 7:00 p.m. or later, they became CH's after-school family. He had begun to object to a sitter as babyish;

and even the mini-playgroup I arranged finally began to pall. So almost every weekday afternoon, my sister-in-law Valorie welcomed CH (*plus* a couple of his classmates) into her home. Often he stayed for dinner. CH still loves their son Charlie as a younger brother. Since both are only children, I hope the brotherhood continues throughout their lives.

I don't think that I'm unique in these family relationships. Many of the divorced single parents I contacted in person or by questionnaire find their relatives neutral or supportive, by a count of about 2 to 1. This is particularly true of the male single parents. The widowed, on the other hand, are much less enthusiastic about their relatives; perhaps they expected more support than divorced parents do.

The most frequent problems. Those most commonly mentioned are criticism of the single parent and a "poor little kids" attitude toward their children. How do you handle these situations? Here again, I think that straightforward communication is the best answer. Why not be as frank as the Staten Island teacher who says right out: "I need to be told that I'm bringing the boys up 'right' or well. Was unsure at early teenage stage." It's no disgrace to admit that you need and want praise. You can also gently point out specific remarks that hurt. Your relatives may not even know when they're bruising your feelings. You may also have to explain to them (as you may to grandparents) that your kids don't benefit from constant doses of "I feel so sorry for you." Suggest some practical ways relatives can help your kids instead—by inviting them for after-school visits, by occasionally including all of you in a family outing, by remembering birthdays with a card or phone call. Many families have never dealt with single parenthood before and they're going on guesswork. If they really feel warmly toward you, they'll appreciate learning what your needs are.

Less common but more serious problems. A few single parents are flagrantly abused by relatives. One young mother with a 6-year-old son mentions an uncle who has made sexual advances to her since her divorce. A young widow, now remarried, told me that her former father-in-law tried to rape her while she was widowed. A business friend I've known for a long time mentioned that after her divorce, her cousin's husband started calling to invite her out for drinks. These situations rarely happen. When they do, they are sickening to face and heart-wrenching to hear about. They prove that even within her own family, a singled woman can be seen as fair game. Anyone can handle coy little phone calls with a firmly worded "no." But if physical advances or attacks occur, I recommend that you contact the nearest chapter of NOW for advice and help. Or call a local community service organization. Most importantly, remember that these abuses are no reflection on you personally. Direct your feelings of anger and disgust toward the predator, not toward yourself.

Friends: You Win Some, You Lose Some

Who said "You can't choose your relatives, but you can choose your friends?" Who cares—this old saw is very valuable advice for single parents, particularly when relatives are behaving like nerds. In his book *Marital Separation*, sociologist Robert S. Weiss puts it this way: ". . . assured membership in a valued network is necessary for a satisfactory life; it is this that fends off social isolation, with all its deficits and discomforts." A single parent from New York City puts it more bluntly: "Friends have been my only support system."

Straightforward communication is the best way to deal with problems concerning the kids.

Single parents
need new and differ-
ent kinds of friends.

Most of us rapidly discover, however, that we need new and different kinds of friends when we start living singly. I'm not talking about lovers—that's the next chapter. I mean friends—even acquaintances—with whom you have a basis of understanding; with whom you can share your ideas, experiences, sorrows and pleasures. Also—very important—friends and acquaintances who live by the same timetable you do, so that they're free when you are.

I've never met a singled parent, for instance, who didn't feel that she or he had begun to lose touch with former married friends shortly after becoming singled. The best I was able to achieve was a straddle—one foot in the world of the married through friends who went back to school days, the other in the singled world with friends made after my divorce. There are lots of reasons for this falloff, some due to our reactions, some to theirs; some quite understandable, others foolish or cruel. As I see it, they break out this way:

Sexual free float. Married people are publicly committed to sexual monogamy. They see singled parents as free floaters, bobbing around the social scene, no longer anchored by former sexual ties now severed by divorce or death. This can create three reactions—fear or envy or both.

Married women are afraid of husband-hunting. Married men are suspicious of wife-raiding. Even when they believe that *we're* completely well intentioned, they're not always that sure of their mates. As Erica Abeel put it in the book she wrote about her own divorce, *Only When I Laugh,* married sex can become a bit settled, sort of "comes with the dinner." We represent a new and delicious bit of dessert (or so some believe), spiced with the unfamiliar and sauced with hey nonny nonny.

The other attitude, envy, can produce a desire to punish. "I'm stuck with my klutz. Why should he/she be racketing around free to take another grab at the gold ring? Single is what he/she wants, so single it is." And they enforce their attitude by leaving you alone.

There are only two ways to handle this fear/envy, as far as I can see. One: be careful *not* to violate your married friends' territorial rights. Two: deliberately bring up the whole topic in conversation and make it perfectly clear that you're not interested in anybody else's mate, with reasons. "The last thing in the world I need is somebody else's guy who comes complete with children and support and alimony payments" is how one divorcee I met at a single-parent group explains it. "Broken marriages are painful. And I've had all the hurt I need" is the explanation another singled friend of mine uses. Your married friends may not believe you, but you can try.

Sex is part of the reason singled parents are uncomfortable with married couples. As one medical secretary from Pennsylvania, the mother of two young sons, puts it, "Wives found me a threat and husbands tried to get me into bed." Singled men also mention not-so-subtle advances from wives. If you're really trying to maintain a friendship, this can be angering and embarrassing. Also, almost impossible to deal with, except by severing the friendship if the mate-on-the-make is really determined.

Some married people also show a kind of wet-lipped curiosity about our sex lives that can be very unpleasant. Since I don't ask married friends how many times a week they have intercourse, why should they ask me? One strong-minded single parent I met told me how she'd silenced a familiar question about *her* sex life. At the top of her lungs, in a diner, she announced flatly, "With a broomstick." No more questions.

I'll take up some of the other ways sex makes it difficult to share social time with married couples in the next chapter.

Different life schedules. This is a pure and simple reason for our drifting away from married friends. Most women who become single parents start or return to jobs. So they're not available during the day for lunches, bridge games, shopping jaunts. And after being out of the home all day, many feel they should spend evenings with their children. Fatigue, a workday that starts early and sitter costs also cut down on midweek socializing. Weekends are often a problem for singled males because this is when children come visiting. Very few married couples include children in a dinner invitation.

The suburbia syndrome. This, too, works against continued friendships between married couples and singled parents. There's a strong tendency among the married to forget that single-parent families are just that—families. And they would appreciate being included in *family* activities their married friends plan. Many of the single parents I spoke to voiced this wish. And, in fact, only one single parent who responded to the questionnaire mentioned that she has some married neighbor-friends who invite her young daughter over to share activities with their children. So we single parents head for each other and start to plan family outings of our own. Or we join single-parent organizations that provide us with these opportunities.

Keep in touch with old friends by phone or note.

The contagious-disease theory. Some marrieds act as though single parenthood were catching. When I discussed this reaction with two single parents, both social workers who daily deal with other single parents and community attitudes toward them, they came up with some interesting sidelights. One mentioned male fear and distrust of women who are making it on their own. Dolores felt that some husbands want to keep their wives from recognizing that they could function independently of a husband. Ruth mentioned some marrieds' fear of the "single-parent under-ground"—a single parent may hear about an extracurricular affair from other single parents and pass the word along to a previously unsuspicious married friend.

Envy plays a part in this reaction, too—not envy over supposed sexual freedom but, sometimes, the recognition that a singled friend or acquaintance has grown, blossomed, developed new capacities and a new sense of self. This can be very threatening to someone who's married, particularly if he or she is feeling trapped or cramped in marriage. All you can do is continue to show that you want to be friends and hope the friend manages enough inner growth to make you less threatening.

Are we sometimes at fault? Some single parents recognize that their own attitudes have contributed to broken friendships. One child psychologist from New Jersey, with three children aged 4 through 21, wrote that she'd experienced some rejection the first few years. She also honestly admits, "I was defensive too. Needed this space I guess to heal up and maybe I created it as much as others did." My friend Mag wrote me that "At first I thought my friends could have been more supportive. But then as the same thing happened to them one by one, I wasn't any better. I discovered that you're a kind of embarrassment to those who are married. And those who are not are too busy trying to keep their own heads above water."

Purely practical problems: the easiest to solve. There are a few do's and don'ts you should hold on to if you really want to maintain a circle of married friends:

- Recognize that you *are* going to lose some. Face that. Then don't bore the others with nagging or self-pitying stories about how rotten your friends have been. Spend that time showing the true-blues how much you appreciate them.

- Realize the exigencies of differing life schedules. Keep in touch by phone or note when the timing prevents seeing each other. Mel Krantzler (*Creative Divorce*) describes one woman who sets aside an occasional evening hour just for calling old friends. She keeps the chats short but she keeps in touch! She relaxes with a martini while she phones, but I'd add a caution to this: keep it to one or you'll end up with some phone bill!

- Recognize financial realities. Very few marrieds can (or want to) keep paying your way in restaurants or bars. It's much easier for single men to chip in when the bill comes than it is for women. If you're close friends, you can hand the husband whatever you figure your share is (including the tip) after he's paid the bill. But don't pull your money out and slap it down on the table while he's figuring! Tell the waiter that you want to settle up your share separately, before the rest of the bill is presented. If the host or hostess notices the discrepancy, just mention quietly that you're "already taken care of."

Look around you . . . The odds are in your favor.

- When you invite married friends to a party in your home, make sure they're not the *only* marrieds. Think about how you feel when you're the only single in a group. If it's a big party make sure it's about 50-50—marrieds and singles. And skip any singled friends who are apt to get plastered and act hostile or (even worse) get lovey toward marrieds. Skip any married friends who are apt to do the same. Believe me, I speak from experience. I once had to separate a woozily affectionate Bronxville husband from an irate lib friend of mine who was not at all amused by his antics. Nor was his wife, I might add.

Single Friends: Who, Where and How

If you're freshly singled, gradually losing touch with former friends and still not sure of how this new world you're living in shapes up, you can get pretty depressed. One single parent wrote that "the loss of my friends hurt as much as the divorce." But she adds, "I've made almost all new friends." If the rest of us can do it, so can you.

Start with a positive attitude. I usually grind my teeth over self-help advice like this. But here it happens to be true. You have to want to meet people, and you have to feel that you have something to give. I was very shy as a child but my mother drummed this truth into me: most people are just as afraid of taking the first step as you are. Keep telling yourself this. And remember, there are almost 153 million adults over 20 in the United States for you to meet, but only one of you. So the odds are in your favor. Learn to look at it as wisely as one single parent from Long Island, New York, does. "Make new friends. You have a new life to lead," she advises. And she's right.

Start with where you are. Take a look around you. Look at your neighbors, at your co-workers, at the parents of your children's friends. But don't just look. Think and feel. How many of them are singled, too? Marriage puts blinders on us. We tend to see only other marrieds. And we tend to choose friends that *both* sides of the marriage can get along with. But you're on your own now, so you're free to reach out to people *you* feel drawn to.

When you start to look at people as possible friends, the thought gets across to them. You see them in a new light; they see you. Maybe some of them wanted to be friends all along. But you were so enmeshed in your marriage that you never noticed.

The first step doesn't have to be a giant stride. It can start with an exchange of words or a shared laugh, or by volunteering a few facts about yourself. And you don't have to be afraid of taking the first step. Very few people rebuff a friendly gesture. They may not follow up on it, but they won't slam you down there and then.

Start with parents of your children's friends. Particularly if you find out they're singled, too. Remember, they're in the same boat you are! And they're easy to reach—many schools provide class lists with parents' names and addresses. Or approach the school principal or a student advisor frankly. Tell them you're singled and that you want to build up a network of friendships with other single-parent families for your sake and your children's. Single parents have had some pretty horrendous experiences with school personnel (which I'll talk about later in this chapter), so be sensible. If the school *is* a horror show, skip this bit. But if they seem generally supportive in other ways, it's worth a try.

When I first moved to Bridgehampton, where I still live, I didn't know anyone. Furthermore, I was freelancing, so I had to make frequent trips into New York City, which cut down on the time I could spend seeking out Bridgehampton acquaintanceships. CH, meanwhile, was making friends at school, and I honestly felt that I should have at least a nodding acquaintance with their parents. I also felt they should have a look at me. So I gave an open house over Christmas vacation for all those parents, explaining why when I called to extend the invitation. Most accepted, and several have become staunch friends whom I treasure.

Start with your own interests. If you already have a hobby or there's a new interest you'd like to develop—bird-watching, needlework, archeology, whatever— see if there's a club or organization in your town based on that interest. This has become such a well-recognized way for singles to meet that you can hardly miss. I joined a national conservation/hiking club, with a New York City chapter. I learned a lot about bird banding and bird flight patterns. And I did make a couple of rewarding friendships. (I also beat off an occasional barracuda who thought friendship meant a one-night stand in a tent.)

Support Groups: The Pros and Cons

Some of us are "joiners," others are not. So how you feel about support groups, particularly those that exist specifically to serve singled parents, depends upon your own personality. In *Marital Separation,* Robert Weiss calls these groups "supplementary communities" and describes their advantages and disadvantages:

- *One of the most important plusses,* he mentions, is the fact that it's easy to form a network of friendships within the group. Usually, other members have developed a philosophy of friendliness toward newcomers. Because they have faced, or are facing, the same problems and experiences you are, they are often more understanding than the general community and more willing to share your doubts and fears. Often, too, they have amassed a "store of experience and [are] equipped to provide … useful advice … and services tailored to potential members' needs."

- *On the debit side* (and this is true of any group or organization) is the fact that you do not personally choose the other members as you do personal friends. So you'll find a wide variety of personalities, social and economic levels represented. Also, if you're a very private kind of person, you may feel that membership in a self-help group implies that you can't make it on your own. But if you approach the group with the idea that you don't have to become close personal friends with every member and also realize that everyone needs help at some time in their lives, participating in these groups can be a very positive experience.

Parents Without Partners

Here's an inside look at the largest single-parent group, the group that I've had the most personal experience with. As individuals and as an organization, I've found them friendly, supportive, extremely knowledgeable about single-parent problems and very practically oriented in helping to solve some of those problems. The idea for forming the group was conceived by Jacqui Bernard, a writer, and Jim Egleson, an artist, both single parents living in New York City. They got the idea off the ground with this ad in the February 13, 1957, issue of the *New York Post:*

Everyone **needs help at some time in their lives.**

> PARENTS WITHOUT PARTNERS: Whether you have your children full time or "on visitation," wouldn't you like to know others in the same position—talk over common problems, to develop a fuller life for both yourselves and your children, to hold discussions with psychologists, lawyers, etc.? We'd like to hear from you.

In response, 25 people showed up at the first meeting, on March 21, 1957. From that start, the group has grown to its present membership of 180,000 in more than 900 chapters in the United States, Canada, Australia and South Africa, with affiliated groups in several European countries.

PWP now publishes a monthly magazine, *The Single Parent,* and has also formed an International Youth Council (IYC) open to single-parent children (12 to 19 years of age.) The council's purpose is to provide contact with other youths who are experiencing life in a single-parent family.

Each chapter of PWP develops its own schedule of adult social activities, discussion groups and family outings. Larger-zone conferences and a yearly International Conference offer workshops given by professionals who specialize in matters relating to single-parent living. The PWP Information Center represents the single largest collection of educational and informational material on single parenthood in the country. And the organization is often consulted on single-parent issues by legislators, researchers and writers.

These are the bare-bones facts and statistics. But what is a meeting really like?

Orientation

You'll find your local chapter of PWP listed in your phone directory. When you first contact them, you'll probably be invited to an orientation meeting. In smaller chapters, this can be a simple discussion of the PWP setup and what it offers. In large chapters like the Suffolk Chapter #64, with a total of several thousand members, it may include several sessions with trained member-speakers discussing basic topics like "Overcoming Depression" and "Achieving Emotional Separation." When I attended the Suffolk meeting-series for background information for this book, I was honestly impressed with the humanity and depth of understanding these speakers offered. In fact, I was so impressed I joined up! And you don't have to worry about feeling like the new kid at school. These are all people who've experienced loneliness, so they're ready and willing to meet you more than halfway. During the coffee-and-cake social time after the discussion period, you'll find members coming up to you, introducing themselves and starting friendly conversations.

To give you an idea of the PWP activities available, here's a partial listing from the newsletter of the Peconic Bay Chapter #308, which I belong to: a "bring your own supper" beach party for members and their kids, an afternoon of family bowling, a Sunday brunch, a showing of a March of Dimes film on "Teenage Pregnancy," a "Car Care" workshop conducted by a professional auto mechanic. This last is typical of a "Practical Skills" workshop program that grew out of a conversation between Helmut Lecke, who is an international director of PWP and head of their education program, and a professional psychotherapist. When Helmut asked how PWP could be more helpful to members who were experiencing "separation distress," the therapist said, "I can help them deal with the psychological problems during a therapy session but I can't offset the frustration and feeling of defeat a woman suffers when she goes home and finds a blown fuse she doesn't know how to deal with, or a father, when he burns up a pot roast he's trying to cook." With this clue, PWP started encouraging chapters to schedule workshops in which members shared practical know-how—simple auto care and appliance repair for women, cooking and other homemaking skills for men. Presented in a friendly, sharing way, these workshops are a practical contribution to single-parent living.

Your Own Life-Saving System

If you're not group-minded, take the advice of many single parents who mention the value of developing a special "distress pal"—someone you can phone when the walls are closing in or you're struggling with one of those "it's the pits" days. Naturally, it's a reciprocal arrangement. It can also be helpful to start an informal discussion group with your own single-parent friends. I've found this works best if you keep it to a straight information-swapping system. "What are you doing about baby-sitting? How do you handle sharing the family car with your teenagers?" That kind of thing. Stay away from the "let's analyze each other" approach. Face it— you're not therapists and you can do more harm than good if the discussion gets out of hand. If you make a rule that you're there to share information, not to judge others' attitudes, meetings like this can be very supportive.

"The family of friends: collected, constructed, chosen." I'm quoting from an article by Mel Ziegler, "Friends Are the New Family," in the October 1977 issue of *Apartment Life* magazine. Here he discusses one of the developing extensions to the nuclear family—a friend group that becomes as intimate as family, but without blood ties. Since we ourselves represent a modification of the nuclear family, which in its pure form consists of a mother, father and their children living in one residence not shared with any other kin, we may often have to search out and explore new social groupings. What do you do about holidays, for instance, if you have a strong sense of family but live too far away from your own blood kin to share these special times with them? What do you do if you find family genuinely unable to comfortably accept your separated status? How do you handle holidays when your children are visiting their other parent? These are all situations where a family of friends can become meaningful.

My own family is very holiday-minded. But after I was divorced, I began to discover that CH and I were falling into a pattern of celebrating holidays in my mother's or brother's home—in other words, outside of our own home. While I appreciated the sense of sharing and of coming together, I felt that we should develop a tradition of celebration within our own environs or they would become just a place to eat and sleep, a kind of permanent hotel. So we began to spend part of each holiday in our own home, inviting special friends in to share the occasion with us. Since these were *chosen* family, people whom I loved because we shared common likes and interests, I found we often created special happenings that would never have occurred with my own kin. One memorable Christmas Eve, a dear friend who specializes in extemporaneous drama sparked a spur-of-the-moment pantomime of the Nativity scene. It was a robust performance with one of the visiting children turning in an academy-award interpretation of a cow licking baby Jesus' hand (this role played by another young visitor) as a sign of love and welcoming. Each of us will rely on a special circle of friends in our own way. But the sense of family and the support gained from such a grouping can be one of the pleasant surprises of single-parent living.

Schools vs. Single Parents, or, "Who's Learning What?"

Judging from interviews and from answers to questionnaires, it's obvious that our school systems have a lot to learn about single parents and about how to deal with us and our children. But it's also apparent that there are some things we can do to help schools adjust to this new lifestyle that so many of their pupils are living. Again, communication and cooperation are essential.

General Gripes

Statements like this one, from a Kansas optician with two sons 12 and 14, about negative school experiences are typical: "School staff—negative attitude toward single female parents. Too much advice, not enough confidence." A receptionist from New Jersey puts it more strongly: "School staff (in this community) tend to treat the *divorced* parent and her children like 'fallen angels.' If something minor goes wrong in school they attribute it to 'the family situation.' This attitude is detrimental and caused me to avoid school functions." The most extreme situation was reported by a Texas mother: "[Single parents] are discriminated against in the 'Bible belt.' My son's school counselor criticized me for being divorced and being a member of a church that permitted divorce, so I contacted the American Civil Liberties Union which helped me." Congratulations, lady, for your courage and determination!

Specific Gripes

These range from pragmatic matters to very serious discriminatory attitudes. Some of the complaints single parents voiced to me are completely practical problems. This doesn't mean they're not serious—they are. But they may be easier to deal with than deep-rooted, subliminal prejudice. I'll cover the major complaints and add possible solutions that could be suggested to school authorities.

Parent-teacher conferences scheduled during working hours. This is a frequent complaint, and one that schools are going to hear more and more frequently as more and more mothers join the labor force. Two-parent families, even where both parents are working, can share this responsibility of meeting with teachers because one parent can cover for the other. In single-parent families, it's the custodial parent who must try to shoulder the whole load. One eastern Long Island father, bringing up three sons on his own, puts it bluntly: "I find most teachers don't give a damn. They won't help. There are exceptions." If you work in a tightly organized office or are dealing with a particularly busy work schedule, you may just have to skip the conference.

Possible solution: You might suggest a telephone conference. Arrange a mutually convenient time, then *you* place the call. One single parent mentioned that her school had in fact suggested this to her.

Not recognizing the money squeeze single parents face. Two single mothers describe this very succinctly. The first: "I wish the school staff would ask for a little *less* financial support from *me*! Not enough notice when the kids need money or materials; like they need it yesterday and the only store that carries it is 10 miles across town." Special school activities can be a particular burden, as this mother from Herkimer, New York, notes: "I think schools expect too much. For instance, a trip someplace and eat on the way. When I had three in school, in the band, and they each needed $2 it was a crunch on the budget. Or when they needed new color guard boots, gloves, etc.—things they need or be left out of the crowd."

Possible solution: Be perfectly frank with the school administration, individual teachers and with your kids. Tell them all that you're on a limited budget in terms of both money and time. Stress the fact that with enough advance notice, you may be able to handle the "specials" but that unexpected demands cause problems. If you can't handle extra money demands, be frank about that, too. Maybe the school has access to special funding. If not, you'll have to plan out with your own children which extras you *can* cope with. But all of this means that you must have some idea of what's involved *ahead of time*.

> Be frank with the administration, teachers, and your kids.

Stereotyping you and your children in the two-parent family mold. This kind of thinking creates situations that range from the sad to the ridiculous. Starting with the ludicrous, there's the school that adamantly continues to address parent mailings to "Mr. and Mrs. Zilch" even when it's a matter of record that you're divorced and your child lives with *you*. Or as one widowed parent puts it: "School letters of recognition (run off from form styluses) saying 'Congratulations to the parents of . . .'."

Much more serious is the school habit of preserving special Mother's Day and Father's Day activities. Kids spend crafts time making gifts for mothers or fathers whom they never see—or who may be dead. When I mentioned this point to CH, just to let off some steam, he laughed and said, "Yeah, they did that to me. I thought they were retards." So at best, our kids see it as asinine; at worst, it can be very painful.

Sometimes you *and* they go through the agony of rounding up a stand-in for the missing parent when the school schedules "fathers'/mothers' visiting days." One of the strongest reactions against this came from Nina, a friend of mine who has two sons and has been happily married for 12 years. The school scheduled a fathers' day; her husband was going to be out of town on business. The kids got upset, so Grandpa agreed to stand in. Grandpa comes down with a tooth infection the night before the big day; the kids are hysterical, so is Nina. Finally she cons a busy but willing brother-in-law into making an appearance.

Possible solution: After the dust settled, Nina and several other mothers (some singled, some not) issued a formal, strongly worded statement to the school protesting this kind of holiday. And the school agreed to stop! Sometimes you just have to get vocal to get results.

Insults and "bull in a china shop" insensitivity. Eileen Herlbert, an International Director and head of Parents Without Partners' Children's Activities Committee, has single-handedly raised 10 children of her own. She was the first (but not the last) single parent who mentioned how frequently school staff use the outworn description "broken home" to describe our households. Many other single parents share her resentment. Some have solved the problem by telling their kids to politely mention that "My home isn't broken. The roof's on, the sides are tight. And the porch is freshly painted." (Translate into apartmentese if necessary.) A Minneapolis mother puts it this way: "I get very tired of school people referring to single-parent homes. I get very defensive about the assumption that every home needs a man." Fathers who are raising their kids themselves get equally defensive about remarks like "Men can't raise kids" or "Kids need a mother." Actually, this whole question of mother-father image and single-parent vs. two-parent care is being reexamined and revised in research circles today.

Solution: Educate the teachers!

Schools are sometimes quick to judge single parents without really checking on the facts. One Des Moines mother who's working 70 hours a week to support three kids says that her "school staff thinks I'm neglecting my kids when I don't stay home with a slightly sick 14-year-old." Even more sobering is the case of the Minnesota mother whose "school accused me of condoning or pushing drug sales in my house. (My home was near the school and I worked during the day.) They gave me no opportunity to try to handle the situation myself but notified other parents before telling me."

Possible solutions: More and better communication, more education about the realities of single parenthood can help. Parents Without Partners often provides speakers for PTA sessions on one-parent households. Your local community service group may be equipped to address such a meeting. But the meeting won't happen unless you get up and ask for it! I also think it's time we began to bunt back some of those brickbat remarks. What's wrong with saying "I object to phrases like 'broken home' and 'broken family.' They're inaccurate and insulting." That should put a cork in their mouths even if it doesn't put brains in their heads.

Prejudging: single-parent kids are problem kids. "School blamed single-parent environment for child's problems and it developed that child had a learning disability." This simple statement from a mother just about sums it up. Learning problems and social problems, too, are sometimes attributed to the single-parent situation out of sheer prejudice. One mother from Ontario, Canada, mentions that her son's fifth-grade teacher suggested the Big Brother organization during a counseling meeting with him. (This was a standard meeting held with every student in the class.) "He told her I belonged to Parents Without Partners and their activities satisfied our needs. He was adjusted and normal, but she was assuming otherwise." However, the teacher never felt out a subject of this type on him again.

Possible solutions: Elizabeth Hormann suggests a very positive step in her article "Family-Making for Single Parents" (*Our Family* magazine, November–December 1978). She describes what happened to a friend who told the school of her recent divorce. The teacher "marked Diane's folder 'Broken Home' and shoved it into the drawer." The author continues:

> Forewarned, I was able to short-circuit this negative approach when my own marriage ended a year later. My children had visibly relaxed when the tensions were eased at home. I told their teachers to expect them to be happier at school as well.... Encouraging their teachers to think of our family's restructuring in a positive light made it easier for them to look for good things instead of problems.

A quick visit with each new homeroom teacher, in person or by phone, could accomplish much the same results. It helps to attend school functions, too. Many are held in the evenings so working fathers and mothers can attend. This can show school staff that you don't have horns and a tail but look just like any other hard-working, home-oriented parent in the crowd. (For the young and the young-at-heart: leave the disco pants at home and show up in something conservative. You're not doing this just for fun, remember.)

How Some Single Parents Have Eased Edgy Situations

It's unfair to give the impression that all schools are at war with all single parents. Many parents who answered my questionnaire indicated that schools had been very supportive for their kids. For instance, Joan English, whom you met in Chapter 2, mentions that the small private school her daughter attends is "very much in tune with this sort of thing." Sandra Morse, the young decorator, also sends her daughters to a private school in New York that is sympathetic and understanding of the single parent situation. Other mothers, from Suffern, New York, Hartford, Connecticut, and Platteville, Colorado, mention that the school staff "made special arrangements to attend functions missed due to other commitments. Phone conferences rather than meeting in person"; "My children's teachers and principal

Your involvement allows the school to see you as *you* really are.

in their grammar school have all been very understanding and have even gone out of their way to help"; "School counselor very helpful in providing a book about divorce written for children." Singled fathers, from Worcester, Massachusetts, Staten Island and Selden, New York, also report that "school staff has been excellent"; "supportive at principal's level"; and (this from the young teacher who has custody of his sons) "my principal reduced my work load the first year."

Some parents are very definite about how they've created good working relationships with schools. One mother from Island Park, New York, says that there's an "excellent school district here. *I was always in touch with school staff who knew my circumstances and helped a lot.*" Another single parent explains that the school staff (some, not all) "has been very understanding and helpful to my children. Mainly because I had a working relationship with a goodly number of teachers, having been involved in the PTA." Another: "I often go to school to help with school plays and have done some health-teaching in my daughter's class. Her teacher has often praised my efforts to her and has gone out of her way to make my daughter feel good about herself."

Keeping in touch, getting involved in PTA or other school activities, sharing a special talent with the class or school—all these avenues give the schools a chance to see you as you really are, instead of as the stereotype they've been stuck with. And this involvement and sharing gives you some real clout if trouble does arise.

Churches and Church Groups: A Special Source of Help

From pioneer days on, our churches have occupied a special place within our communities. Besides providing religious guidance and a place to worship, they traditionally function as social centers—a hub around which many different kinds of individuals can come together and share themselves with others. For us as singled parents, they can offer an established and comfortable way to make contact with a community. In fact, in many areas, churches have been the first social institutions to recognize our special needs.

As an example of this singled-awareness, one mother from Kenai, Alaska, very kindly shared information about a special church-supported situation that was started in her area about six years ago. Called the Beginning Experience weekend and sponsored by the Episcopal church, it is designed to help widowed, divorced and separated people. In her words, "It is well run, very supportive. It helps its participants deal with viewing themselves, trust, guilt, sex, closing the door gently and beginning a new life. There is also a Beginning Experience weekend for kids. When my son returned from his experience he declared it was the best weekend of his entire life."

In my own area, just within a radius of 15 miles, there are two examples of church involvement. The First Presbyterian Church of Bridgehampton provides office space for a non-sectarian community service group that offers help and guidance to many singled parents, as well as other members of the community. The neighboring town of Southampton offers a special group for Separated Roman Catholics.

Some church organizations have equipped themselves to offer group therapy sessions. One single parent I interviewed mentioned that her own group, run by the Unitarian church, offered this kind of help. She said it helped her come to terms with the very difficult decision to separate and to give her ex-husband custody of their three sons.

Several single parents I'm in contact with mentioned establishing groups within their own churches. "I started a single-parent group with the help of a campus minister. It has been very beneficial—a great way to meet and support others." That's from a Missouri university professor. A mother from Phoenix, Arizona, mentions that she would like to go to a singles-oriented church because "seeing families worship together makes me depressed because I am there alone."

I'm not attempting to lead you into joining any of the church denominations I've mentioned, nor even church groups in general. However, so many of the single parents I've talked with have found churches to be an important part of their own support systems that I wanted to share this information and possible option with you.

Neighbors, Neighborhoods and the Community-at-Large

Single parents' reactions to their neighbors are very mixed. Some find neighbors nosy and supercritical, some have had both good and bad experiences and some, like this parent from Nassau County, New York, have found that "My new neighbors have been super—and since their children play with my daughter, I am lucky." One Texas mother sums up the good and the bad this way: "Some of the neighbors help with my kids. However, a few are supercritical about a single woman raising children alone. I am expected to do a *better* job of parenting as a single than two parents. Some disapprove of any hint of a social life—having guests in or my going out."

The same mixed reactions hold true for communities-at-large. The single parents who seem happiest with their communities are located in areas where there are a great many other parents in the same situation. Joan Russell, head of Single Parents on Campus in Boulder, Colorado, specifically mentioned that both she and her children felt much more comfortable since their move to Boulder, which has a large single-parent population. Others have touched on the difficulty of living as the *only* single-parent family in a community. Often, joining up with a single-parent organization in a neighboring town has meant salvation for these people. Membership in one of these groups is particularly helpful when it gives their kids a chance to meet and interrelate with other children from single-parent families. As one parent described it, "My kid was the only child from a single-parent family in her whole school. Most of the school books she uses, and most of the popular TV shows too, present two-parent families as the *accepted* family setup. When I joined a single-parent group (in a town 20 miles away) it was her first chance to see that there *are* different styles of family living, that we're not freaks."

Developing Good Public Relations with Your Community

This wisdom was gathered from other single parents and from my own experiences:

- Give relationships a chance to develop naturally. Don't push too hard at first.
- Maintain an open, friendly attitude and don't brood over rebuffs. Neighbors (or a whole community) sometimes have some very practical fears about becoming too friendly with single parents. They may be afraid that you'll try to use them as

Give relationships a chance to develop naturally.

baby-sitters, or that you'll constantly come running to them for help with small household problems (fixing fuses, jumping a car that won't start, etc.). And then there's the bugaboo about "wild singles parties." I know it's a laugh, but it's a real fear to many people who've never associated with single parents before. If you handle your own problems and don't let your life spill over into theirs, you'll allay these fears. Give it time. If some remain hostile, well, that's the way it is—as one mother put it, "their problem, not mine." You can't be friends with everyone.

- Make your first overtures casual and family-oriented. Ask a neighboring family over for a picnic or an early supper. This gives them a chance to see you as a family. And many times those parents want a chance to size you up before allowing their children to visit freely. Again, sad but true. This kind of introduction is particularly important if your children don't live with you but visit regularly. Your community needs to know that while your children are in residence *you're a family!*

- Be realistic about the kinds of children's activities you plan. Howard Cain, the widower who has raised his two children on his own, mentioned that kids' sleep-over parties were popular in the neighborhood he moved into after his wife's death. His daughter Candy was often invited to these. But he held off on reciprocating until he was well-established in the community. He had sense enough to realize that many neighbors would be uncomfortable with the idea of a singled man in charge, overnight, of a group of young girls. Whether you're a man or woman, it's probably best to be cautious about overnight invitations at first.

- If a baby sitter is going to be in charge while neighboring kids are visiting, tell their parents so. And tell them something reassuring about the sitter. If it's a daily after-school arrangement, you may want to introduce your sitter to those neighbors whose children will be visiting regularly.

- If at all possible, sign up for some community activity. There are some volunteer jobs that don't require a lot of time—making a few phone calls, for instance, doing some typing or Xeroxing. You may be the only one in the neighborhood with ready access to a typewriter or duplicating machine. But be specific about how much activity you can handle. It's better to underestimate than risk disappointing the group you're volunteering for.

Some final gems of advice from three single parents. These remarks are so practical and so pointed that I feel we can all benefit from them.

- From a mother in New York City: "Problems with family and community arise when you are dependent upon them helping you. You have to have your own systems set up. Other people can be brought in when the system occasionally fails. But they can't be the whole answer."

- From a single parent in New Jersey: "I've always been very independent. But when I get beyond my capabilities due to illness or whatever, I'm not afraid to seek help. I've always been gratified by the response."

- From a widow in Baltimore: "*You* have to go out and find your own help. There are groups everywhere, with everything to offer. Libraries for small children, entertainment for adults. If you don't have someone to go with—go alone. And talk to someone else alone. It works!"

6/Your Social Life: Entertaining, Dating, Sex

When you're married you don't have to create and maintain a personal social life. It's a package deal. You and your mate develop mutual friends, entertain as a team, date each other and provide an assured supply of sexual gratification (in theory anyway). As a singled adult, you suddenly discover that you're back where you started as a teenager. But—you've picked up a little baggage along the way: a career, a lifestyle that centers around your home, perhaps a few extra pounds and some grey hairs and, most importantly, your children. And for all of us, there's the overriding fact that we haven't functioned *separately* in the social context for quite some time.

Is it necessary to do so? Yes. You are living as a separate human being now. And it's just as important to develop your own personal social life as it is to maintain your place within the general web of human relationships. However, I'd like to emphasize the word "personal." Single parents come in all sizes, shapes and flavors. When I attended the 1979 international convention of Parents Without Partners, I shared a breakfast table one morning with a dignified, grey-haired grade school teacher who'd been married for 20 years; an industrialist who'd had three grandchildren by the time his marriage of 30 years had dissolved; an energetic young widow in her mid-thirties with three children ranging from a 7-year-old son to a preteen daughter; a mechanic in his mid-forties, twice-divorced and about to try again; and a secretary in her early twenties, divorced after two years of marriage. The secretary had been exploring the Atlanta discos the previous night and brought the rest of us up to date on the local scene.

"My God," I thought, "how can I write anything about a social life that will be meaningful to all these people?" To talk about one-night stands and whether you do or don't bring your sex life out in the open in front of your children seemed ludicrous in terms of that settled, sedate-looking school teacher. And advice on how to give a dinner party for friends was obviously not what Ms. Disco needed or wanted. As I thought about it, however, I realized that a social life can exist on a number of levels. What works for one may not work for another. But we *all* need some interaction with other people on a purely social level—some people-centered *recreation*. Sitting home with a book or sharing activities with your kids are both fine as far as they go. But kids grow up and leave home. And while books can amuse, provoke thought, provide a mystery to solve, they can't share a drink with you, shake hands or argue back. So, yes, you need a separate and personal social life! As one mother from Indianapolis with two preteen daughters put it: "I need time with other adults and often feel guilty about leaving the girls alone so much." But—"I figure I'm happier doing what I feel is best for me—so I will be an easier parent to them in the long run."

Don't Get Lost in the Parenting Process

Psychologists, therapists and counselors all stress this point, for married as well as singled parents. Traditionally, it has been a "woman's problem." Our society considered it normal for men to hold down jobs and support the family. Women stayed home, ran the household and brought up the children. And that was all they did. This view of family and society has begun to develop some pretty grim results—summed up in the phrase "displaced homemaker."

Slowly and painfully we're learning that raising children is not a lifetime job. Biologically, it's programmed to occupy about a third of our lifespan. Figuring that you spend the first third growing up yourself, physically and socially, and the second third raising your children, you're still stuck with that last third—which we can expect to get longer all the time! And if you're a singled parent who doesn't remarry, you won't have the option of walking gracefully into the sunset, hand in hand with a lifepartner. Listen to one mother with two grown daughters who's been there: "I made the mistake of avoiding social contacts with men when both my children were home because I really didn't have much time and I was determined not to get intimately involved because of my kids. Now, when I would welcome it, there don't seem to be any single men in my age bracket." I know this woman well. What's really happened, I feel, is that she's lost the habit of socializing—the technique of dealing with social peers as a form of fun. There's always somebody there. He or she may not be "standard" in your terms—may come from a different background or a different economic level, but broadening out is what it's all about.

The same thing is true for single fathers, of course. As more and more men share custody of their children or assume full responsibility for them, they begin to tussle with the same problem: How do you balance out parenting with the need to maintain a separate personality apart from your children?

Linley M. Stafford, who now has custody of both his children, and who wrote the book *One Man's Family,* says that he has compartmentalized his adult social life into daytime occasions because his children became so hostile to his friends. I have two serious reservations about this "put it off until the children are grown" approach. First, I don't feel that you can turn life on and off like a faucet. You run the risk that it won't be there when you decide to turn on the tap. Second, I've seen what happens to children who grow up believing that they can control their parent or parents. What you get is a frightened tyrant, a personality that has no sense of set limits, and so has no yardstick by which to measure or limit his or her own behavior. You also get a personality who deals with all other people as though he or she owns them; because the child did quite literally own the first human beings with whom he or she came in contact—parents.

The best way to bring up children who can interrelate successfully with other people is to do so yourself. That means recognizing a double set of needs—your own and your children's. It also means that your children learn to recognize double needs—theirs and yours! One mother from California, a waitress who's sharing a large studio apartment with her 10-year-old daughter and 11-year-old son, did *not* list living space as her major problem in combining a personal social life with single parenting. She put children's jealousy at the top of the list. And in answering the question "How do you cope with the problem?" she wrote: "Not very well. Accept it. A little resentful sometimes when the children can't see my needs." Resentment is an honest response to unreasonable possessiveness. Setting limits to possessiveness is the next positive step.

Breaking Back in to Society

How do you get started on this new social life? I feel there are a few general pointers it pays to keep in mind.

Plan some social engagements that don't include the kids. Go to a movie with a friend, join co-workers in a Dutch treat dinner out, go to a friend's house for dinner or to watch TV. Just make sure there's something you do occasionally that involves you with other friends and does not include the kids. This is different from maintaining contact with family and relatives and from planning family-style outings with other single parents or married friends. This is adult recreation. You need it. Your children must come to see these occasions as part of the fabric of family living.

Save personal problems for close friends or therapy sessions. There's some truth to the old saw that "Laugh and the world laughs with you; cry and you cry alone." These get-togethers with friends are supposed to be fun occasions, remember? That means fun for you and for those you're with. Pack along your problems and you ruin their evening as well as your own. Of course you're not a Barbie doll with a built-in laugh tape. Anyone can slip into depression and find it hard to shake off. Helmut Lecke, whom I've already mentioned, and who's a very human and honest person, described a Parents Without Partners dance that he went to and "fell apart" in the middle of. I really frightened some social friends one night by suddenly sliding into a complete Slav depression. And when a central European goes down, I want to tell you we go down! These friends had never seen this side of me, and honestly didn't know how to cope with it. Sure, it can happen, but what I'm saying is: don't look at purely social occasions as a chance to dump your problems on others. You'll get more out of the occasion if you look at it as a time when you step away from the pressures.

Use social occasions to step away from the pressures.

Proud parent, yes—but have something to talk about besides your kids. I'm sometimes amazed at single parents who start an evening by saying how glad they are to get time away from their children—and then proceed to talk about nothing else! On some of these occasions I was shooting part of the food budget just to get away from the whole topic of kids! I really do understand what it's like to face your first big party or your first date as a newly singled. You're scared. So you mentally carry your kids with you as a security blanket. They're your identity, proof that you were once attractive enough to become someone's sexual partner and insurance that you're not "just another single on the make." Think about all that. What are you really telling yourself? That you don't have any value as a separate person? It's not true.

This may sound like a course in "How to Win Friends and Influence People," but you *can* practice up on general chitchat. It's a valuable social skill that may have gotten a little rusty over those married years. To start, read a book, develop an interest. And begin to open your ears and hear how other people start conversations with each other. If they can do it, so can you. It doesnt' have to be brilliant dialogue, just anything that allows you to build a bridge of words between yourself and another human being. Generally, it's been easier for a man to open a discussion with a woman, but that's changing too. With the advent of women's—and men's—lib, there's an increasing feeling that both sexes share the responsibility for making contact with each other.

Develop friends of both sexes. Try not to make your social occasions unisexual. It gets to be a habit. We've all seen women who remain eternally one of "the girls" and men who are only comfortable talking to "the guys." That's really pre-adolescent. We've also seen adults who have *no* social system other than the eternal "sexual hunt." They see the world as a collection of possible or non-possible bedmates. This is also immature. And limiting. And boring. Men and women can relate to each other on a sharing basis. We can be friends, share experiences and points of view, learn from each other and enjoy being with each other—as well as experiencing each other sexually. And having both male and female friends is the best way to show *your kids* that this kind of relationship is possible.

Don't hang on your kids—they deserve a social life of their own! You can buy this concept in principle and still violate it in little ways, particularly if you've centered your life around your kids. There comes a time when that close family life you've worked hard to achieve begins to break up. Ten-year-olds make weekend plans that don't include you. They'd rather go to the movies with another youngster or spend the weekend at a friend's home than go on a family outing, for instance.

Teenagers disappear completely. They take weekend jobs, start dating, prefer grabbing snacks on the fly to showing up at regular mealtimes. When they *are* home, they hole up in their rooms with teenage friends or by themselves. You begin to get the feeling that you're running some kind of boarding house. In a way you are. Much of this is part of the natural separation process. Your adolescents are struggling to break free, trying out how far away they can get on their own. But they're not mature enough yet to cut the ties completely. If you try to contain children within the old patterns of family sharing, they rebel. Or they lose the chance to take the growth step their own maturing dictates.

Understand, I'm not talking about kids running wild. I really believe in that radio-TV question "Do you know where your children are tonight?" I don't have to know exactly where CH is all the time. But I do expect him to phone in if he's going to stay out for dinner or overnight. I'm really adamant about this and I've explained why. I don't want to spend the night imagining a car crash with his mangled body

Don't try to contain children within the old patterns of family sharing.

lying on the road somewhere. And I do have a lurid imagination. I also don't want him to worry about *me* if I suddenly have to make a business trip into the city. He understands this. There's no behavioral judgment involved, just a simple, practical reason.

I've also learned that teenagers' friends don't have last names, nor do they have phone numbers—unless you ask! They have a beautiful way of telling you that they're at Joe's house. "Joe who?" "You know—the guy who drives the '65 blue Camaro with the air scoops." That tells this aging mother a lot. So as each new face floats in, I do a whole introduction number: "Hi. I'm Carol Murdock—CH's mother." Then I wait for the answer. "I'm Joe." "Joe who?" Joe looks at you as though you've lost your mind (he's driving the hot-shot Camaro with the air scoops, remember?), but he eventually dredges up his last name. Then I bird-dog the phone number out of CH. And I keep a list. I have a whole page in my phone book for "CH's friends." The laugh is that I've now become an information center. *They* call *me* to track down friends' phone numbers. Never mind. If I had to call CH in an emergency at Joe Blue Camaro's or Pete With The Army Boots' house, I could— because I put down the name, and the phone number *and* the thumbnail description on my list.

This growing-up process can be very hard on weekend parents, by the way. Since you're not around all the time to witness the progress of this development, you sometimes don't understand. When your children begin to dig in their heels about visiting, it doesn't necessarily mean that they're rejecting you or that the other parent has turned your children against you. They're just growing up. And in residence or out of residence, it's a process you have to face. It also doesn't, and shouldn't, mean that you never see your kids. But you may have to adjust visiting times to mesh with their burgeoning social life (see Chapter 7 for more on this topic). The whole process is much easier on you if you've already developed a separate life of your own.

Remember, It's Your Home Too!

Living with wall-to-wall kiddy litter makes any kind of personal social life impossible. Most guests don't want to stumble over pull toys, navigate around playpens, or try to outtalk a TV set that's droning on at one end of the living room. It's true that cramped quarters are a problem for some single parents (although I was surprised at the number who returned questionnaires stating that this was *not* a consideration). But kids have a way of spreading out to fill any amount of given space. And it gets worse as they get older. The bikes get bigger; sports equipment sprouts up in unexpected places; intricately wired stereo equipment snakes from room to room; more friends appear, stay longer, eat and drink more and fill ashtrays to overflowing. Your "space" in the home and your right to adult-time can gradually get squeezed right out of existence. It creeps up on you.

When you're first singled, and lonely, it's kind of comforting to see the children's things around. They're a reminder that you are indeed a family. You're happy that they're making friends. And when your pens, pencils, Scotch tape or whatever start to disappear into school crafts projects you're so pleased to see them involved with their schoolwork that you overlook borrowing without asking first. But there comes a time when "It's absolutely necessary for a mother's sanity—a room of her own!"

That's a busy full-time elementary school teacher from Detroit who copes with two teen-age children and a drama/dance studio she owns and runs. Many of the single parents I interviewed and contacted by questionnaire had practical suggestions for dealing with space problems and personal privacy. I've melded their thoughts with some hints from professional decorators and my own experience into the following Sanity Suggestions.

Make it as easy as possible to keep public spaces like living/dining rooms ready for adult entertaining. If you can give your kids enough play and recreation space of their own somewhere else in the house, fine. Then it's understood that you share the living room with them at "family time" but they don't take it over as personal play space. If they do have to use the living room for most of their activities, then have set rules and stick to them: toys get picked up; games and crafts supplies, ditto. Keep any multi-purpose room simply furnished but provide shelf space for the kids' playthings.

If your kitchen or bathroom is big enough to hold a foldaway kitchen or bridge table, schedule messy crafts activities for these rooms. Or tape sheets of newspaper to kitchen or bathroom walls and let younger kids paint, crayon or paste-on standing up. It's actually more comfortable for early graders to work this way.

Plan a party "just for us" from time to time. Everyone in the family pitches in to clean up the living room and then enjoys a formal party in it later—complete with their favorite food, a cake with candles, whatever makes it seem festive and grown-up to the kids. It's hard to stay interested in constant tidying up if you never get to enjoy the end result! And heap on the praise for what a good cleanup job they did.

One secretary from Oklahoma who has been divorced twice and has her teenage son with her mentions another good idea: "Our apartment has points of interest or conversation pieces because my son has hobbies." Older children *do* enjoy seeing their collections or creations on display. And it helps strengthen their feeling of sharing the home, both pleasure *and* responsibilities. She also makes another important point: "A big house wouldn't make us happy. Ourselves would still be with us. Happiness and contentment within is the key." It's true. Space alone won't solve your problems. It's how you live in the space that matters.

Make sure each person has some space all their own; if not a whole room, then a corner. Connie Spencer, computer expert from Kentucky, has a six-person household which includes two teenagers. "I sometimes feel we are coming out the windows, but we do the best we can." Recognizing that each family member *really* needs personal space helps immensely.

You can stretch existing space by dividing one bedroom into two with a folding screen, a room divider or curtains hung from a ceiling traverse rod. If bedroom space is really tight, put in bunk beds and screen off separate quiet-play corners in the room with panels of translucent fiberglass hung from the ceiling or hinged together into a folding screen. Or use standard folding screens or translucent floor-to-ceiling curtains. If you can afford it, have loft beds built. The space underneath the sleeping platforms can be enclosed to create a room within a room. Kids love this kind of enclosed environment. Gives a feeling of back to the womb, I guess.

But don't forget—this personal space applies to you too. To get personal space where space is a problem, most of the single parents I've contacted use one of two solutions. They turn their own bedroom into a complete living environment where they can retreat to "think, cry, read, talk on the telephone." One mother from Colorado "made my bedroom look like a den with desk, pictures, and the bed made up to look like a couch." Another mother from New Jersey, busy working as a state manager for a major distiller, says, "My room is my sanctuary and I try to keep this one room totally mine." Some parents reverse the process and carve a bedroom for themselves out of the living room area. This can be as simple as a "single bed with a cover and bolster so it appears to be another sofa," or it can be "a sofa-bed so each child has their own room upstairs and I sleep downstairs. I like the additional privacy to read, watch TV or whatever. I really do not mind the inconvenience." If you take this route, as I did, just make sure you give yourself enough drawer and hanger space for clothes within the living room. Otherwise you'll do a lot of scantily clad tripping back and forth to the clothing source. I finally bought a secondhand office cabinet (the kind you hang coats in), spray-painted it Chinese lacquer red and treated the hinges and lock to a little gold leaf. It didn't look too bad. In a real bind, you can screw cup hooks into the back of a wooden paint-it-yourself chest of drawers and hang hangers on those. One of the most creative ideas I've heard came from a career counsellor for women entering non-traditional jobs, in California. "I divided a large living room with a wall of melon crates to make a bedroom where none existed. It really looked *great* when I got done, creative as hell." The worst thing you can do is "just crowd everything in and walk carefully, as one mother described it. Some single parents have made very far-reaching solutions. "My son has gone to live with his father, primarily because of space." It's the will for your own space that counts. Just want it. You'll find it.

None of the singled fathers I've contacted seem to have any special problems with space. Chapter 9 shows how one single father with two preteen children arranged his living quarters when his children came to live with him full-time. Some suggestions for living/sleeping arrangements for children who visit weekends or for a brief school and/or summer holiday are included in Chapter 7.

Set up a timetable that recognizes and protects adult time. Some of my more child-oriented friends used to proclaim scornfully that the children's hour has turned into the cocktail hour in many homes. And I'm afraid I agreed for awhile. With a few more years' experience under my belt, however, I developed an answer: "So what!" To insist that children must have an hour or hours of undivided adult attention *every* single evening is as impractical as saying that you must *never* break a promise to a child. Both are good general maxims but not meant to be followed out the window. Children have to learn to share—their time, their attention. And they have to learn to share yours. You won't always be able to plan an overnight visit to a friend's or Grandma's house when you want to have adult friends in. So you and your kids had better come to a definite understanding about your rights to entertain in your home. This bill of rights should include: no whining, sulking or showing off in front of guests; no stereo that can be heard in the living room. Booming amplified music through the house till the walls shake is a favorite passive-aggressive way for preteens and teenagers to intrude on adult time—"What's wrong? I'm only playing music, ma!" Add these to the list, too: no kitchen raids before the party and no bedtime scene.

Here are some practical suggestions that will grease the wheels of compromise: provide a portable TV that can be moved into a child's room (if the only other set is in the living room) or, as a very special favor, into your room. This suggestion came from Matt, whose living arrangements you'll come across in Chapter 9. Allow older children to invite in one guest each (if it doesn't crowd up the house too much). Allow your kids to stay up an hour longer than usual on party nights. But it must be a quiet time—spent reading, drawing or watching TV. I also believe this is a good time to provide a treat—a new comic book, game or put-together toy. Some call this bribery. I prefer to think of it as "creative problem-solving." Anyway, it works!

The most effective time-tabling is reversible. You occasionally schedule the use of the living room for each child. To watch a TV special he and several of his friends are particularly interested in. To accommodate "slumber party" sleep-overs (in sleeping bags, not on the couches). To provide floor space for building a super-city of blocks, which can be left up overnight as a special treat. Whatever. Just so long as it's a special use of the room geared to the child's wishes. In planning the occasion, make the point that you're *scheduling* his or her use of the room so there'll be no interruptions—just the way you plan your own grown-up times!

Special teenage situations. You'll find it's easier to enforce music-free hours for yourself if you schedule specific times when they can play it as loud as they want. You may have to check this out with neighbors.

Teenage entertaining can present special problems, too, known as sex, drinking and drugs. It's hard to give advice about this, because standards are different for everyone. Some households are much more tolerant than others. I just think you ought to start from the base that all three are definite possibilities and decide ahead of time what your attitude will be.

Intimate parties of two in your teen's bedroom are another special situation. I've read all kinds of complicated systems for dealing with this, like insist they keep the door open, put a time limit on the visits, keep a list of OK visitors. There's an easier way. Just make the rule "No sleeping together in this house. Or he/she never visits again." Let them figure out how to show you they're not. There's more information about teen attitudes and the psychology of adolescence in the next chapter. Right here, though, I'd like to make the point that, whenever possible, it's better to tell a teen "I can't let you do that" than "No, you can't do that." You're still saying "no," but the first at least admits of some dialogue and/or explanation while the other just dares them to try!

Lack of Personal Privacy: The #1 Problem

Answers on my questionnaires listed lack of privacy as the biggest hindrance in trying to combine a social life with single parenting. It topped children's jealousy, sitter problems, guilt feelings and lack of time, money and space. In fact, many of you mentioned that you felt a lack of privacy even when living space was fine.

Privacy really covers two areas: your personal space and your personal possessions. Invasions of space probably seem the more serious problem for single parents because they're directly connected with the sexual side of your social life. If your kids are in the habit of opening a bedroom door and walking in, that's a factor you have to deal with in deciding how you'll handle your sexual situations. If a closed door is considered the same as a "Do Not Disturb" sign, you have different options.

Even if your life is as celibate as a Trappist monk's, however, you need and deserve an area of privacy. Social anthropologists stress the importance of maintaining our personal circle of space—the area of empty space we need around us to keep from feeling crowded. If that circle is constantly invaded, even by those we love, we get irritable and feel threatened. We can't take complete isolation, but we can't handle constant companionship either. The woman from Kentucky who spoke out for each member of a family having a personal place, even if it's only a corner, has some more good advice to share: "My children have been raised to respect my rights as an adult. I taught my children personal privacy from the year 1. Each member of our family respects the privacy of others through habit. I raised them that way on purpose. And it pays off!" It sure does.

You need and deserve an area of privacy.

Developing Privacy Awareness in Your Kids

You don't develop this kind of awareness in kids overnight. They may have a strong sense of *their* personal rights. But you, as the parent, are the "sought-after object," so they have a tendency to bounce in on you, cling to you, almost physically possess you whenever they feel the urge to. They have to learn, by example and reminders, that *everyone* in a family has a need for privacy and that this has nothing to do with rejection. Obviously, there's a happy medium. Parents who live in the same home with their children but are as physically remote as the Alps don't raise well-adjusted kids. And of course, you're prepared to give extra time and attention to a child who's going through an emotionally difficult or insecure time. But you have a need and a right to define and to maintain your own personal space. There are several steps involved.

Be realistic about the changes children make in your life. You don't have the personal freedom and privacy that a person living singly without children does. You probably became aware of this while you were living as part of a couple—spur-of-the-moment dinners out and spur-of-the-moment lovemaking both became more difficult when there were children to consider. You swapped more extensive freedom for the pleasure of having and raising your children. The same limitations are true now. It's natural to look wistfully at single friends who come and go as they please. But read some of the articles in the singles magazines and you'll begin to realize that they suffer through desperately lonely hours too. Those of you who have your children part-time are often more aware of this than custodial parents. You've faced the emptiness of rooms after children leave. And you also face the intrusions they can make. Part-time or custodial, we have to recognize both our responsibilities as parents and our rights as individuals.

Start establishing privacy in small ways. Even toddlers can be made aware that grown-ups have areas of personal privacy. Steering a 2-year-old gently around you while you're sitting with another adult, instead of letting him bull right between you, is a beginning lesson in personal space. Closing a bathroom door is another; this isn't "modesty" as much as it is an experience that doors *are* closed sometimes and don't get opened until the big person chooses.

It's never too late to start training like this. If you have older children, even teenagers, who've fallen into the habit of ignoring your personal boundaries, start establishing them. Set an hour when family time and togetherness is over. They go their ways (to bed or into their rooms to read or whatever) and you have this time to yourself. If you choose to stay in the living room, then that room is off bounds to them during "your time." The same applies if you retreat to your bedroom. You can get tough about it without getting nasty. Put up a big, gaudy "Do Not Disturb—

This Monster is Resting" sign. Kids love physical symbols like this. And it helps them remember. Lock your door until they've acquired the habit of knocking before they burst in. Privacy isn't built in a day.

Don't be afraid to say "me" and "mine."

Personal possessions are personal. You do exist as an individual and your possessions are part of your personal space. Again, you don't have to get nasty. Just make the statement "That's my Scotch tape you're using. I don't mind borrowing but ask first, please." If borrowing really drives you crazy, establish a flat rule: "This desk, or this dresser, is mine. Don't touch anything on it or in it." I got really lax about this and, believe me, I regret it. Since I work at home, I have a toothsome supply of office materials—paper, pens, tape, labels, paper clips, a stapler. Heaven for sudden crafts projects. They're also the kind of diddly little items I never need until I *need* them. CH got to be a real raider. And when he laid a hand on anything—goodbye. He never put anything back! I finally decided to help him break the habit instead of flaring into attacks of rage when I couldn't find something I needed. First, I bought seconds of everything. (This doesn't work, by the way. A habitual borrower goes right on borrowing.) Then I sat him down and gave a really heart-rending description of *why* I needed to find my supplies intact: "I finish a chapter at 10:00 p.m. I've promised the editor I'll put it in the mail that night. I open the desk drawer for a manila envelope and sealing tape. They're not there! The editor will hate me. I'll never get another freelance assignment. We'll starve." (This brought on glassy-eyed boredom. I'm not cut out to write soap operas, apparently.) Finally, I simply said, "They're mine! Don't touch them." That got through. He'd just never associated the concept of ownership to desk supplies.

Realize that privacy is a two-way street. Make rules about personal space and possessions—and keep them. The rules you adopt apply to everyone in the household—to your children in their dealings with you, to you with the children *and* the children when they're dealing with each other—or the whole thing's a waste of time.

Children learn by example as well as by being told. If you want them to knock on your door, always knock on theirs before you enter. If you want tools and supplies put back where they belong, learn to do the same yourself. If you want private times, allow them theirs. And be consistent. They can learn to respect your privacy only if you respect theirs. And they can learn to respect yours only if you do too. If you think it's important, then it's important *every* time!

You're Living in a Two-Sex World!

You're a sexual human being and so is everyone else you meet. No one takes a vow of chastity when they become singled. And no one suddenly switches from conservative, middle-class thinking into swinging single, either. That's reality. Right now, you've probably got pretty much the same basic beliefs and attitudes about sex that you brought into marriage, no matter what they were. But your behavior may change because you begin to interpret those beliefs differently, by looking at the marriage experience itself, the separation process, through therapy or through the day-in, day-out living of single parenthood. Or this "living-through" may simply reinforce the beliefs you incorporated as you were growing up. The problem is to keep our behavior lined up with our beliefs. And that's not always so easy.

We usually kind of mush around in the middle, trying to meld the beliefs we were brought up with and the realities of single parenthood. Most of us developed our ideas about sex during pre-liberation days. Now we're living in a sexually free world. Even if we buy the concept of sexual freedom for ourselves (and many of us don't), we still worry about the effect our behavior will have on our children. In an article called "A New Man in the House" (in the July 1979 issue of *Working Mother* magazine), Jane Adams describes the single-parent tug of war this way:

> They may have learned that a divorce decree (or death certificate) does not sever them from their need for love, companionship, affection and sex. They may have accepted, at an intellectual level, the new sexual freedom. But for most single parents, these new theories are difficult to translate into behavior that meets their needs as sexual human beings and also fulfills what they perceive as their parental responsibilities.

We're really asking ourselves "Will I?" and "Should I?"

While you're battling out the answer for yourself, just remember that we're all different. First, we have different levels of sexual need. Maybe celibacy gives you a headache. Or maybe it's sexual activity that does. Either way, it's no big deal as long as *you're* comfortable—and as long as you stick with partners who are as comfortable with your needs as you are with theirs! Needs have a way of getting met.

The trouble is that we also have expectation levels which are very individual. Some of us can be easy on ourselves. We can tolerate lapses from standards we've accepted and view these lapses (our own and others') as growth situations. Or you may be much harder on yourself. You may set a standard, expect to maintain it, work hard at meeting it and become disturbed when you don't. You must recognize this kaleidoscope of beliefs and needs and expectations in yourself—and in others—when you start creating a social life as a singled parent. I said earlier that men and women can be friends. They can share social times together without sexual involvement. This may not be what you want. If it is, it may not be what someone you meet wants. Or you may want to put both friendships and sexual experiences into your life. But understand that you are free to make the choice. Each one of us has to respect the needs and expectations of others. And we have the right to insist that they do the same.

How you feel about your actions affects your children.

I'm really belaboring this because how we *feel* about our actions affects our children much more than what we actually *do*.

Well, Will I?

The statistics show that most of us do. I don't expect anyone to live by the numbers or to feel pressured if they happen to decide against the statistical norm. Personally, I never felt any better or worse about a relationship because I know that I was one of the 75% doing it at that particular time. That's the figure Morton Hunt gives in his book *The World of the Formerly Married* for those who become sexually active within a year of their divorce. Dr. Graham B. Spanier, Associate Professor of Human Development and Sociology at Pennsylvania State University, very kindly made available to me a research study he had conducted with Margie E. Lachman, a doctoral candidate in the Division of Individual and Family Studies at the University. Their research showed only one-sixth of the sample group reporting that they did not date at all. There were 91 men and 114 women in the group, ranging in age from 20 to 67, and all had been separated no longer than 26 months. "The majority of the respondents (59%) dated at least once a week, with 19% reporting that they either dated someone daily or were currently living with someone other than their [former] spouse. Only 7% of the sample reported that they were dating less often than once a month. Dr. Spanier concludes that "... in this sample of recently separated individuals, dating appears to be an accepted activity.

Aha—but does dating mean sex? This kind of brings us back to where we started. For some of us it does, for some it doesn't. Robert Weiss found that "The role of sexual need in the initiation of dating would appear to be secondary for most among the separated." In fact, he believes that sexual desire may be so enmeshed with other needs that it may not be possible to decide just how large a part it does play in the desire to date. Those other needs are:

- need for emotional as well as physical contact
- need for security of attachment
- need for assurance of worth

Weiss quotes from a discussion between two women, both separated after long-time marriages. I'm including part of this dialogue because I think it sums up our sexual needs so well.

> *First woman*: You know, physical deprivation is one thing. What I miss at this point is just being held and cuddled.
> *Second woman*: I've been celibate for a pretty long time, so I've learned to cope with it. ... Being alone in that sexual manner does cause hurt, if you are a normal human being and have desires and wants. But you know you want to be with someone who wants you.

One singled woman, just about my closest friend in fact, recently met an attractive, sophisticated and singled television producer. On their second date, he was frank about the fact that he was becoming very attracted to my friend, but also frank about his belief that sex wasn't purely physical but involved emotions as well. And he did not want to make a sexual commitment until they had grown closer to each other. (He'd flown from Canada to New York City just to keep this date, by the way.) This sounds admirable to some of you—the way things should be. To others it seems a colossal waste of time. "Sex *is* how you get close to each other." I can hear some of you saying right now. Actually, my friend would agree with you. We Sagittarians have a tendency to go to the point directly. But once again, it's the kaleidoscope. He looks at life through one set of needs, beliefs and expectations; hers are slightly different.

Sex: It's part of parenting and it's here to stay.

OK—Should I?

What most of us are really asking ourselves with this question is "What effect will my sexual activity have on my children?" Even those of us who are freebooters tend to be much more conservative where our kids are concerned. Jane Adams makes this point in that same article for *Working Mother* magazine. She's talking about a study done for General Mills called "Raising Children in a Changing

World": "...the study reported while some parents may have established new values and behavior for themselves, they are still not certain enough of the moral validity—or usefulness—of these new attitudes to want to pass them on to their children."

There's so much ambivalent claptrap handed around about sex that it's easy to lose track of the two major points: sex is here to stay and sex is part of parenting. Granted that we're in a peculiar position. We have, quite demonstrably, "done it." Now, do we go on doing it? As married couples we really never had to explain our sexual lives or needs to our children. As singles we often do. It can make us very uncomfortable.

How Do the Children Handle It?

The traditional psychological view is that it's difficult for kids, particularly at certain stages, to accept a sexual view of their parents. They just ignore the whole thing even while they're busy learning the facts in general. It's a blanket "My folks don't do that." This is partly because their own emotional growth involves having to learn that we cannot be *their* sexual partners. Therefore, it's hard to handle the fact that we're *anyone's* sexual object. Nevertheless, they do have to resolve this oedipal conflict (for the final time as adolescents) in order to become mature themselves. It *may* be harder for children of sexually active single parents (and no one's sure about this) to do so, but it's not impossible.

In fact, when I interviewed Dr. E. Gerald Dabbs, Associate Clinical Professor of Psychiatry at Cornell Medical School and Chief of Mental Health Services and Training at the New York Foundling Hospital in New York City, he indicated that some children can find it reassuring that their parent has a sexual partner. It *helps* them resolve the oedipal conflict. If you belong to someone else sexually, you're not a possible partner for the child.

Now understand that here we're talking about the most basic subliminal workings and development of the human psyche. In response to my questionnaire, singled mothers and fathers mentioned a range of obvious reactions—some good, some difficult—to their own dating and sexual activity. Here are some of the responses, grouped by the children's ages.

With children 6 and younger. One nurse from Connecticut who has a daughter 4 years old (as well as three older daughters) mentions that the attention demands her children make "can sometimes be overwhelming." A medical secretary from Pennsylvania describes a problem we've all been through. Her boys (3 and 6) "keep getting out of bed and horsing around. I do my best to have them into a routine so by 8:30 they are settled and the rest of the evening is mine." And one mother from New York City knows that she's caught in what she calls "a vicious cycle of my own making." She has a 5-year-old and a 4-year-old and finds that her own guilt feelings make it difficult "to leave them if they are not at peace with the baby-sitter, if I feel I'm interfering with their awake time, if they're sick, etc. They seem to have picked this up and react accordingly—trying to keep me home. I end up angry but still guilty." She's perfectly right about that guilt cycle. And there's some expert advice on guilt in Chapter 9.

With children 6 to 12. A New York City executive, sales manager for a publishing house, describes how he handles the whole question of personal privacy and a social life with his 9-, 8- and 5-year-olds who visit frequently: "I found a two-bedroom apartment. Informed my children I socialized. They were glad to hear it!" He also maintains "a bedtime for children, leaving evenings (after 9:00) for myself." Another Pennsylvania parent (her children are 7 and 10) has also opted for a fairly open approach, but worries: "It is so hard to know whether I'm doing the right thing for my children when my boyfriend stays over. I have been seeing him steadily for over a year and my kids like him. He seems to enjoy all children and is a very easygoing person; also he is not very demonstrative. What the children mostly see is our friendship, so perhaps it is a good thing for them to know two people can be close, love each other and be good friends without making a lot of demands on one another." Another mother from Iowa who has a 9-year-old daughter (as well as two teenagers) finds that her 9-year-old grows "extremely attached (emotionally) to my dates." Another version of this reaction comes from a magazine editor in New York City: "I do not like combining my private life with my time with the children [two daughters 7 and 10] because they immediately feel cheated unless the person pays a lot of attention to them which usually doesn't happen." A nurse with a 10-year-old daughter reports that "if I date I tell her that I have a date and will be going out. She will often ask questions and will want to meet him. I have not found this to be a problem." And one secretary in upper New York State has been able to achieve an open and guilt-free relationship with her 9- and 12-year-old daughters: "I have never really sacrificed for my children, and have been able to be open and honest with them about my needs. They balk occasionally but sense from my lack of guilt reaction that it is of no use. My well-being is pertinent to theirs and they have even robbed their piggy banks to contribute toward a night out for me. They're super."

With teenagers. Here the reactions seemed to be mainly positive, although one Staten Island mother mentions that her 15-year-old daughter makes it "very difficult" to achieve personal privacy. "No easy answer," she concludes. Others, however, find their teenagers very supportive. A Long Island teacher with teenage sons who've learned about her steady relationship, finds that "At first I was nervous about what they'd think, but I knew I wanted the relationship and needed it and they accepted it because they like the man and know he won't hurt me in any way." Another, from Maine, who has a 16-year-old daughter at home and an older son in the army, says "My children are no longer jealous of other men or my social fun—in fact, we can talk about dating much more freely." However, this mother feels that if she has "a man over for the evening and am attracted to him physically I cannot take him into my bedroom. I *will not* do that with my children at home. And they're usually home." And one California mother finds that "My problems come from *me*, not my son [15]. He *encourages* me but I'm really afraid of men."

How Open Should You Be?

Whatever you can get comfortable with will work best for you and your children. It's an established fact that just about all singled parents date in one way or another. In fact, the research study that Dr. Graham Spanier conducted showed that:

Those who were dating most frequently were better adjusted [to post-marital separation] than those who were not. Fifty per cent of the sample reported that their dating experience has helped a great deal in adjusting to the separation. However, it appears that dating is most influential in facilitating the adjustment to separation for those separated most recently.

His study actually showed that dating was more important to good adjustment than frequent social interaction with relatives and friends.

In her article for the June 5, 1979, issue of *Esquire*, Barbara Wright quotes Dr. Hugh James Lurie, who is Medical Director of the Child Study and Guidance Clinic of the Tacoma-Pierce County (Washington) Health Department: "The whole question of who's sleeping in Mommy's bed is vastly overrated. The effect of sex on the child has more to do with the quality of the relationship between the mother and her friend; the love, respect, and affection that exist between the mother and her child; and particularly whether the parent-child relationship is maintained." Dr. Gerald Dabbs, whom I quoted before, also feels that the more comfortable the parent is, the more comfortable the child will be. And finally, Robert Weiss writes in *Marital Separation* that "It would seem that . . . children are as able to accommodate to parental frankness as they are to parental dissimulation."

Judging from my questionnaires and the interviews I conducted, many more single parents are comfortable with dissimulation than they are with openness. Most are willing to admit that they do date but don't spell out just what dating may entail. And they live openly with a sexual partner only when they're reasonably sure it will be a stable relationship. Those who *are* willing to be frank with their children seem to find it beneficial both for them and their kids.

Here's an "attitude" test you can take. Jane Adams opens the Introduction to her book *Sex and the Single Parent* with a very real, very explicit incident that sums up a fear many of us carry into our singled sexual lives.

> The first time I had sex with a man who was not my husband was a test. As a woman, I passed; as a single parent, I did not.
> The "test" was the embodiment of a recurring fantasy/nightmare: [she then describes a nightmare about taking a college exam for a course she's never attended].
> The nightmare ends in a sweat-drenched awakening. And so it ended when my child called me from her room while I lay naked, a few feet away, in the embrace of a man nearly as unknown to me as the fantasy professor whose lectures I had never heard.

How you react to this tells you a great deal about how you will be able to deal with your sexuality with regard to your children. If the thought of being seen in bed with a man panics you or makes you deeply uncomfortable, you're probably not cut out for the frank approach. If you feel that it's unfortunate but not earthshaking, or that Jane Adams should have prepared her child for this eventuality by openly acknowledging that she occasionally shares her bed with a man, then you're better suited to openness with your own children.

Some of the singled parents I've contacted frankly state that "no way" or "never" will they risk this experience. They carefully arrange their sexual lives around times when their children are away visiting. Or they go to their date's home. Both men and women feel this way. A woman from New York State who has teenage sons says, "I cannot bring a man home and enjoy sex in my own house when my sons are there." A Brooklyn father whose son visits on weekends wrote that "I will not have a woman stay with me when he is here." Another mother solves the problem by having the man "leave by 5 or 6 in the morning, before my son wakes up." Another New Jersey parent says, "I feel you just can't have a private life in your own home, a lover sleeping over (never). Visit him at his place. It's the price you pay."

Others deal with their sexuality differently. "My kids learned to see Cy in bed with me. Mornings, they were free to come in, cuddle with us, share the loving feeling we had for each other. When he left our lives, I told them that he had been part of our family, that we all gained in love from the relationship, and that love was a growing, sharing experience." This mother, whose children are 6 and 10, describes their family relationship as "very huggy and kissy. Lots of physical interaction." But she says that she was careful to include this sharing of a lover with her children only when "the continuance of the relationship seemed positive. Then I gradually told the kids that I would be seeing more and more of him and that he would be staying over."

Another single father, whose children visit regularly, describes how he handled the kind of situation Jane Adams experienced. "I had an established relationship with a woman. My children had met her, spent time with her as part of their visits with me. They were accustomed to seeing her in my apartment when they went to bed, and seeing her there the next morning. But they had never seen us in bed together. One night, my 5-year-old woke up after a bad dream and headed into my bedroom. Instinctively, I simply acted 'normal,' invited him into bed with me, cuddled him, and carried him back to his own bed when he fell back to sleep. The next morning he had no recollection of the incident. Nor has he ever shown any recollection or reaction to it with me, his mother or in school. I was concerned and I checked."

The pros and cons for each approach: hidden vs. open. There are advantages to both and you have to weigh them for yourself. If you decide to keep your sexual life a private matter, there are certain practicalities involved. You have to arrange dates for when your own children are away or when your partner's are. This gets pretty complicated. If you can afford it, you can stay at a motel overnight or plan a weekend trip. But this involves overnight sitters. And you also run the risk that your children will begin to resent your absences if they're frequent.

If you invite a date in, there's always the risk that you'll get caught. If this happens and you handle the situation badly, acting frightened and guilty, you're giving your kids some pretty negative input about sex. In fact, one husband and wife therapy team, George and Sally Finger of the Staten Island Family Forum, believe that hidden sex generally creates negative attitudes in children. As one of them put it:

> If sex is always hidden, if children never hear anything positive about sex—that it's warm, and sharing and communicating, and feels good—how are they going to develop that attitude themselves? If you sweep sex under the rug, you're saying that it's dirty and you don't want to deal with it. Since children grow into sexual beings themselves, you're telling them that their own desires are dirty and not to be dealt with.

Hiding can make for rotten sex, too. It's pretty hard to concentrate on yourself and your partner if you're trying to listen for the patter of little feet and are scared to death you'll hear them. And if the sex is unsatisfactory, it can damage your self-image or your partner's.

The open approach lets you gradually accustom your children to the idea of you as a sexual being. And it allows you to get across the view of sex you would like them to develop—that it's part of loving. But with this approach you also run the risk of overestimating how comfortable you really are about your own sexuality. You may start out fine and then come to a grinding halt under the cool, open eyes of a child. So if you have any doubts about your ability to carry it off; don't try!

There's certainly one fact that I think we can't ignore. When children become aware of their own sexuality, sex is *their* discovery—they feel it belongs to them and their generation, just as we felt it belonged to ours. They don't share their attitudes easily, if at all. So even if you present a very open view of your relationship with another adult, the emphasis should be on the *relationship*, not on the sex. As one 20-year-old told me in an interview: "I know my mother enjoys her lover, and that's OK, but I don't want to hear about it." Our children go through a long process of separating from us. In order to succeed they have to create a generation divide. And it's realized sexual potential that finally makes that boundary possible. We don't have to cross it. We can coexist.

Being open enables your children to think of you as a sexual being.

Practicalities that reduce the risk factor. Since few parents want to be completely open about sex with their children, here are a few practical steps you can take to help sexual situations go smoothly:

- If you can manage it, try to arrange your first few sexual dates when your children are away. This gives you a chance to get easy with the whole idea yourself, and probably makes for a more enjoyable experience. If you decide later on to bring the relationship out in the open, you'll handle it more easily.

- If you decide to spend the night at a date's home or at a motel—plan ahead. Make sure you've got a reliable sitter lined up who can and will stay through the night. A mature person is probably best. If a teenager knows you're going to be away overnight, he or she may decide this is a great time to get in a little sex of their own. Be sure to leave the sitter a telephone number in case there's an emergency. If you don't know the number where you'll be staying, leave a friend's number or a relative's. If you want to check in back home by phone, that's OK. But don't get compulsive about it and start calling in every hour. Your kids may get the idea there's something seriously wrong and start yelling for you.

- When you plan your family living arrangements, be realistic about the fact that you may occasionally have a date who comes home with you. If there isn't a door to your sleeping quarters, put one up. And think about adding a latch. Some parents feel a locked door will frighten children. But if you make a habit of it, they'll take it for granted.

- Remember that you have the right to lay out some ground rules in your own home—what time your date must leave, how freely he or she can move around the house, whether you want real tiptoeing or just normal quiet. If a date doesn't recognize your concern for your children—is this a good relationship for you?

- Most importantly, decide how much you're going to tell your children and how you're going to phrase it—ahead of time! Many experts suggest simple explanations like: "Mommy/Daddy sometimes wants a friend to sleep over, the way you do." Or, "Mommy/Daddy gets lonely and needs another grown-up around sometimes." One single parent who's involved with a parenting group advises. "Don't talk about dating in terms of 'maybe this will be your new daddy or mommy.' Instead, mention that 'he or she will be around a lot.' Always make it clear that a lover is not taking the place of the other parent and is not taking the child's place in your love. "Yes, mommy loves George (or daddy loves Harriet) but that's different from the way I love you." If your child has sensed that there's been someone in the house the night before (and they sometimes do) and asks about it, you can always say, "Yes, a friend of mommy's or daddy's stayed very late." It's really more the *way* you say things than what you say. If you're calm and matter-of-fact, a simple answer will satisfy.

If your children battle baby-sitters. Some children show a great deal of anxiety about being left with sitters. This can be true particularly if they're having a hard time dealing with the parent separation. It's called separation anxiety, and in extreme forms you may need therapy or counseling. But there are steps you can take to relieve milder problems:

- First, believe that you have a right to get out of the house and to plan social occasions that don't involve the children. If you feel guilty or are worried about leaving them, they'll sense it. And they'll feel worried about your leaving.

- Make your first few trips out of the house short ones. And come back on time. This helps overcome their fear that you're disappearing for good every time you leave.

- If you're going to be later than you'd expected, call and tell the sitter so. If a sitter begins to worry about time, your kids will begin to pick up on his or her nervousness.

- Don't go in for lingering farewells with your kids. And don't become dramatically affectionate. This is *not* the final goodbye. The easier and more natural you are about it, the more easily they'll accept it. Just put on your coat, kiss them goodbye and go! If they tend to be "clingers," just wave goodbye and skip the kiss. In other words, don't give them a chance to physically grab you. Struggling toward the door with an octopus child hanging onto your arm or leg is an unpleasant experience. And your emotional reaction feeds back to the child and makes him or her more frantic.

- If they start a scene, keep on going. Nine times out of ten they'll settle down happily as soon as you're out of sight. Children accept the inevitable and can deal with it.

- And finally—make sure that you're not using their anxiety as an excuse to avoid facing the job of building an adult social life of your own.

7/How's Your Ex-Rating— As Partner, As Parent?

The day that you separated from your husband or wife or that your divorce decree became final was the first day of your new life as a singled parent. On that day, you became part of the singled-parent statistics: 7,666,000 children under 18 living with a separated or divorced parent in 1978 (426,000 of them with separated or divorced fathers); divorce rates approaching one-half of recorded marriages (in 1975 10.0 of every thousand people were married, 4.8 of every thousand were divorced). But neither the physical separation nor the divorce papers nor the statistics really free you emotionally.

Achieving Emotional Separation

It takes time, a mourning process and gradual healing to achieve emotional separation, what psychologists and other single parents call "the emotional divorce" or "a divorce in fact." Edith Atkin and Estelle Rubin, both psychiatric social workers who have practiced extensively in the mental health field and who co-authored the book *Part-Time Father*, point out that "achieving a divorce in fact as well as in name is a slow, painful, resistant process." Whether you were married for many years or for a short time only, you shared a large part of yourselves and your time with each other and you shared the experience of parenthood. Atkin and Rubin describe the emotional difficulties:

> Cutting the bonds of matrimony in no way means cutting the emotional bonds that weld together a man and woman, especially if they have once been in love. Mixed-up feelings of love, hate, guilt, anger, resentment, spite, and jealousy can hold a divorced couple in bondage to each other for years. Sometimes for life.

Both men and women feel a sense of loss. Let's face it, you're putting a lot of your life behind you, even if you left to start up with a new partner. Words, printed politely on a divorce decree or hurled at each other in anger, don't scrub out shared activities and memories—first dates, the flush of sexual pleasure, furnishing a home, steaming a kid through a croup attack. Good or bad, these experiences are built into you. And they're deeply emotional ones. No matter what you want your attitude to be, you're still hung up on feelings.

You're also shackled by habits. "Joe always took out the garbage" or fixed the drinks or took care of servicing the car. "Kathy picked all the furniture" or helped the kids with their homework or had dinner ready when you got home. Any two people who live together work out daily routines that become so ingrained they don't even have to discuss them. Who ever has a summit meeting every time the table needs clearing or the lawn has to be mowed? Suddenly *you* have to work out new patterns for getting all those diddly-squat jobs done. And each time they come up, you're reminded of the other person.

We tend to have highly selective memories, too, controlled somewhat by how we're feeling or what we're experiencing at the moment. Joe suddenly calls to ask how Junior is because "he seemed kind of logy when I had him last Sunday." Kathy says, "Why don't you stay for dinner?" when you're dropping Junior off and are dreading a solitary meal in your empty apartment. You feel a rush of warmth and gratitude. All the good memories come crowding in. Never mind that Joe arrived home bombed out of his skull almost every night of your married life or that Kathy's compulsive neatness finally drove you out of the house. You tend to remember how much fun Joe or Kathy could be when they weren't bombed or compulsively picking up. You're kidding yourself, of course. Because for that moment it's more rewarding for you, or easier, to think of your ex as you would have liked him/her to be. It's also just as unreal to go on picturing each other as total monsters once you're removed from the arena of an unworkable marriage.

Some of us don't want to lose the love—or the hate. We carry it around with us like a security blanket. We seem to enjoy living in an emotional maelstrom. These are the single parents you meet hanging mournfully in a corner at a social gathering, or over the end of the bar, waiting to tell you, "I'll never get over it. I'm a one-man/woman person." Or who, with bared teeth, begin to recite the list of wrongs they've suffered that they'll never forget. I get the impression that they're afraid to let go of these emotions because they fear they may never be able to replace them. It's not the absent partner who's precious (or hateful), but the emotion that's centered around that partner. As long as they hang on to this baggage from the past, there's no need to find a replacement; in fact, there's no room for new emotions.

We have to realize that emotions result from the way each individual perceives an event or a situation. This perception can sometimes have very little relationship to the event itself or to the actual situation. Kathy mourns the loss of Joe because she sees divorce as personal failure, irreligious or irresponsible. She feels badly about herself and interprets this as grief for the loss of Joe or as love that she can't shake. Her best friend may perceive the divorce as the best thing that ever happened to her and feels relieved that Kathy no longer has to deal with the klutz.

How Do You Start Separating Emotion from Reality?

That's what you must be able to do to achieve emotional divorce. I attended an orientation discussion on achieving emotional divorce given by Suffolk Chapter #64 of Parents Without Partners. The advice seemed practical and sound so I'll pass it along.

Achieving emotional divorce: Start by looking at your expectations.

- Start by recognizing how you got where you are. First, ask yourself, "Why did I marry in the first place?" The answer could be love, security, the fulfillment of a fantasy, social pressure, to get away from your family—any of a number of reasons. Try to pin them down for yourself. These reasons were really expectations; you expected to *get* something for yourself through the marriage. What was it?

- Then, recognize the fact that as you grew up you learned labels for people— Father, Mother, Wife, Husband, Family. And you began to expect people who wore the labels to act in certain ways.

- When you became a Husband, Wife, Father or Mother, you accepted that label and expected certain actions from yourself, and you expected your partner's actions to match his or her label. But recognize that the actions you attached to the labels Father/Husband or Wife/Mother may not have been the same as your partner's! You expected behavior from each other that may have had nothing to do with the way each of you would actually behave.

- However, the rewards you expected (the "what's in it for me") from the marriage were based on how you expected the other person to act, and vice versa.

- If these expected behaviors didn't match, or at least mesh, each side felt cheated. You weren't getting what you thought you'd get. Usually, both sides begin to tell each other so by hurling oblique negatives at each other: "You're a rotten cook" (implied: bad wife); " You never take me out"(implied: selfish, lousy lover); "Why the hell can't you keep the checkbook straight"(implied: idiot, irresponsible); "You never get a raise" (implied: ineffectual, failure).

- Some of those negatives and their implications stuck with you. Think about them. Are some of them true?

- Probably. But take these negatives and match them up with the way *you* think about labels, the way *you* want to behave. Sure, you're a lousy cook. But you didn't hire on as a chef. *You* expected to give affection to your spouse and a lot of mothering to your children. That's how you interpret the label Wife/Mother. Okay, you spend evenings bowling, beering or playing poker with friends. But you didn't hire on as a dating service. You're a steady worker with a good paycheck, and you work hard around the house on weekends. That's the way you read the Husband/Father label.

- You may never change your definitions. But you can start to realize that you didn't fail *your own* expectations. There was nothing wrong with your reading of the labels. You simply failed to recognize or meet *someone else's.* And vice versa. This meant that neither one of you was getting what you wanted out of the marriage.

- Now each side is free to act in his/her own way. Each has the right to do so. You're no longer trying to meet each other's expectations. You have only to

When one parent
disappears, the
other faces the
effect on their
children.

meet your own. So how can you hate or hurt each other? You still think your partner isn't living up to expectations? Why should he or she? If it didn't happen while you were married, it isn't going to happen now. Do *you* want to have to keep meeting the other side's demands? Let go! And most of us eventually do so.

Children: The Continuing Contact

Single parents can have a very hard time disengaging from one another because they still have a point of contact—their children. Even when one parent disappears, the other still faces the effect on their offspring. And that can keep the wound from healing. Or one or both parents may use the children to manacle themselves to their ex-partners. The book *Part-Time Father* describes it this way:

> The emotional shackles of divorce are generally so well disguised that both parties may be quite unaware of them ... frequent telephone calls or letters, ostensibly about the children's welfare, never-ending legal battles claiming violations of the contract regarding support or visitation rights. Or they may take the guise of "let's-be-civilized-about-this," with Daddy coming to dinner once a week, supposedly for the sake of the children but really to keep tabs on the ex-partner.

Single parents describe these situations in their own words. Those who answered the questionnaire delineated a variety of situations designed to bind.

- From a draftsman in Louisiana: "We hardly speak except through attorneys. We could save so much money if he would communicate with me directly ... the lawsuits have caused me to build up bitterness and distrust."
- An inventory control specialist from New Jersey: "Terrible. We can't discuss anything without winding up in an argument."
- From a secretary in Oklahoma: "I have to ask him if he will have my son over; then have to drive him 45 miles there. Each year I care a little less if I make the effort."
- A bookkeeper from Texas: "He always gets his way because I am afraid of him. He threatens to stop paying support or doesn't take the kids for a while. This hurts *them*."
- From a Canadian real estate broker: "My second wife is jealous of my third wife. My third wife is jealous of the child of my second wife. They change (visitation) times sometimes and I'm caught in the middle."

Other single parents have been better able to achieve detente. The circumstances vary, however, and reactions include:

"Never see him. Hooray." This single parent from New Jersey then explains: "Really believe that since he remarried and we (kids and I) formed a separate unit it's been much warmer and stronger than when we had to adjust to the weekend 'duty' visits, etc. For me? Great. I have complete social space. No ex around or *inside* anymore."

A medical secretary from Pennsylvania declares, "I have no relationship. He packed his bags 3 years ago and I haven't heard from him yet. He is no longer the man I married so long ago. It's better for all of us that he stays away." The women's career counselor from California, whom you met before, believes: "It's good in that there is *no* relationship. It was so intense before that this is better." A technologist in the computer field, from Kentucky: "We are both concerned about the kids' welfare, but we do not see each other and haven't spoken in 3 years. I like it that way."

"*Wish my ex-wife would visit more.*" This father with custody of his sons represents the other end of the axis—those single parents who would like to see *more* contact between their ex and their children. (Incidentally, he also feels that there are very few special problems in raising his boys that he can't handle. However, he feels that "Children respect father more for discipline but lack the motherly communication.")

A mother from Indiana who has two daughters 12 and 13 thinks that "visitation should be mandatory for fathers." And an accountant from Minneapolis, with long experience as a single parent (she's been divorced 13 years and her children range in age from 17 to 31) wishes "it had been written in our divorce decree—that my husband had to see the kids. As it was he saw them about twice a year until just before he died. I think both he and the children missed something."

"*It is neutral. The only relationship I want is as a co-parent.*" This teacher from Alaska, who shares custody of her two sons with their father, sums up what roughly one quarter of those who answered the questionnaire have managed to achieve: careful neutrality. A father with custody of his son and daughter puts it this way: "She is cooperative and has very little emotional effect on me." A university teacher from Missouri, whose son is 8 years old, says, "We talk to each other on the phone once a week. It is very superficial, but the contact is there for my son's sake. I have no desire to see him."

"*Continues to improve. More honest communication and respect.*" This New York father, whose three children visit with him for six weeks out of the year, represents an opinion shared by another quarter of those who sent in question-naires—that their relationship with their ex is steadily improving, or is better than their married relationship. A mother from Florida, divorced for one year and living with a 2½-year-old son, describes her relationship as "good at this time. Talking more now, no more hostility. I know I could call on him in an emergency." A Massachusetts mother with three daughters feels "It is a good relationship. He is remarried and once I was able to accept that (it took about 6 months) I learned we could have a good workable relationship with the girls. If he wants the girls for extra time I never refuse and it also works the other way."

A secretary from upstate New York sums it up: "We communicate openly. Have spent many enjoyable Holiday meals together with his parents, his girlfriend and her children. Our divorce has allowed us to be the friends we never were during 10 years of marriage. We live and let live."

Quite obviously, this last group of single parents have managed to find true emotional freedom from their former partners. Each has rounded out the physical separation with emotional estrangement. And each finds that this is rewarding for both sides.

A Code of Behavior for Ex-Partners

Based on the experience and advice that so many singled parents have been willing to share:

Caution: Don't confuse separate/friendly with a revival of interest.

- Be willing to disengage emotionally.
- Allow your partner to lead his or her own separate life.
- Respect the decision you have made.
- Share the parenting of your children as generously as possible.
- *Never* use your children as a weapon against the other parent.

Kids and the Code

Keep your attitudes toward your ex clear-cut in your own mind and crystal clear to your children. This is one area of single parent/child relationships where all the experts agree. Children are resilient; given time, most can come to terms with their parents' separation. In fact, for some it is an actual relief— it's easier for them if they're not subjected to constant or continued wrangling by parents.

Also, your relationship with your ex shouldn't be so close that your kids begin to think you're headed for a reconciliation. Young children in particular will seize on any chance to feed this fantasy. They'll become seductive, manipulative, demanding, in order to fulfill this apparent possibility. Other children become confused. You're just making it harder on yourself, and on them, if you allow your relationship to slip into this marginal area.

"Things got very mixed up." Take it from Margery Mulcahey, an attractive young mother who'd been divorced about five years. Her relationship with her ex had been polite but disinterested when he came to pick up her 11- and 18-year-old daughters for visits. Then he joined AA and successfully arrested his alcoholism— and she found their relationship beginning to change subtly. She and her ex-husband began noticing each other as individuals—"starting paying attention to each other." There was an immediate reaction from the girls. They became jealous of *both* parents. These children had worked out a way of relating to each parent in the separated situation. When they sensed that situation beginning to change, they felt threatened. They saw growing attention of the parents toward each other as taking away from each parent's relationship to them. Fortunately, Margery realized this. Since she had no intention of reviving the marriage, she returned the meetings to a more formal footing.

Detach, but Not from Your Child

This is good advice for both mothers and fathers, custodial and visiting parents. How can a custodial parent detach from a child? It can happen. In fact, it commonly does at a certain stage in the divorce-adjustment process. Robert Weiss, in *Marital Separation*, says:

> There appear to be two fairly distinct phases in movement toward recovery. One is a period of *transition* in which the pre-existent pattern of life has been disrupted and a new pattern not yet integrated. The first few months of this period of transition are for many a time of disorganization, depression, unmanageable restlessness, and chaotic searching for escape from distress.

For many women, this restlessness and search for escape from distress drives them out of their home and away from their children. They feel guilty, but they're driven by impulses they don't understand. Eventually they restabilize, and a new pattern of home-living begins to take shape.

This post-divorce trauma can be even more severe for fathers, because most don't have the company, comfort and stabilizing influence of their children around them. Their new home seems empty, desperately lonely. When I interviewed Helmut Lecke, an international director of Parents Without Partners, he told me: "I used to be harsh on fathers who dropped out of the picture. But now I realize the difficulties. To drop off the kids, after the visitation, and return to the dead silence of that empty home is simply too difficult for some to take. They protect themselves from this pain by gradually sliding away from the visits."

How to Beat the Visitation Blues

Helmut was kind enough and open enough to share some of his own ways of coping with this loneliness. He has three very sensible suggestions:

- Go to a movie. It's quite possible to feel lonely in a crowd, which is the problem you may face if you dive into a bar. But in a movie you're relating to the screen. You don't have to relate to those around you.

- Make social plans for yourself. Arrange to have dinner with friends or family. But go straight from dropping the children off to your social engagement. If you stop off at your apartment you may get so depressed you won't make it to your date.

Beating the visitation blues: Make social plans.

- Invest in the most complete sound equipment you can afford—whether that's a simple radio or a complete stereo set. What you need is noise in that apartment.

Advice from the Experts: How to Stay in Touch

This advice is culled from a research report done by Joan B. Kelly, Co-Principal Investigator of the Children of Divorce Project of Marin County, California, and Judith S. Wallerstein, Principal Investigator of the same project. Their article "Part-Time Parent, Part-Time Child: Visiting After Divorce" appeared in the Summer 1977 issue of the *Journal of Clinical Child Psychology*. Here's what their information seems to suggest:

- You may find that under a visiting arrangement, you and your children get along better than you did before.

- Experience suggests that at first, you should try to keep the visits short—a few hours. Then move up to a day-long visit, then overnight. Or you may find that short but more frequent visits work better for you.

- The authors found that among the group they sampled, significantly more girls than boys in the 2- to 8-year-old group suffer from infrequent and erratic visiting. If you have daughters, bear this in mind. Their research also showed that the most difficult visiting age appears to be from 9 to 12 years old. At least that's the age where visiting was least frequent. Remember, this is an angry age, but cutting back on visiting just increases their anger, setting up a vicious cycle.

- Be prepared to have children begin to visit singly as they grow older, rather than having all the kids visit together. This may make for some pretty fancy scheduling on your part— and you have the right to keep it within limits.

- Also be prepared for shorter, less frequent visits from your teenagers. Don't get huffy. It's part of their need to separate themselves from both parents. I've found that telephone calls with his father seem to be deeply satisfying for CH. Adolescents are phone-minded anyway. And it's a way of staying in touch without having to deal with the physical presence. Greeting cards—the gaggier the better—also work well.

Especially for Fathers: Understand Your Children's Growth Patterns

This is a very brief, coarsely defined map of the stages of development all children go through, with special emphasis on the role fathers play at each stage. I think it's helpful for both parents to understand the interaction of the fathering and mothering roles. As part of this development synopsis, I'll give some specific information about the way separated parents, particularly fathers, can help their children. The material is drawn from the book *Part-Time Father*, from other research reports and books, and from interviews with practicing psychiatrists. (By the way, I'm going to use the words "he" and "him" in referring to a child here, not out of sex prejudice, but because the he/she convention becomes very awkward for this kind of review.)

Infancy

At this stage, the child's view of the world is totally dependent on how quickly and how completely his needs are satisfied. Because he's so dependent on the nurturing figure (usually the mother), he is very aware of changes in her moods and attitudes. But the infant also needs a "constant figure" to relate to, because the constancy of the figure largely helps the infant to make the distinction later on between "me" and the outside world—i.e., to develop a sense of self.

Fathering. From *Part-Time Father:*

> It has always been taken for granted that during this period the father contributes indirectly to the child's well-being by giving the mother emotional support . . . which in turn helps the mother satisfy the infant's needs . . . But fathers make a more *direct*—and essential—contribution . . . Daddy looks different, sounds different, smells different [from Mommy]. He provides the child with variety . . . This early variety enriches the child's capacity for warmth, feeling and responsiveness to other people.

Dr. Gerald Dabbs suggests that during the ages of 6 months to a year, experiences with a figure other than the mother help the infant begin to develop a concept of self as apart from the mother. He also makes the point that infants at this age often resist separation from the mother. You get a clinging, demanding infant (which makes this the most dangerous stage for child abuse). "The more external supports the parents can have, the better. Outside people are also important for the child."

Single-parent fathers can help by visiting frequently. This gives the infant the stimulation he needs. And it gives the mother some relief from the infant. Since these visits usually take place in the mother's home, the visiting father should respect the fact that *it is her home.* Don't make snide remarks about housekeeping standards, react jealously if a phone call comes in suggesting she is dating someone else, or give advice that's not asked for. You're there to maintain your contact with the *infant,* not with her.

You're visiting to maintain contact with your child, not your ex.

1 to 3

During this stage the child begins to develop his sense of self. He's able to move about physically on his own, recognize that he's separate from the rest of his environment, and control that environment to some extent. He can move toward things, away from them, throw. He also begins to talk—which gives him the ability to say "no."

Fathering. Atkin and Rubin, in *Part-Time Father,* have this to say:

> The "No" so characteristic of the two-year-old is his way of demonstrating that he has a will and a mind separate from his mother's. Often both mother and child have mixed feelings about this independence. Father's presence and his active contact with his child can encourage the child's independence, lessening the chances of a child's remaining too tied to his mother.

If a father takes an active role in the child's "civilizing" (toilet training, weaning from the bottle, etc.), "he can give his child the opportunity to see that, like Mother, Daddy not only satisfies but also frustrates his needs ... [This helps the child] view his parents realistically, ultimately seeing each of them as neither all good nor all bad."

Dr. Dabbs raises another point:

> During the second and third years, where you have a single parent with a single child, there's the question "Should there be more stimulation" than this relationship affords. This can affect the child's speech development and his development of a sense of "rights"—what his are and what other people's are. And the fact that they have them!

Single-parent fathers are given this advice by John A. Rohrlich et al., in the Summer 1977 issue of the *Journal of Clinical Child Psychology:*

> When children are developing autonomy they require firm but reassuring outer controls, [they] must not feel that their need for choice or their need to demand appropriately will mean the end of their existence. Consequently the parents' reaction to the child is more important than the separation of the parents per se.

Obviously, this shows the importance of maintaining father visits on a regular basis if you're going to do them at all. Particularly when the 2- to 3-year-old acts up, he needs reassurance that he hasn't driven one parent out of his life by his very real need to assert himself. If you have a bad time with the child, be firm about your decision (whatever it is), but let the child know after the incident is over that you're still "in touch." Call him on the phone just to say hello. And be sure to show up when your next visit is due.

3 to 6

Around the beginning of this period, the child enters the oedipal stage. This is the first step toward achieving a true, separate identity as an adult. The child learns that he or she cannot possess the desired object (mother or father) and that it is possible to exist without doing so. This is also the first step in sex-typing: if the child cannot possess the desired parent, he will begin to pattern himself after the parent who *does* possess that desired object.

Fathering. This is the stage when daughters say, "I'm going to marry my daddy;" sons say, "I'm going to marry Mommy." Each sees the other parent as a rival in this relationship and becomes frankly hostile to that rival. Fathers can help their daughters by reassuring them that "Daddy loves you because you have a very special role—you're Daddy's *daughter* and he loves you for yourself." Here's some advice from *Part-Time Father:* "From her father's attitude a little girl develops feelings of worth and acceptance of herself as a female." Fathers can help a son through this difficult time by accepting him "with all his rivalrous and angry feelings ... The little boy can be helped to reconcile himself to the fact that, though he cannot be Daddy, he can be like Daddy."

Single-parent fathers are told by Rohrlich and his colleagues:

> If the child is fantasizing the death or elimination of the same sex parent (due to oedipal conflict) and divorce or separation occurs the child may develop very powerful guilt feelings. That is, the child may actually see himself as the cause of the separation. This can of course be felt at later stages as well, for example if the child has been the scapegoat of many arguments.

Again, it's obvious that steady contact between father and child is important. Sons must know that they cannot and did not get rid of Daddy—because here he is, visiting. Daughters must know that Mommy didn't get rid of Daddy as a jealous counter-move against the daughter's wish to possess him. Mommy hasn't gotten rid of Daddy—here he is, visiting. And it would seem very important at this stage for fathers not to criticize mothers in front of their daughters. This will only encourage daughters in their oepidal longing. Traditionally, separated parents have worried about the effect on boys of living in a mother-headed single-parent home. Dr. Dabbs (along with most of the other experts) feels that "there's not too much to indicate that single-mother sons have more difficulty sex-typing. Civilized joint custody would be an advantage here. Other male family members can help, too. And entering into a pre-kindergarten or kindergarten (a small group) can reinforce sex roles." Single-parent fathers could help with this last item by kicking in financially toward pre-kindergarten or kindergarten tuition if no public facilities are available.

6 to 10

Up to this point, the child's world has been largely bounded by his immediate family. At 6 he begins to step out into the world of school and other children—peers. This outside world becomes important to him. He begins to value peer and teacher approval more than that of his parents or the rest of his immediate family. Psychologically, it marks the period of early latency: the child has solved his oedipal conflict for the time. He shelves it in favor of all the new outside experience he is having. He's still a sexually developing human being, but sexuality does not precipitate a major conflict at this stage.

Fathering. From *Part-Time Father:* "While the child is discovering life outside his home, his father's role takes on another dimension. In addition to being a protector and a model of manliness for both boys and girls, the father becomes the transmitter of social, cultural, and ethical values; he helps the child learn what the world is about."

And this from the Rohrlich article: "Part of the interaction with peers (at this age) includes comparisons of oneself and one's family. This can present an additional burden for the child whose parents are divorced. During this time of moving out into the world and establishing relationships it is important that the child's energy be kept free for these purposes."

Let your child know it's OK for parents to be divorced.

Single-parent fathers: battles between ex-parents, particularly if the children are involved in them, exhaust kids and keep their attention focused on the disturbed family situation rather than on the outside world. You can help by showing more forbearance than usual toward your ex.

This is the stage where fathers can bring their children down to their business place and show them "what Daddy does." When the kids visit, take them on trips around town—to different kinds of shops, to different areas, anyplace that expands their experience with the outside world. Very few custodial mothers have the time or energy to do this.

You can help with peer pressure, too. There are still many communities where the reaction "Your parents are *divorced?*" uttered in tones of horror is common among children. Give your kids something to fight back with. Sample: "Daddy, are you and Mommy divorced?" or "Why are you?" Answer: "Sure we are. And we're a lot happier this way than we were before." Or the child says, "Johnny doesn't have to visit his father. His father lives at home." "That's nice. But Johnny doesn't get a bus ride *every* weekend to the other side of town. Or get to visit an apartment building and talk to the doorman. Or go out to a restaurant to eat." Whatever. Just help your child realize that it's OK for parents to be divorced and give him some way of telling this to his peers! Or, as Edith Atkin and Estelle Rubin put it, "Consistent contact with Father will reassure the child that he has not been deserted and that he can fall back on paternal support, should he need it. Reassured, he can march ahead toward mastering the tasks of middle childhood."

Preteen

This is the last stage of latency and/or the vanguard of adolescence. Children have entered that no man's land between childhood and adulthood. Preteens can no longer avoid issues through fantasy. Peter Blos explicates this in his book *On Adolescence: A Psychoanalytic Interpretation:*

> They know where babies come from but they are mystified about how this relates to their own bodies. Among girls open curiosity is replaced by whisperings and secrecy; and to share a secret the content of which is usually of an undisguised sexual nature remains a form of intimacy and conspiracy during this phase. This situation differs from the latency period when merely to have a secret as such— about any topic—is the source of delight and excitement.

The pre-adolescent girl is beginning "the prolonged and painful severance from the mother [that] constitutes the major task of [adolescence]." For boys:

> Any experience can become sexually stimulating—even those thoughts, fantasies, and activities which are devoid of any obvious erotic connotation ... it is not necessarily an erotic stimulus which causes [erection], for it can be provoked by anger, fear, shock or general excitement.

Blos continues with an additional explanation of some of the emotional complications of pre-adolescence. Both boys and girls, he explains, are beginning to break the last ties that bind them to the initial nurturing figure (the mother image). But they do this in differing ways. Boys assert their independence by associating almost exclusively with other boys their age. Girls, however, begin to be interested in boys. The herd instinct begins to take over, too; at this stage, expect youngsters to be most comfortable with large groups their own age.

Fathering. Fathers generally set higher goals for their children than mothers do, and are more concerned about how well the child does in school. This can be both a help and hindrance during pre-adolescence. It's a stormy age, almost as stormy as adolescence itself. Poor behavior at home and school is typical. If fathers stand firm on their goals for their children, but present these goals with love and without too much pressure, they'll provide a beacon by which the child can steer his course.

Single-parent fathers: Once again, it's important to be patient, both with your children and your ex. Resist the impulse to say, "The kid is behaving like this because you've loused him up." The child would show symptoms of stress at this age if he'd been brought up by Earth Mother herself.

Stand by teenagers with first-aid and encourage them to go forward.

Running away is a characteristic way kids of this age deal (or fail to deal) with their problems. This reaction becomes much more possible for children from divorced families—they have the other parent to run to. Psychiatrists, including Dr. Dabbs, tend to take a very cautious view of requests to live with the other parent at this stage. If you're picking up this request from your child, you and your ex might want to talk it over with a counselor before you take any specific action. And *never* at this stage (or at any other, for that matter) tell a child, "If you don't like living with Mommy, or she doesn't treat you right, you can always come and live with me." That's inviting disaster.

Teenagers

Combat troops—what else can you say—torn between the desire to advance with the rest of their battalion (at risk to themselves) and the temptation to retreat to safety. Assaulted by physiological changes, sexual drives, the feeling they want to go and still want to stay, these war-weary troops hang in with their peers, cuddle up to their security symbols (parents), get drunk, dope out, daydream and, eventually, inch their way through to the target area—separation and maturity, to take their place with the rest of us battle-scarred veterans. How to help them? Stand by with first aid and encourage them to go forward.

Fathering. Part-Time Father comments:

> A father can make a very definite contribution at this stage in his child's development ... In the march toward independence, adolescents desperately need a father with whom they can disagree, yet upon whom they can rely for firmness and limits ... Boys at this stage often become very hostile to their fathers ... a father needs a great deal of tolerance, forbearance and humor to accept the onslaught and to recognize his importance in his son's life.

The same can be equally true of daughters.

Single-parent fathers: there are very specific ways in which you can help both sons and daughters. Show that you respect their emerging maturity by discussing visits with them ahead of time. But make sure you don't get lost in the process—they *do* need to see you and they need to know that you want, and *insist*, on seeing them.

Teenagers need the security of a home. But they're God-awfully difficult to deal with within the limits of a small house or apartment. Sometimes, tragically, a custodial parent simply finds the situation impossible and in a fit of rage and frustration turns them out. If you see that your kid and your ex are heading into serious trouble, you might discuss the possibility of that teenager coming to live with you (bearing in mind the foregoing cautions). What you're trying to prevent is the adolescent being physically separated from home and parent before his time. Anything you can do to be supportive to your ex at this time will be appreciated and will make her better able to deal with the adolescent.

The Ultimate, All-Time Visiting Code

There are do's and don'ts that can make visiting arrangements and the visits themselves easier and more successful for all. When I interviewed Helmut Lecke, an international director of Parents Without Partners, he offered the following advice, based on his work within PWP and his own experience with his two sons.

Pickups and Returns

Helmut's sons are with him every weekend. He picks them up at his ex-wife's home on Friday nights and returns the boys Sunday evenings. Here's what they've learned.

- Set a definite timetable and hold to it. Everybody then knows what to expect.
- Don't be overly concerned about discussing which parent is in charge of the children during the visit and at exactly which point the transfer of authority takes place. Just avoid the whole issue and any "testing" of the children.
- Don't use the time to discuss "issues" with your ex. Save them for another day when the children aren't around. Make this meeting as brief and as routine as possible.
- Have the children packed and ready to go. Some families keep double sets of clothing, one at each home. Even if this is true, children usually have some extras (clothing or equipment) they want to bring with them. Make sure they've packed or gathered together whatever they want to bring so there are no last-minute hunts.
- If you're going to be unavoidably late picking up the children, phone and say so. And try to be specific about how late you're going to be.

Helmut summed up these suggestions as "plain old-fashioned courtesy." And courtesy does make awkward situations easier.

Plain old-fashioned courtesy makes awkward situations easier.

Suggestions from Other Single Parents

Most of you were quite verbal on the questionnaires about what you consider important for children's visiting. I've sorted out your responses into those that deal with practicalities and those that relate to behaviors and attitudes. Since there are many more mothers with custody of their kids than fathers, the advice tends to reflect the mother's point of view.

Purely practical:

- *Pick up the children and leave!* Don't hang around your ex's home. And don't snoop. As one teacher from Indiana puts it: "Keep your nose out of my bedroom and other rooms you no longer have business in. Do not feel you can drop over without calling first. Spend as little time as possible with me alone."

- *Be careful with clothes.* "Don't lose precious clothes carefully packed for the weekend," a New Jersey mother advices her ex. Another from Pennsylvania wishes her children "did not come home with a suitcase full of dirty and clean clothes mixed up."

- *Make the reentry as easy as possible.* If it's a weekend visit, remember that the kids have school the next day. Bring them back on time. The New Jersey mother above sums it up: "Bring the children home early so that I don't have to be policeman and see they are bathed, etc. for school the next day. Let me enjoy the reentry time instead of having to do the disciplining."

Don't make kids feel like ping-pong balls.

- *Pick your children up at a neutral place.* School is the most usual choice. Several parents mentioned to me that they'd found it useful, particularly when the separation was brand new. It gives both sides a chance to work into the new situation without the trauma of facing each other in one home or the other.

- *Recognize that older children make dates on their own.* They'll appreciate this, along with a little flexibility on your part. The Oklahoma mother who drives her son 45 miles to visit adds, "I'd like the father to call me (or son) and *ask* what days and holidays he could have son. It makes the visit more special if the father shows awareness of child's needs, and that he is thinking of him." Another makes this point: "Fathers should negotiate directly with teenagers. If they aren't ready, change plans, etc., that is *their* responsibility in relation to the father, not the mother's."

- *If you live out of state,* try to check with your ex before you visit, and allow enough time for plans to be changed. "My ex writes when he's coming in, he *never* asks if we have plans for those dates. Everything must be cancelled to suit him or he makes it very unpleasant for the kids."

- *Remember that transportation is expensive,* and getting more so all the time. Try to be cooperative about splitting these costs. Or, perhaps offer to increase your share.

- *Don't bring along dates.* No one seemed to object to dating *during* the visit, but several parents mentioned that it would be easier if the dates weren't there while the children were being picked up.

- *Special note to custodial parents:* Visiting time is limited, so respect it. One Canadian father wishes that "Wife wouldn't expect me to take time I'm supposed to be spending with kids running errands—taking her shopping, picking up beer, etc."

Constructive attitudes/behaviors

- *Try to work out consistent rules and discipline.* "This takes cooperation, though," as one mother put it. Others suggest: "Abide by the rules I've set" (an Ohio parent). "Don't spoil the child. Try to follow my suggestions for limitations and eating habits" (a custodial parent from Florida). "Don't neglect discipline. That, too, shows a child he/she is loved." This last, and wisest, advice comes from a mother in North Carolina who has a daughter 4 1/2—an age when consistent rules are extremely important.

- *Neither a good-time-Charlie nor a dropout be.* That about sums up the advice sent in by live-with parents in terms of visiting plans and activities. On the good-time-Charlie question: "Visit-with parents shouldn't feel the need to be the good guy. They should realize it's not necessary to spend money on materialistic things. It's the caring and attention that's needed." Another mother wishes "their father didn't buy them materialistic things when I don't have enough to pay the bills each week." A Texas parent puts it very fairly: "The weekend parent sometimes puts a burden on the custodial parent, by not disciplining, or by treating *all* the time. I can't live up (full-time) to the excitement of occasional visits with him." It can come across to the kids as "Daddy is fun—Mom makes me do things." One Florida parent describes what the result of this can be: "My daughter always asks for her daddy when I go to punish or reprimand her. Her father never does it. Daddy is a 'good-time-Charlie' because he buys her toys and takes her to McDonald's and Mommy is the bad one because she teaches her right from wrong."

Some fathers, however, feel they're pushed into this super-good-time position. A Massachusetts engineer says it's important that the non-custodial parent "can feel at ease with the children and not feel he/she must entertain them or supply them continually with gifts." Another suggests: "Don't tell kids that Daddy has the dollars, so ask *him* to take you there."

Others feel some plans should be made: "I wish he'd just plan on doing *something* on the 1 day a week he has them. They hassle me on the phone to come get them. 'Daddy watches TV and makes us just sit.'" "Spouse should take the kids to a movie, eat, fishing, walking, talking, for a drive—anything—just *don't* hang around." "My ex has been taking the girls every other weekend for 3 years and it has worked out well. However, he brings them to his mom's but spends very little time with them. This I wish I could change."

- *For both sides: Keep in-laws in line.* There was a lot of comment on this from both mothers and fathers. From a mother of three (ages 3 to 12), divorced four years: "Dad shouldn't allow his family to 'bad mouth' mom to kids." A Canadian father wishes that "wife's parents would stay out of the act and not rehash things, stirring up arguments."

- *This goes for your own mouth, too.* "Each side speaks fondly of the other—or shut up! (That's the biggest problem and it makes kids feel like ping-pong balls.)" "Forget the past hurt and pain and let the child look forward to seeing and staying with the other parent. Don't knock each other down to the children. They want to love both of you and don't need to hear negative, degrading comments." This mother has a split-custody arrangement. Her 8-year-old son lives with his father and stepmother, her 6-year-old daughter lives with her. Her son visits summers.

- *Respect each other's rights as parents.* "Each side accepts the need for the other side to *be* a parent, custodial or otherwise, and butts out. (No manipulation just because it's 'your turn' to have the kids.)" "Everyone respects a person's right to make a mistake. You each made mistakes when you were married—it didn't result in Armageddon!" "Parents should stop arguing over small things. If the father or mother wants extra days with the children—let them go. It might be all one-sided at first (the giving-in) but in time the other will see how nice it can be and will do the same. If you can't make it one day—it should be no problem. The kids will understand and enjoy you even more the next time."

Respect for privacy is a factor, too. "Neither parent should question the children about what's going on in the other parent's life and make the children carry stories back and forth." And a mother from Alaska feels that respect for each other should be expressed this way: "Try for joint custody. My children don't visit. They live in two separate homes with duplicates. The only things that go back and forth are cub uniforms, skis, skates and bikes."

- "*Realize and accept the kids' love for the ex-spouse.*" That's advice from a New York parent. Another mother of four (ranging from 14 to 21) beautifully sums up the basics about children's attitudes: "Remember, your children learned 'their way' of dealing with your ex-spouse when you were married. The way your ex-spouse treated the children during marriage probably bothers you more now that you 'don't have to put up with it.' It probably bothers *you* more than the children." She also offers this after-visits advice: "They may have feelings about the visit (sad, hurt, confused, disappointed, etc.). They may act on these feelings, but don't assume it's difficult for them to deal with ex-spouse—assume they have strong feelings about leaving the other parent. Also realize that *you* have to put up with children's acting out their feelings when they return from a visit."

A close relationship with both parents is certainly the most desirable. But visits work best for children as well as parents when both adults are able to focus on the needs of their children. Remember—your kids weren't the reason your marriage failed. Why should they be used as weapons in a war that's over?

8/How to Deal Positively with the Negatives

Loneliness, guilt, anger, dependency: these emotions are part of the single-parent experience. There's no magic wand that will make them disappear. A Pollyanna attitude that they don't *exist* won't work. And a "grin and bear it" approach won't do much for you either. But there are two basic realizations that *do* help. First, accept the fact that your lifestyle and your emotions have both taken a battering and that it's perfectly natural to react with an assortment of powerful negative emotions. Secondly, recognize that you can learn to deal with these emotions realistically and constructively, as they relate to both you and your children.

I'm going to present a wide spread of advice from experts and from other single parents because no two people react to stress in exactly the same way. As you read through this, pick up on whatever seems most workable for and sympathetic to your own situation and personality. Notice, however, that there are some general approaches that almost everyone agrees are helpful. Some of the advice may seem simplistic, but it's offered because considerable numbers of us ignore it or merely pay lip service to it. For instance:

Believe That You Need a Healthy Body to House a Healthy Mind

The holistic approach to health, recognizing the interaction of mind and body, is gaining increasing acceptance among medical experts. Emotional stress does take its toll physically. Conversely, an abused body saps your mental and emotional reserves. In Chapter 1, I mentioned Dr. Roy Kern's advice about developing a physical program for yourself that includes walking/jogging at least 15 minutes a day (taken from his workshop "Maintaining Sanity in a Single Parent Family," presented at the 1979 International Convention of Parents Without Partners in Atlanta). Dr. Thomas Forrester, who is a professor of physiology at the St. Louis University School of Medicine, also stresses the importance of regular exercise in helping to develop a feeling of well-being and mental alertness and in overcoming depression: "It is a common observation that after regular exercise a person usually has a feeling of well-being. They are relaxed mentally, and they can once again think about problems they didn't want to think about before . . . I have observed that very active people are generally not depressed." (From an article in the February 27, 1979 issue of *The Star* newspaper.)

"Tend to your life on the level of daily maintenance."

Author Shirley Smith spells out advice in this area even more specifically. In her article "Deeper Valleys . . . Higher Mountains," which ran in the April 1979 issue of *The Single Parent* magazine (published by Parents Without Partners), she states: "This is a time when your health is in danger. Loneliness and isolation lead to emotional deterioration and then physical deterioration. Lonely smokers and drinkers will smoke and drink more. Overeaters and undereaters will get fatter and thinner, respectively." What does she advise?

- "Find a physician who understands the holistic approach to medicine. And don't be afraid to ask him for help in getting through the early stages of your experience."

- "Tend to your life on the level of daily maintenance: meals, rest, exercise, work, recreation. This will force you into routine activities and daily decisions and short-range plans."

Daily Maintenance

In my own experience, the "daily maintenance" approach has been very helpful, particularly when it comes to meals. I tend to be an undereater and stress numbs my appetite. But it's important to recognize that "appetite" and "hunger" are two different things. The first has to do with whether or not you feel like eating. The second is a real physical need for nourishment. You can be hungry without feeling appetite. The reverse is true for overeaters.

When you're busy working out new living arrangements and coping with the emotional aftermath of separation, it's easy to begin skipping regular meals and settling for snacks here and there. This is particularly true for non-custodial parents who don't face the necessity of providing meals for children. It's important to develop the habit of eating at fairly regular times. Any book on basic nutrition (ask your library to recommend one) will tell you what your body needs to take in, in order to maintain and restore itself. Follow this advice. If you find it's lonely eating by yourself, try to set up dinner engagements, or turn lunchtime, when you're eating with business friends or associates, into your major mealtime and settle for a dinner snack. Just don't let yourself slip into the lethargy and letdown feeling that hunger can provoke.

Dealing Positively with Sleepless Nights

Insomnia is a common reaction to emotional stress. It's uncomfortable but not crippling. Most people can get along on less sleep than they think they can, for a while anyway. Lying in bed worrying about your lack of sleep isn't going to produce slumber. Again, Shirley Smith (in "Deeper Valleys . . . Higher Mountains") offers some sound advice:

- "Don't scare yourself with fears that the loss of sleep will harm you … Your sleep patterns are disrupted temporarily, along with other patterns and habits that are now in transition."

- "This is the time to indulge yourself in things that your [former] bedmate did not like. You can have the light on and read … You can turn on your favorite music … let the cat or the dog sleep on your bed … eat crackers … watch the late show … try sleeping in the guestroom, or on the sofa."

- "Start planning what you will do on the next wakeful night … Purposeful activities—not just time-fillers—can see you through the night … You could make a model airplane … work on one of those fiendishly difficult jigsaw puzzles … write long letters … clear out your closet and go through the stuff in your desk."

- "At night, decide how long you will wait for sleep (I finally settled on 25 minutes). Then get up and do something that carries out a plan previously made for the next time you could not sleep."

In an article in the July 1979 issue of *Working Mother* magazine, Susan Selinger outlines three simple steps for meditation, a method of relieving stress that increasing numbers of people are finding useful:

MEDITATION MADE EASY

1. Sit in a comfortable position, back straight or supported, in a quiet room. Tell the children not to come in, take the phone off the hook, dim the lights and close your eyes.

2. Be still.

3. Concentrate on an object, a sound or simply on your breathing. When you find your mind wandering to the worries of the day, focus again on your slow, regular breathing and repeat softly, i-i-i-i-i-n-n-n-n-n with the fresh air—ou-u-u-u-u-t-t-t-t with the tension.

The article suggests that you try this twice a day for 15 minutes. It can really help, particularly before you go to bed or during a sleepless night.

The question of tranquilizers and sedatives. Most experts, both medical and psychiatric, agree that these may be helpful for some as a stopgap measure. But they also warn that these medications are a crutch that you will have to learn to do without at some time. They can, of course, be habit-forming, and they can actually work to delay the healing process by simply putting off the grief and mourning periods that are a normal part of separating. Taken in conjunction with alcohol they can be lethal; one increases the effect of the other. Certainly you should never start using either a tranquilizer or a sedative unless it's been prescribed for you by a professional. Well-meaning but misinformed friends will sometimes offer theirs to you "just to see you through." Thank them, *but refuse.*

Coping with Emotional Stress

When you decide to care for yourself physically, you've taken the first step toward recovery—toward living a life that recognizes *your* wants and needs and is organized around them. Now you can start coping with the emotional stresses.

Physical care is the first step toward a life that's organized around *your* wants and needs.

Loneliness: The First Concern

And it can lead you into some bad decisions. Parents Without Partners spells out the greatest danger you face in the first few months or year. Their pamphlet *The Single Parent* advises:

> An amoeba may enjoy being single. Most single parents do not . . . [but] in many ways society imposes barriers against parents who are divorced, widowed, separated or unmarried . . . Hence in our single-parent role we assume that finding someone else, someone to replace a lost partner, will solve our problems . . . will free us from our islands of fear, insecurity, loneliness and isolation. Will it? Not necessarily. Locating a new mate is not the first order of business. It should not even be on the agenda at the beginning. The question is, have we the will and the courage to adjust to change, to face a new life?

PWP continues with some general recommendations for dealing with the separation reality:

- "First, learn to understand yourself. You can turn out to be far better company to yourself and your children than you first thought possible."

- "Become more concerned with the world about you for a shell can be cracked . . . Seek to expand and improve your relationships with others. Become more interested in the health and well-being of your children."

- "Pursue a purpose . . . establish that purpose for it is an essential element in our reconstruction process. Purpose has meaning . . . provides direction . . . is a design for living."

- "Accept change. Most people are afraid of change . . . we must accept change for survival itself, for whether we like it or not a change has taken place. A marriage is dissolved. We are directly affected and so are our children."

Set a goal for yourself. We've already talked about the importance of maintaining yourself within the web of society (in Chapter 5) and of developing a personal social life apart from your children (see Chapter 6). But this advice about developing purpose and accepting change is equally important. When you set a goal for yourself and work toward achieving it, you're putting something into your life that's more important than your loneliness—so the loneliness eases. When you accept change, you open the way for new and different ways of relating to people and situations. This can eventually replace the need for the former relationship.

Realize that your purposes may change. Singled women may find, for instance, that achieving in a job becomes one necessary and fulfilling goal. Even if you worked before the separation, that job may be much more important now. It can mean financial security, a sense of self-esteem, a way of meeting new, congenial people. Many singled men, on the other hand, find that they reevaluate their previous drive for business success. They may find that emotional attachments (to their children and to a new life-partner) are now much more important to them than they were before. It's a common saying among single-parent families that the children spend more time with their fathers *after* the divorce than prior to it.

Both men and women may find that in restructuring their lives they want to pursue an interest or talent they'd let slip before. And this can now become one of the goals they decide to pursue. Maybe it's singing or theatre or a handcraft. One recently divorced man I know decided to indulge his secret hankering for ballet lessons. Where his ex-wife had scoffed, friends now encouraged. If you've always wanted to play the piano but were blocked by your mate's remarks about "Paderewski here," now's your chance. Play away!

One of my own goals, developed since I divorced, is to own a house, for both financial and emotional security. And once I own it, I can satisfy another craving— to build a stone wall. (Don't ask me why. I just want to do it. They fascinate me.) Or you may decide you want to get rid of the house you own, find a good rental situation and be freer to travel.

You may decide that finding a mate is important for you. There's nothing wrong with that if you've given yourself a chance to function on your own first. But be sure to think out exactly what kind of person will fit into your life *as it is now*. It's different and you're different than you were when you married the first time. Sounds obvious. But a lot of people think that with another mate their life will automatically go back to where it was before. It won't. The experience of living as a single parent creates changes for both you and your children. Recognize those changes and look for a partner who can happily share your new strengths, capabilities and attitudes toward daily living.

Other healthy ways to deal with loneliness. These suggestions were developed by Betsy Nicholson Callahan as part of a series of Workshop Models for Family Life Education published by the Family Service Association of America. In the workshop model developed for *Separation and Divorce*, the author makes these points about loneliness:

> Being alone is viewed as unacceptable and a fearful situation. . . . Most experts on the subject feel that many of us create our own loneliness and that lonely people, instead of taking responsibility for having needs and filling them, try to manipulate others into filling their needs or blame bad luck or circumstances for their own failure to relate. . . . The truth is, everyone gets lonely sometime or other. Loneliness is, and always has been, part of our human condition. It is not limited to the unacceptable. . . . Running away and not facing our loneliness squarely makes our self-confidence less and our needs seem overwhelming.

So what positive steps can you take to make loneliness less terrifying—and perhaps even enjoyable? Callahan suggests some possible approaches:

- We all become lonely at times. Admit this to yourself and learn to recognize when you yourself are lonely. Really, all you're saying is that you need human relationships to make life meaningful.

- Start right now. Decide on two activities you think you might enjoy doing by yourself the next time you feel lonely. But don't stop there; write them down and put them into action the next time loneliness strikes.

- Then begin to treat yourself as your own best friend. Use the lonely times to analyze what loneliness means to you, what circumstances seem to create the feeling and what you can do for yourself to get through the lonely times.

- Learn to distinguish between being lonely and being alone. Our mass-market culture tends to condition us to believe that we can't enjoy ourselves by ourselves. Learn to constructively use times you're alone with your best friend—yourself.

- Recognize that you must take risks in order to achieve happiness. You have to be

Distinguish between being lonely and being alone.

brave enough to reach out to other people and tell them how you feel and what you need. This is the only way you can really get to know others.

- Get specific in your thinking about loneliness. What are the times and the circumstances that seem most apt to cause it? Weekends and holidays can be difficult, so plan ahead. Arrange to share a special treat or outing with a friend. Plan some physical activity (a walk, yardwork, an exercise class) to boost you out of the blues.

- If you refuse to face loneliness (alcohol and one-night stands are favorite ways to accomplish this) you'll never know whether or not you can cope with it—and you'll miss a very important chance for personal growth.

Guilt Rears Its Ugly Head

"Scratch a working mother and what will you find festering right under the skin? Guilt." (From *The Working Mother's Complete Handbook*, by Gloria Norris and Jo Ann Miller.)

With single parents, you usually don't even have to scratch to find the guilt. It's right out there in full sight—a squirrel cage filled with scampering, nibbling little nasties that keep circling back to eat away your energy and confidence: "The children will suffer. They'll fail in school, they'll develop personality problems. They'll become delinquent." "Poor things—they see so little of me (because I'm working, or because I see them only on weekends). Every minute I spend with them must be fun time." "I know they're behaving badly but I mustn't scold/discipline/stop them because *it's my fault.*" "They want new bicycles and I really can't afford it. But I'll have to get them bikes somehow—I've taken so much else away from them." And so you skip the winter coat you were planning to buy. Or give up free time you wanted to spend on yourself to schlep them to the movies. Or stamp across your own rights in some other way to meet your children's demands—because you feel guilty. You are also, incidentally, convincing them utterly and completely that something dreadful indeed has happened to them and that it *is* your fault. That's what you keep telling them in word and deed, isn't it? Why shouldn't they believe you?

On the other hand, you could take the tack that the divorce was the divorce, it had to happen, it was your business, you're perfectly capable of providing the children with a secure and satisfying life (within limits), and they are just as responsible for their own actions as you are. In fact, more so. Which attitude will work out best for the child?

This is one field I have really tilled. First I felt guilty. Then I felt guilty about feeling guilty. Then I felt guilty about not feeling guilty. The last big attack came when I was working out the stages of child development for the preceding chapter. Great! I divorced during CH's first oedipal conflict, went back to work full-time during his late latency stage, physically transplanted him to a new community when he was a pre-adolescent and conducted a major love affair during his early adolescence (final oedipal stage). Perfect timing, all round. I created what could be considered traumatic changes in his life at each of his major developmental stages. And he *is* immature for his age in many ways. And he *is* having trouble finding himself. And he *is* insecure in some situations And what's done the most to make him that way is the overprotection of his rights vs. my own that I insisted on giving him because I was feeling so God-damned guilty all the time!

Recognize that logically, you have to feel guilty. Dr. Roy Kern believes that it's impossible for any of us not to feel guilty at some time. So just relax and try to deal with it, he advises. Accept the fact that you feel guilty for the following reasons:

1 You wonder whether you made the right decision about the relationship.

2. You wonder about the effect on the kids.

3. You worry about whether or not you'll be able to spend enough time with the kids.

Just keep giving yourself these answers:

1. You've made the decision; it's over and done with.

2. Research indicates that there's nothing terribly damaging about living in a single-parent family.

3. You're never going to have enough time with your kids, whether you're a single parent or a married parent. It's *how* you spend the time that counts. Try to set aside just a few minutes each day when you can give your kids your full attention, interest and affection. Joan Russell, in Colorado, has a very busy work and school schedule. But she starts each morning with a few minutes of cuddling time in bed with her two children. The whole family carries a warm, affectionate experience through the day.

> **It's impossible not to feel guilty at some time, so just accept it and try to deal with it.**

How to handle guilt. More from Roy Kern's workshop, "Maintaining Sanity in a Single Parent Home":

- One talk-to-yourself approach goes like this: Assign a certain time each day when you *want* to feel guilty. Go ahead and get guilty about everything you can think of. Then try to release yourself from guilt at all other times of the day.

- Or talk to yourself the other way around. And talk out loud. Ask yourself, "What's the worst thing that could happen as the result of my actions?" The kid's going to grow up to be Dillinger? If this answer comes back to you seriously, you've got a right to be worried (never mind guilty). Get help fast! Usually, however, you realize that you've been packing around a lot of unfocused worry: "Oh, I don't know exactly what's going to happen but it's going to be terrible." Why not quit with the worry/guilt until you at least know which worry to feel guilty about.

- And always remember that growing up means finding other sources of parenting. You will not be all-important to your children forever—they'll eventually replace you!

Further word for chronic "guilties" like myself. Dr. Roy Kern isn't the only expert who feels that the available research seems to prove that life in a single-parent family can be OK. *Separation and Divorce* (part of the Workshop Models for Family Life Education) describes the effect on children this way:

> Studies have shown that children in troubled but unbroken homes are probably worse off than children whose parents recognize that they are unhappy with each other and separate. Children are amazingly resilient and usually bounce back to normal much sooner than adults. Most children of divorce who were not already having problems before are fairly well-adjusted within a year. Children do not need a two-parent home to feel secure and loved by both parents.

A 1978 study on divorce and the preschool child, conducted by Dr. William F. Hodges, Associate Professor and Director of Clinical Training in the Department of Psychology at the University of Colorado, and doctoral students Ralph C. Wechsler and Constance Ballantine, came to some new and interesting conclusions about the effect of divorce on young children. They surveyed 52 preschool children (26 from intact families and 26 from mother-custody homes) all from the Boulder, Colorado area. Their findings showed:

- Even though both parents and teachers who, along with outside observers, evaluated the children's behavior said they believed that divorce does have a profound impact on child behavior, there were statistically few significant differences in behavior pathology between the two groups of children. This included problems with aggression, withdrawal, dependency and other signs of immaturity and emotional upset. The only observable difference was that the children from divorced families were found to be more withdrawn in structured situations (e.g., "show and tell" and directed games) than the children from intact families. In unstructured situations (e.g., spur-of-the-moment games or activities like block-building), the reverse was true.

- There was no relationship between the length of time since separation (this ranged from 5 to 48 months) and behavioral problems. (Previous literature tends to indicate that the longer the time since separation, the lower the degree of maladjustment.)

- The more visitations made by the non-custodial parent (always the father in this study), the lower the child's score on mother-rated cooperation. The more hours the child was visited by the father, the greater the amount of teacher-rated aggression and parent-rated aggression. (This finding also conflicts with other literature, which usually suggests that frequent contact with a non-custodial father would alleviate the negative effects of divorce.) The Colorado researchers feel that the increased aggression may develop because the children are patterning themselves to a greater extent on the adult male/father role (which they usually perceive as more dominating and aggressive than the mother figure).

- Limited financial resources, the relative youth of the divorced parents and the number of moves made in the last five years *did* indicate negative adjustment for the children from divorced homes.

So as far as this study is concerned, if you're going to feel guilty, direct it toward your lack of money, your age and the number of times you've had to move.

In a seminar paper submitted to the Graduate Faculty of Bowie State College, Ann P. Parks, Director of Publicity for Parents Without Partners, studied "The Relationship Between Perceived Adjustment and the Self-Esteem and Social Interest of Adolescents Following Parental Separation or Divorce." She researched a group of 24 parents and 32 adolescents. Her conclusions indicated that:

- Adolescents with high self-regard and strong feelings of closeness to others have adjusted better following their parents' separation or divorce than those with lower self-esteem and lower social interest.

- The older the adolescents, the better they will adjust after their parents' separation.

- Adolescents in families whose parents perceive serious or long-lasting problems with any of their children tend to adjust less well (to family changes following divorce) than those in families where few or no problems are perceived.

Among her recommendations, she states: "A major source of strength for adolescents of divorce may be the expectations by the adults surrounding them that they can handle the situation of family changes. The notion that divorce is deviant or permanently disabling cannot be encouraging nor foster the self-esteem of the children involved." None of this last bit leaves much room for running around beating the breast, moaning, "You'll never be able to cope and it's all because of this dreadful divorce thing I've done."

Recognize your right to anger, and tell others that you're angry.

Recognized Anger Is Normal, Healthy and Healing

Many of us feel badly when we experience anger—our own or other people's. We may feel particularly badly when we experience anger from our children. Usually it's not the anger that's making us feel badly—but what we've been programmed to feel about anger. "Many of us have been taught that anger is bad and that an angry person necessarily alienates and offends others. To feel angry, however, is not evil; it is a normal feeling, a normal reaction to a stimulus." This is from the Family Service Association of America's Workshop Models on Family Life Education: Separation and Divorce. However, the workshop points out, there is a difference between feeling angry, recognizing that anger, telling someone else that you're feeling angry—and expressing that anger in violent or aggressive *actions*. One of the safest ways to avoid such actions is by recognizing your right to anger and by telling others that you are angry.

What happens when you block off this emotion? You'll probably begin to develop a whole set of indirect behaviors that are not particularly healthy or helpful:

- We may completely deny being angry and substitute feeling sad or hurt, because we've been taught that those are more acceptable feelings. This leads to that God-awful "more in sorrow than in anger" posture, which is guaranteed to send everyone you're dealing with up the wall. *You* may be piously sorry; they're angry!

- Depression is another by-product of unrecognized anger. It's usually described as "anger turned inward." Eric Dlugoskinski, Associate Professor in the Department of Psychiatry and Behavioral Sciences at the Oklahoma Health Sciences Center, points out that:

    To counteract these feelings [of depression] an individual must once again assume active control over his or her life. In some cases it means sorting out the anger, sadness, and joy and experiencing each of those feelings independently. Anger and sadness are experiences of the real world that can be specified, experienced and left behind whereas depression has no such healing features.

- The Workshop for Family Life Education notes that you may also experience "anxiety (generalized anger with no one specific source), guilt (self-punishment for not obeying 'shoulds and oughts' from childhood), self-destructive activities (drinking, eating, gambling to excess), and aggression (bottling up feelings until they explode at others in a damaging way). Learning to express anger appropriately makes these negative behaviors unnecessary."

How can you express anger constructively? The Workshop model gives some specific advice:

- "Take responsibility for your own normal angry feelings. Admit that you are angry when you are and don't blame your anger on another; no one but you can make you feel angry."

- "Express your angry feelings at the time you become angry. Don't build up hostility toward a blow-up. This helps keep anger in control so it is not destructive to you or others."

- "Express your angry feelings honestly and assertively so that no one is hurt in the process. This means effectively communicating your feelings in a way that does not put the other person on the defensive and in such a way that he has a possibility of understanding the problem and changing his behavior as you request."

- "When anger is intense and you feel like exploding, try nondestructive physical activity to blow off steam—beat up your pillow, run around the block, shred papers, write down what you're upset about then tear it up."

- "Learn ways to express your feelings as they are developing—the use of 'I' statements are especially good as this avoids blaming or putting down others. For example:

  > I am getting angry.
  > I'm getting very upset.
  > I really don't like what you're doing.
  > I get mad when you do that.

Combining an 'I' statement with a request is often a helpful way to keep hostility from building up. For example:

> I get angry when you're 15 minutes late every time we get together. I would really appreciate your being on time from now on.

Let's see how all this would work in everyday life. You come home and face a disastrous kitchen: pots on the stove, half-filled with food; a carton of milk left out on the countertop; a pileup of dirty dishes in the sink. The kids and a few of their friends have fixed themselves a quick snack! You take one look at this mess and begin to seethe. Now how do you handle this anger? Let's take the workshop advice, point by point.

1. Recognize that you're angry. Say it out loud. "Boy, am I angry." I find that it also helps to tell myself exactly why I'm angry. "I get angry when I see a pile of pots and dishes left for me to clean up." Aha. Right away I realize that I don't have to get angry over part of that statement. I don't have to clean up those dishes and pots. But I have a right to be angry that they were left there. That's something I can handle.

2. The time to express this anger is now. March right in and tell the kids, "I'm angry because there's a pile of dishes in the sink and food left out of the refrigerator." If they're not home, wait till they get home and tell them. But *don't* clean up the mess in the meantime and bottle up the anger until the next time. You're not really getting rid of the emotion and the kids aren't learning anything.

3. When you sound off, tell them why and what they can do about it. "I'm angry because those dishes and pots are here and I'm going to stay angry until you clean them up." Avoid statements like "You're making me angry because you're a dirty slob." That's not specific, and it focuses your anger on the child as a person rather than on the *actions* that caused this particular attack of anger. In the meantime, you can relieve your feelings by punching out your pillow, dancing up and down with rage or any other non-destructive way of expressing yourself that appeals to you.

Hang a punching bag from the ceiling and whack it until you're tired.

When you're feeling angry about a situation that you can't control. What do you do? Single parents face a lot of these, particularly in the first few months after separation. You're angry because you feel abandoned or because you've been forced to move out or because your ex has remarried. There's really nothing specific that you can do about any of these situations. But you *can* get the anger out of your system. George Finger of the Family Forum, Staten Island suggests that you hang a punching bag from a hook in the ceiling (use a pillow or a pillowcase or an old duffel bag stuffed with rags) and whack it with a tennis racket until you're tired. "Take that, and that, and that!" "But," he warns, "you must direct that anger toward the person who is causing your emotion." That way you're really working it out.

Widowed persons feel anger too, he reminds us, but usually their anger is directed toward the abandonment itself, rather than toward the person who caused it. Once again, recognizing your emotion for what it is and expressing it physically can help you grow through this phase of separation.

Children, too, feel anger and need to express it. "Anger is a normal reaction most children feel about separation. Often it is directed at the parent that they feel is responsible for breaking up the home, or their anger can be visited on both parents." This statement is taken from the "Children of Divorce" section of *Separation and Divorce.*

How do children deal with anger?

> The young child may become aggressive in play, be belligerent, and so on. Older children may be more verbal about expressing angry feelings by talking back, being negative or by refusing to see their father when he visits, disobeying their mother, and so on. Difficult as it may be for you, you do need to encourage your children to express their feelings and to recognize anger as part of the grieving process over the loss of a two-parent home. Children feel threatened by the separation and may want revenge for the insecurity or embarrassment it causes them.

How do you handle your child's anger? By accepting it and by dealing with it. Easy enough to say—but what do you actually *do* when you're faced with a belligerent kid, red-faced with anger, and shouting! Or with kids who sullenly dig in their heels and refuse to cooperate in the simplest ways: "I won't brush my teeth," or "go to school," etc. Here's a roundup of practical advice from a variety of experts.

Don't meet anger with anger, George Finger advises. "When your children hurt you, it's usually because you're not accepting them as they are, not because they're rejecting you." In other words, accept the fact that they're angry. Tell them so. "I know that you're angry. That's OK." Or,"Boy, are you angry. I can see that!" Encourage them to talk about why they're angry. Explain that their anger cannot change the basic situation. Show them some way to deal with it themselves. "You know what I do when I'm angry. I punch my pillow." George Finger explains it this way: "Never push back. Join them and then turn them around. The minute you stop pushing you can move forward."

Dr. Nancy Catlin a marriage and family counselor, offered this advice in her article "Some Do's and Don'ts for Single Parents" which appeared in the July/August 1979 issue of *The Single Parent* magazine:

> If you have nobly retained your objectivity and sense of humor in the face of your child's misbehavior, do the unexpected: think about what you would typically do (explain, spank, yell, cry, etc.) and do the opposite. A kiss for example, when a spank is expected, can in some cases work wonders. Once when my son had a tantrum I waited for him to catch his breath and then I lay down on the floor, kicked and screamed, exclaiming "It's my turn now!" When I began my tantrum he stopped his and after taking turns a few times we both "broke up." Needless to say, your unexpected response has to be changed often and can only be used when you are relatively unshattered by the preceding event.

Remember that some of your children's belligerence may stem from their age. It may be part of the normal process of growing up and away from you and may have nothing to do with the death or divorce separation. Dr. E. Gerald Dabbs made a special point of this in an interview: "As the child matures and moves away from the mother, it's always a difficult time. Especially for single mothers who may feel they're experiencing rejection from the child."

It's OK for kids to feel angry, but not OK to act it out on you.

Dr. Dabbs points out another special problem for single parents in dealing with children's anger. "Either parent acts as a buffer between the child and the other parent. This relieves the intensity of the reaction between parent and child. Other people (i.e., relatives, babysitters, day care personnel, teachers) can perform this same buffering function." When you're the single custodial parent, it all comes down on you. All the love, all the anger, all the thrashing to break free. The child is much more attached to you, so he or she has to struggle that much harder to separate. Think of it as a compliment to the good care and emotional support you've given.

But remember—while it's OK for your children to feel angry, it's not OK for them to *act out* their anger on you. We all have to learn that we can't express anger by striking out blindly at those around us. If you let your child run roughshod over you, that's the way he or she will treat other people. You may take it, but others won't. That's one of the valuable lessons a child learns from being in a group and from dealing with another adult authority figure like a teacher. The other children in the group won't stand by and act as punching bags for your child, nor will the teacher. They'll accept your child's right to feel angry, but not his angry actions against them. Dr. Wayne W. Dyer suggests the following ways of dealing with disrespect, rudeness or insolence from your children:

- "First, ask yourself, 'Why am I allowing myself to be treated this way?' Yes, that's correct, you do get treated the way you teach others to treat you. If you are going to end the insolence, then don't come up with excuses for the child—such as blaming your husband or yourself for wrongdoing when the youngster was an infant. Retracing your earlier steps will not change the child's behavior today."

- "When you receive a crude reaction from a child, tell the child: 'I have a great deal of respect for myself, and I will not tolerate anyone treating me the way you do. I can't really force you to change, but I won't stay here and listen to this kind of talk from you.'"

- "Then remove yourself from the child's presence and allow time for your remark to sink in ... when you receive crass treatment from a child, that's the worst time to discuss the matter. Have a discussion at another, calmer time."

- "Be consistently firm in your reaction to rudeness from your children. Don't gloss it over as if it were simply a mistake ('The poor dear is under a lot of pressure and couldn't help himself')."

- "Don't let yourself become immobilized with anger ... This often happens, and the problem then becomes your anger rather than their disrespect. But this is avoiding dealing practically with the problem."

- "The most effective strategy is to stop performing services for the child who's nasty toward you. When a repeatedly abusive child asks, 'How come I don't have any clean underwear, Mom?' respond directly and say, without malice, 'You don't really expect someone you called a *dummy* to wash your clothes?' He will soon get the message: If I treat Mom with disrespect, then she won't wash my clothes ... At first he will react with anger and possibly even more disrespect. Eventually, though, he'll learn about reciprocity. ... While you may feel pangs of guilt when you behave this way at first, remember that it is important for you to serve as a model, for your children, of a person who possesses self-respect."

Dr. Roy Kern also offered advice on dealing with children's anger in his workshop, "Maintaining Sanity in a Single Parent Home." First, he says, "Be systematic in any behavior pattern or style of parenting. If you're an ogre about something, *always* be an ogre. Kids will only remember the *one time* you were inconsistent." If you decide that you don't like the way your children are behaving and that you want to help them change that behavior, "pretend that you're not the same parent. And pretend this for at least two months. Try and act like this new parent at least 10% of the time with them." Personally, I've found this *very* effective. In fact, I got back home from the trip to Atlanta and put it right into practice. I figured that I was going to need a lot of help around the house while I wrote this book—help with the housework and with errands like marketing, trips to the post office, etc. I have a tendency to do all this myself, carry the world around on my shoulders, and feel that I'm coping *successfully*! I decided that I'd try to be a parent who saw each chore that I (rather than CH) did as a *failure* on my part—a failure to myself (because I was letting all this little stuff get in the way of something more important for me) and a failure to him (because I wasn't giving him a chance to cope). And boy, it's working, I'll tell you!

How do you deal with children's anger toward each other? This can be a real problem when there are several children in a household. Here, Dr. Kern advises:

- "Don't get involved in your kids' fights." Retreat to the bathroom. Turn on the shower if necessary to drown out the noise.

- "Do the unexpected. Tell them: 'I know you have to fight and it's OK. But please fight outside. It's the noise that's driving me bananas.'" The result? "If you say that it's OK to fight, they'll often stop it. Because most of it was for your benefit, anyway. If they go outside to fight, they'll probably forget what the fight was about."

- "When your child gets involved in a fight with a child from another family, recognize that you have a responsibility to protect your child from undue damage, but not to stick up for him at the expense of the other child. And recognize that you'll get repercussions from the other parent. Give them the same advice you're following: 'Let's stay out of the kids' fights.' "

Dependency: An Unrewarding Relationship

The word "dependency" actually covers a lot of territory. It can refer to any escape mechanism you regularly use to avoid dealing with reality. What we're talking about here is the kind of dependency that creates an overly strong need between parent and child for each other—a need that prevents either side from functioning as an individual or at an appropriate age level, or that interfere with the normal "growing out of the nest" process. Single parent families are particularly prone to this type of dependent syndrome. Dr. Eric Dlugoskinski, in his article "A Developmental Approach to Coping with Divorce," describes it this way:

> One of these escapes is a fusion of parent and child identities. A child oriented to see only his mother's needs or pressures as important may neglect his own. Similarly, mothers may live only for their children and neglect their own needs and planning . . . Unfortunately, some children develop an adult role that neglects their needs as children. They protect their mother or father and try to assume the responsibilities of the absent parent without realizing their own needs and developmental restrictions. For adults the process is similar as mothers or fathers silently enslave themselves to the needs and, at times, whims of their children.

Children are not an emotional substitute for the missing spouse.

How to Avoid Dependency

All children and parents feel dependent upon each other at times. That's part of family structure. You *are* there to fill each other's needs. But you're also there to see that your own needs are met. And both sides must be able to fill those needs on their own.

For parents. We must recognize that children are not an emotional substitute for the missing spouse, for other adults or for our own sense of self. We musn't lose ourselves in our children. This means:

- Encouraging children to be independent—allowing them to learn to dress themselves, be responsible for their own belongings, manage their time, begin to make decisions on their own.

- Encouraging them to develop their own social lives—having other children in, visiting friends, dating —even if all of this leaves you sitting at home by yourself. That's your problem, not theirs.

- Above all, in the words of the Family Life Education Workshop, "not sharing a bedroom with a child and burdening him or her with your problems . . . [this] will eventually lead to emotional problems for the child."

For children. They must understand that they are acceptable as children—that there is no need for them to try to fill the absent parent's shoes. Sure, you may have to ask them to do things around the home they never did before. But ask them to pitch in "because I think you're old enough and smart enough to do this now—and I need the help," not because "Daddy (or Mommy) isn't here to do it anymore." One rule of thumb is: "Would I be asking the child to grow into this responsibility, at this age, if I were still married?" If not, don't ask it.

Kids also have to recognize that you don't exist solely for their benefit. As the Family Life Education Workshop puts it: "You have to say NO when necessary if you want your children to be able to experience achievement through their own efforts." They must also realize that they have to share you with others—and with *yourself.*

This Workshop summed it all up in these words: "Work toward being a competent and self-confident parent; this is the best thing you can do to help your children."

The Special Negatives That Death Creates

"What special problems do you feel widowed parents face that other single parents don't?" I included this query in the questionnaires I mailed to single parents as part of the research for this book. The answers showed a strange paradox. Many (both widowed and divorced) felt that widowhood was considered to be more "respectable" than divorce in our society. Yet many of the widowed described heart-rending experiences of rejection by family and friends.

"After the funeral there was no one who came to call. They said they thought they might make me cry. How nice it would be to cry with someone. I can't remember the last time someone put their arm around me or touched me (I don't mean romance). I feel that people are afraid that I might ask them to do something for me, ask for some kind of help. How nice it would be just to have someone to call and tell a small problem to—or a joy or accomplishment. Things happen here—good and bad—and no one out there knows or cares. I don't feel part of the family. When my in-laws die we will bury them but we really lost them at my husband's funeral. I have not 'talked to' anyone since his death."

That's a 48-year-old widow from Illinois speaking. Twice widowed, she is raising nine children who range in age from 11 to 21. I wish that I could feel her situation is unusual. But based on the questionnaire returns and the talks I've had with therapists who specialize in counseling the widowed, her experiences are tragically commonplace.

I received some very clear explanations for this unfair rejection of the widowed when I interviewed Leonard Tuzman at the Long Island Jewish–Hillside Medical Center in Queens. Mr. Tuzman is a social worker and mental health consultant who is actively involved with the Widowed Persons Service of Queens and Nassau. This special self-help group for widowed persons provides volunteer aides as well as professional counseling to help widowed persons adjust to their new lives. All the volunteer aides are themselves widowed so their advice and support is truly valuable. The following information contains some of the insights Mr. Tuzman provided.

Society's Reactions to Death

Isolation is the most drastic problem widowed persons face. Our society fears and rejects death. So we tend to reject anybody who reminds us of the reality of death. We unconsciously regard the widowed as "spectres at the feast." The cruelest aspect of this attitude is the fact that sometimes a widowed person actually shares in this reaction by seeing the partner's death as a rejection of themselves. Out of this sense of rejection the feeling develops that "there must be something wrong with me. Therefore friends and family will reject me too." And this becomes a self-fulfilling prophecy.

How can you avoid this trap? Try to face the fact of death honestly. Recognize that you had nothing to do with your partner's death, and that it is unfair to blame yourself in any way. Discussions with other widowed persons can be helpful. You might want to join a self-help group like the Widowed Persons Service if one is available in your community. Check out this possibility with your church or community service group. Some chapters of Parents Without Partners have also created special widowed persons groups within their membership. If your feelings of guilt and rejection remain very severe, you might consult a counselor or therapist.

Society can deny your need to mourn. The sight of grief makes us uncomfortable because of our fear of death. We tend to admire those who bear loss stoically, who carry on "as if nothing had happened." This is not a healthy way to deal with loss, however. So recognize that you have a right and a need to mourn—and so do your children. Don't allow friends or relatives to make you feel guilty about your mourning process.

Resentment over your reshaping your life. You have a right to reshape your life. This involves moving on from grief, making new friends, learning to love again. Family, and sometimes your own children, may show resentment when you begin to rebuild your life around new people and new situations. Try to explain your needs. If their selfishness continues, just ignore it and do what you feel is best for you.

Rebuilding Your Life

Don't be afraid to acknowledge your own strengths and capacities. You're not taking anything away from your dead partner by recognizing that you can make it on your own. This can be a particularly difficult area for many widowed persons, who need help with looking back into the relationship and seeing the strengths they contributed to it. Discussions with other widowed persons can help you realize that you can and will survive this experience and that you can rely on your own decision-making capacities.

Don't make hasty decisions. Let yourself recover at your own pace. Some people hurry themselves into selling a home or business or moving to a new area in an attempt to get rid of memories. If you're feeling pressured, slow down. You may feel very differently in a few months. If you're under real financial strain, at least make sure to get some sound advice from a lawyer or banker before rushing into an irrevocable decision.

When your children are involved. The feelings of aloneness and responsibility are particularly heavy if you have young children. You can become completely swamped by the demands on your time and emotions. "I used to resent it when divorced friends of mine complained about custody arrangements—having to share the children on weekends or holidays. I never got a free weekend or holiday." That's how one widowed friend of mine expressed it when we discussed the widowed vs. the divorced situation. She also made the point that many divorced parents can talk over important decisions about the children and thus share the responsibility for those decisions. "There's really no solution to this," she concluded, "except to do the best you can and have faith in yourself."

This woman had had an exceptionally close relationship with her husband. Her son reacted very intensely to his father's death. Yet she slowly made it possible for both of them to pick up the threads of their lives. Part of the adjustment was her ability to recognize the validity of her son's rebellion against a standard education. He is a gifted musician, and he wanted the freedom to specialize in musical training rather than spending time in the usual academic college. She was also able to recognize that it would be better for her to move out of the home she and her husband had occupied on Long Island and return to New York City where she could resume her career as an editor.

It took time for her to arrive at these solutions. In the course of living through the first stages of grief and sense of loss, she became deeply involved with helping other women by joining a support group for battered wives. She had discovered on her own what many therapists, including Leonard Tuzman, deeply believe: giving service to others, working with other people, can help you work through to the final stage of your own development as a separate and successful personality.

"I tell my children that I'm only a phone call away.... I think if you love them and are involved in their upbringing, they're not going to louse up their lives."

"My children confide in me about growing up and share their feelings with me."

"Everyone tells me they don't see how I can bring up three boys alone. Actually, I think it's easy—with a little concern."

9/Fathers with Custody: How Do They See It?

According to Ann Parks, Publicity Director for the International offices of Parents Without Partners in Washington, DC, there are now 1,000,499 single-parent fathers in the United States who are raising their children themselves. In Canada, 17% of single-parent homes are headed by men. The men whom I've interviewed seem to enjoy it and appear to be doing a good job. The fathers you'll meet here all have very different personalities, and all lead different kinds of lives. Their households reflect this. But with all of them I sensed an acceptance of their children, an awareness of their needs and individuality, and a deep love for them.

What do these men see as their biggest problem? "Other people telling me I couldn't do it." "People telling me 'A child needs a mother.'" "Those ladies yak, and I'm amazed at what my kids overhear and bring home. That's when they start asking those questions—'Are you ever going to see Mommy again?' 'Are you going to dump us after the divorce?'"

A Divorced Father Speaks

That last is Peter Burl talking. When Peter and his wife decided to separate last spring, they agreed on a joint custody arrangement that would be very flexible. And they agreed that ultimately the kids would live where they wanted to. The first summer it seemed best for the kids and for their mother, who was trying to get her own shop started, to have them spend the summer with Peter at his home in Burlington, Vermont.

Peter is big—about 6'5'' and broad—with a nose and mouth to match and a wide-open friendliness that warms his eyes. He's an auctioneer working for himself, so he's not tied to regular job hours. I interviewed him just after the kids had returned to Weston, Massachusetts, for the winter. "How old are Ian and Martha?"

I began, because I hadn't seen the kids in a couple of years. "I have five children," Peter corrected me. "Roger, he's in the army in Germany, is 20. Laura and Pat are 19 and 17. And the little ones, Ian and Martha, are 8 and 7." (The three older children are his wife's by a previous marriage, but have taken Peter's last name.) "I had all of them with me this summer, except Roger of course, and they were really with me, all the time. Especially the little ones. It was a good summer for them. I found that routines made things easier. Insisting they dump dirty clothes into the washing machine, or at least somewhere near it, for instance. Then we'd fold up and put away the next day, at some time when it was convenient. I wasn't fussy about their rooms, just as long as I could walk across the floor if I had to. But I did have two rules: no wet towels and *no food* in the bedrooms." Meals? "I've got a theory that the things you want to eat are the things you need. So if they wanted grilled cheese sandwiches for breakfast, that was OK. Lunch was usually a picnic at the beach or outside the house. Or we'd pick up a hamburger somewhere if we went on an outing. I took them to see a lot of things I figured they wouldn't get to see otherwise—a dairy barn, horse stables, a trip through the marshes. Or sometimes the excursion would be *their* idea, someplace they mentioned they wanted to go.

"Dinner depended on who was coming. Even if we had guests, I kept it simple. Grilled meat with a vegetable and a salad. One thing I found, we couldn't eat together if we ate out. The younger kids can't sit that long. So if we went to a restaurant I'd pick someplace where they could move around. Or where the little ones could sit with us for a while and then take themselves down to the sandwich shop and get themselves a hamburger. Then they'd come back and have dessert with the rest of us.

"Rainy days I'd take them to Woolco and let them pick out a rainy day project—a game or coloring books or a model that took a good long time to finish. I also started them on riding lessons. Ian didn't like it but Martha stuck with it. She rode four times a week. It cost $11 a shot but when you stack that up against summer camp it's not that much. And then we have a lot of animals on the place. Two goats, and a pony and homing pigeons, and a cat with kittens. So they had a lot of things to do.

"I also learned that the little ones needed separate attention. So I made sure I split them up now and then and spent time with each one individually.

"Really, I think the older kids have a harder time than the younger ones. Mine both had problems getting jobs this summer. And there's the question of boyfriends. I'd rather have them come home with a guy than stay out all night. Or at least check in. And I always made sure they drove their own car to a party or went with a girl who had a car. That way, they could leave when they wanted to. But I'd have a problem with them moving a guy in. I think parents should preserve that space for them, so they have someplace to go and get away from the guy if they have a fight.

"I also don't 'approve' or 'disapprove' of boyfriends. 'If it takes you six months to find out the guy's a shit and I knew that all along, well, I'm older.' That's my answer. There's no need for me to say 'I told you so.'"

Peter has also stressed to the children that they have a place in both homes. "I tell them that I'm only a phone call away. Call me anytime. And you're always free to come here when you want. But don't decide to come down on your own. Don't run away. We'll always work it out for you."

What did he do about his own social life while the children were with him? "I'd get a baby-sitter. Or the younger ones would spend the night with their grandmother. But I decided not to bring a woman here for the night."

Basically, Peter takes a confident, optimistic view of his five children. "I think if you love them and are involved in their upbringing, they're not going to louse up their lives." He's told all the kids, " 'If something does go wrong, don't lie to me.' I don't pry but I don't want to hear it from someone else. Because that means that *we* can't communicate." He also feels that the separation has made all of their lives calmer. "There's no tension. When married people start having problems, it's the truth that's hurting them. Then they start hurting each other. And when you live with someone you know where to push. Both sides do. So when I visit up there and something comes up that I don't like, I figure it's a short visit, who cares. That's the sensible approach."

The Widower's Situation

Howard Cain's situation is very different. When his wife Peg died 10 years ago, Howard had a big decision to make. Should he send his son and daughter to live with his brother's family or try to raise them on his own? His daughter Candy, whom you met earlier in the book, was only 7, and both friends and relatives insisted that a father couldn't raise a young girl by himself. Howard, a quiet, slender man, was worn down emotionally and financially from the strain of his wife's illness, the responsibility of caring for the children during her final hospitalization, and the pain of her death. "If you could ever say that a man had lost everything he worked for, I had. I'd lost my home, my job and my wife. But somehow I kept putting off sending the children to my brother's. As two and then three months went by, I suddenly realized that I was doing just what they said I wouldn't be able to do. I was keeping a household together. I was raising the kids. So I decided to keep on until something proved to me I couldn't."

Howard contracted to have a house built in Mattituck, a small town on the North Shore of eastern Long Island. He felt that the town, where he and his wife had vacationed, would be a good place for his children. He furnished it through a bank loan, although this took a little doing because he'd lost that "credit identity" mentioned in Chapter 4. In 1971, 2½ years after Peg's death, he and his children moved in and have lived there ever since. Candy attended the local school and is now a senior in the local high school, a National Honor Society student planning to attend Suffolk County Community College next year. She is on the staff of the school newspaper and has been helping her father edit the book he is writing about his widowed experience. Howard's son Chip took time off between high school and college to try living on his own. Currently, he's working and sharing a condominium apartment with two other friends in Hauppauge, Long Island, and has decided to enroll at Suffolk Community College next semester. "If I'd listened to what people told me and sent the kids away, they would have lost the one parent they still did have," Howard says quietly and firmly.

I shared a pleasant dinner with Howard and Candy in their Mattituck home, and thoroughly enjoyed talking with both of them. They have a nice, easy relationship, with a lot of teasing and laughing. When Howard kidded his daughter about being

> **"If I'd have sent the kids away, they would have lost the one parent they still did have."**

a "genius," she whizzed back with "Sure, I had a very intelligent mother," and winked at me.

Candy has had to assure some of her school friends, particularly in earlier years, that it wasn't a goof to talk about mothers in front of her. But her own openness and assurance, based on the love and security Howard has given her, have eased her way. She leads an active life, filled with school, friends, special interests like the school paper, and a summer job as a waitress in a local coffee shop. And she both accepts and encourages her father's dating.

To achieve all this, Howard has had to make some other decisions along the way. His job as a postal employee in a town many miles from where he lives means a long drive to work. It offers security, but it imposes a ceiling on his earning power. However, Howard has come to the realization that his major satisfactions are not money-oriented. His home is attractive and well cared for. He's able to provide for his children by carefully thinking out expenditures. Candy, for instance, would like contact lenses. But Howard feels that she is still too young for this investment, that there is too great a chance of loss. And she accepts this decision.

Howard is happy in the community, having made friends on his own and through his membership in Parents Without Partners. And he takes a deep pride in the family he kept together and is rearing.

Other Fathers with Custody

Phil Matuos is a father who has custody of his son. An expert auto mechanic, Phil lives not far from the Cain residence. Phil is stocky, jovial, with an air of great competence. He's had custody of his 16-year-old son for about six years. "I really wondered how it would work out at first," he admits. "But everything's fine." He's tolerant of his son's typically teenage fondness for flashy cars and cheerfully admits that "he likes to be a big shot. Sure, he'd like to own every car he sees. And all the latest equipment—stereo, color TV. You know, he's a kid."

When I interviewed Phil, his son had just left for a visit with his mother. How long would he stay? "All I can tell you is what he told me: 'I'll stay as long as I can take it. Then I'll come home.'" But this is said with kindness and humor. It's obvious that Phil and his son are able to accept and to deal with his ex-wife's problems.

Sitting with Phil in his home, I noticed the same neatness and attention to detail that I'd noticed at the Cains'. These are efficiently functioning homes, carefully thought out to combine comfort with eye appeal. Decorative extras are unfussy and meaningful: a framed illustrated poem of Candy's hung beside the fireplace, handsome ashtrays Phil's son made in his pottery class at school. Phil had recently bought a wood burning stove for the living room—again, chosen carefully to combine efficiency with pleasing design. Does he feel that he has any special aptitude for parenting that other fathers might not have? "Maybe. I don't know. My mother used to take in foster kids when I was growing up. She loved children. So I was used to having babies around. And I like kids. I always thought I'd have a couple of my own. But it didn't work out that way. It's OK, too."

It's Not All a Bed of Roses

I don't want to imply that solo male parenting is the new wonder drug of divorce, curing all ills. Listen to this father from California whose 9-year-old daughter has just decided "to try living with her mom," and you hear the ache of problems.

Solo male parenting is not the cure for all ills.

John, a construction worker, has had custody for seven years. His daughter was 2 when he divorced and started solo parenting. His problems? Some were job-related, some involved his attempt to mesh his own needs for personal identity with the needs of his daughter. Here's how he answered the section of the questionnaire dealing with simplifying living routines: "Have tried. Doesn't work out. Cannot be spontaneous or take jobs out of town." He also found that school routines, and particularly school hours, didn't fit in easily with a working parent's schedule. He leaves for work early, and has found it hard to arrange for a sitter who would take care of his daughter for those hours before school opened.

What made him feel best about himself? "Went on all the real stomach-upsetting rides at an amusement park. It was the day before my daughter was to go with her mom." What made him feel worst? "That some of my resentment of my daughter's infringement on *my* time probably showed to her. That hurt."

John would like to work out better visiting arrangements for his daughter, with more parental sharing between him and his ex-wife. In answer to the question "Visits would be better if . . ." John said: "They were more often and on a regular basis. There was more of a feeling between my ex-wife and me, and more shared ideas, on what or who we would like our daughter to be. Not that we can necessarily expect her to be any one type of person, but to share in laying out some ground work in her upbringing." He's hurting. But like Peter Burl, he's optimistic about the future. "I believe everything happens for a reason, though, so I'm sure it's all unfolding the way it's supposed to."

Attitudes toward Custodial Fathering

There are wide differences of opinion among the experts about this new trend toward custodial fathering and/or shared custody. Some professionals are concerned about the choices it may give adolescents. There's the chance that they'll try the "geography cure" for their normal growing-up problems—i.e. skip back and forth from mother to father, hoping to outrun the problems—instead of learning to deal with a situation as it is and, ultimately, grow through it.

They're also concerned about the lack of a mother image for growing girls. But this whole question of mother/father image and its importance in child development (especially in sex-typing) is really up for grabs. No available research makes a case for any point of view.

Some of the women's movement leaders, particularly those lawyers who represent the rights of economically disadvantaged mothers, cast a very cautious eye on court decisions that award custody to fathers. Since men generally earn higher salaries than women and tend to move upward on the economic ladder after divorce (whereas many women suffer a loss in economic standing after separation), they are afraid that judges may start basing their decisions on the material advantages one or the other parent can offer their children. This would be manifestly unfair to the thousands of mothers who believe their children are better off living with them, and are working hard to support them adequately if not luxuriously.

Divorce lawyers are also concerned about divorcing fathers who may use the threat of gaining custody to "trade off the kids for cash." To put it bluntly, some fathers may try to blackjack a one-sided financial arrangement favorable to themselves by threatening to grab the kids via a custody suit. As one lawyer put it, "They may not want the kids at all, but who's going to gamble? Particularly if there's a solid precedent set for father-custody and they've got a 50-50 chance of winning." Consider the following story in terms of these concerns.

Careers for women will affect voluntary custody arrangements.

Kevin has had custody of his four sons since his separation. He's an executive with a building materials firm in Colorado, with a salary in the $25,000 per year bracket. When he and his wife separated three years ago, Kevin gained custody of the boys, then aged 11, 12, 14 and 16. The boys spent six weeks each summer with their mother in California. At home with Kevin, they ran the household on a share-the-work basis, rotating the basic chores each week. About four months ago, the three youngest chose to live full-time with their mother.

How does Kevin feel about his sons living with his wife? "I dislike the changes she has forced on my boys." What does he feel is the biggest problem facing solo fathers? "Finding the time to share with them." In terms of his own specific problems as a parenting father, he mentions that "When I had my boys shortly after separation, it bothered me to give up my garage workshop." More seriously, perhaps, was this factor: "Also had to reduce social activities with business acquaintances to care for the apartment and boys." Kevin is career-oriented. "Work with my business almost always produces satisfaction, and results in personal pleasure." He further describes the conflict between personal life and parenting: "When the boys were here, the biggest problem was conflicting events, such as my dinner date and a school function." His solution? "Take the date to the school function, then on to a late dinner."

I feel that Kevin's story is important to us all—both mothers and fathers—because it casts additional light on two considerations in the father-custody area:

- First, does the higher earning power of many fathers give them an unfair advantage with the children?

- Secondly, is the traditional attitude that "boys belong with the father, girls with the mother" really sound? John's *daughter* chose to live with her mother. But so did three of Kevin's *sons*.

Like so much of human experience, there really don't seem to be rules that apply or generalizations that can be made about mother/father custody. Today, many women are as career-oriented as men; more and more, they are breaking into executive salary levels and out of the pink-collar-job bind. And children survive. This will probably have an effect on voluntary custody arrangements in addition to court-decided custody cases.

"Male single parents have more money. It makes a difference."

Father custody: beneficial to women? There's a small but growing group within all branches of divorce-related expertise who feel that more open custody arrangements benefit women. They point out that children may be better off with the father who can provide a more secure lifestyle for them. Or it may be a question of personality; many men have a strong nurturing bent, while some women have little natural aptitude for mothering. There's nothing odd about either type of personality. But up till now, as two young female lawyers I interviewed pointed out, "Let a mother voluntarily 'give up' her kids and she was branded as a social outcast. She might just as well walk around with a big scarlet 'A' on her forehead. With father custody becoming accepted, she's free to make the decision that works best for her, and for her children."

I had a painfully honest discussion with a mother who'd made the decision to leave her three sons, aged 8, 15 and 16, with their father when she and her husband separated five years ago. "I just wasn't going to be able to support them. I didn't have the job skills. My husband had always tried to keep me financially dependent on him. That was one of the reasons I left him. It wasn't easy. There were a lot of rotten remarks made. And it was hard for the boys to understand. But therapy helped me a lot. And now the boys are older, they can accept my decision and respect me for it. In some ways, it's drawn us closer. Because they know I keep in close touch with them because I really love them and want to see them, not because I have to."

I felt tremendous admiration, even awe, in the face of her courage and integrity. This woman knows herself and has fought through to her decisions: "Of course I'm a sexual person, but I don't want to be a sexual *object* . . . If two separated women decide to share an apartment, you immediately hear that they're lesbian . . .

"I'm training to work in psychotherapy. Because I find that I really do have something to give people. Particularly adolescent boys."

Are there success indicators for father-parenting? There don't seem to be, except for the most obvious. The solo fathers whose experiences I shared all wanted their children and enjoyed them. They are all competent human beings with a positive view of life. Even John, who had troubles making custody work for him and his daughter, doesn't give the impression that the shared years were a disaster, nor that the years ahead will be.

I asked Hugh James, another single father I interviewed, about symptoms of success. Certainly he's well qualified to answer. Hugh took on the house and his children when he and his wife separated three years ago. At that time, his son was 5 and his daughter 11. Hugh, a math teacher in a middle-class Long Island community, is a tall, reddish-haired, unbearded Lincoln, who takes his role of father and keeper of the house very seriously. He feels that the development his family lives in is a positive environment for his children. It offers a good, nearby school system, lots of neighborhood kids, and families with high educational goals. It also offers his children continuity and security. They're still living in the same house they occupied before the separation.

It's a pleasant ranch-style home with a sizable backyard equipped with sandbox, basketball hoop, tire swing and plenty of room for running and playing. The house also has a large, finished basement which includes a play section (complete with ping-pong table) for the kids and a fully set-up workshop for Hugh. This was where Hugh's son Daniel and several friends chose to play the afternoon I interviewed Hugh. Once again, I was impressed with the sense of order and design this man's home exhibits. The living room walls are decorated with a collection of antique tools handsomely mounted on pine panels. The slat-back American Gothic armchairs, along with a couch that Hugh created himself by cutting a chair in half and extending the middle section with bed sideboards, have the eye appeal of good design without fuss or clutter. A wall-to-wall cabinet, doored with shutters for storage, is another handyman project of Hugh's. The main focus of the room centers around an old wood-burning stove (Hugh's grandfather's) installed on a round fieldstone slab to function as fireplace and extra heating unit. The room is calm, collected, comfortable and friendly. "It's funny, my wife picked out every stick of furniture that came into the place when we were together. And it always seemed OK to me. But after she left, I eventually wanted to change things. That's when I put the tool collection up. And made the other changes. Nothing's the way it was. A friend of mine dropped in after I'd switched things around and told me that before the room looked as though nobody lived here. My wife really wasn't interested in a home. And I must have disliked the other furniture all along or I wouldn't have wanted to change it." He feels now that the house is large enough and comfortable enough so that he and his children "could stay here indefinitely."

Hugh's biggest problem was cooking and he still doesn't feel that he can invite married couples in for "a big elaborate dinner, the kind they serve in their homes. I just don't have the time for that. Oh, I ask friends over for pizza and beer, but that's about it." Consequently, Hugh found that his contacts with married friends began to wane. "At first people feel sorry for you. But after a while the dinner invitations begin to dry up."

The other concern Hugh faces is finding enough time for his own self-fulfillment. "I take my teaching very seriously. And that takes time. You can't just walk into a class unprepared. Then, the kids are a priority. Finding time to be with them. And there's the house to take care of. I won't let Laurie turn into a little housekeeper. I tell her studies and recreation come first for her. And then, finally, I get around to myself. But I tend to overlook me. For instance, I outfitted the kids for school but didn't buy any clothes for myself. Not because of money but because it would have taken a day's shopping. I still read newspapers and magazines. But I'm reading fewer books."

Are there any similar characteristics of other solo fathers that he's noticed? "You know I told you I tried to get a group started for fathers with custody. I found about 15 guys, but at the meetings they just weren't interested in swapping experiences. I got the idea that they were pretty secure about what they were doing. Or they wanted information from women. Not another man's advice." I mentioned that I'd noticed this sense of "I can do it; I *am* doing it" with the fathers I'd interviewed. "Yeah, I think it's true. In fact, I used to sort of resent it. I figured my wife left me with it because she figured out I could handle it."

Do single men make as good parents as single women? I asked Hugh if he thought single fathers have an easier time with discipline and enforcing rules. Definitely, he said. "In fact, this has been a problem with some of the women I've met. They just seem to be completely helpless in dealing with their kids. The kids are out of control." What about the different self-expectations society engenders in women vs. men? "Men expect to succeed; they're self-confident. When they tell kids something, they expect the kids to comply. If they don't, well, kids will fuss for a few days but they get over it and swing into line. Women tend to hold back on asserting themselves or in expecting certain behavior from their kids." I'd brought the question up hoping for a different answer. "God, he's right," I ended up thinking. And then the thought struck: "You can bet our kids will grow up with a different, and better set of male/female role expectations than we did!" Because single parents *are* succeeding.

Hugh's also aware of the advantage men's earning power give a solo father. "That's something I *don't* have to worry about. I have my salary. And I guess that's one of the big differences between male and female single parents. The men have more money. It makes a difference."

Peter, busy raising three sons, feels there's no difference between a man's or woman's capabilities when it comes to parenting. "Some men make good parents and some don't. Likewise women." And indeed, the problems he mentions are pretty much those that any single parent faces: "Not being able to spend enough time with the kids." School vacations: "I'm having that problem now, but I refuse to leave them unattended. I try to have an adult supervising them all the time." Peter works as a house painter and his sons are an active 8, 12 and 14. "Right now, I'm working on a new business that I can do at home and when I want, so I can spend more time with the kids."

He sums up his attitude by speaking for a growing number of single male parents: "Everyone tells me they don't see how I can bring up three boys alone. Actually, I think it's easy— with a little concern."

"My biggest reward is knowing that I can be so strong and dependable, knowing that I'm capable of loving someone so much ... knowing that I can put me second when it's necessary ... knowing that I am a very important person to someone and that I don't let them down."

"In daily coping with single parent problems *by myself,* I have discovered that I am more capable, more intelligent than I thought before.... I am thrilled to know that I'm not an extension of my husband. For the first time in my life *I like me!*"

10/The Rewards of Single Parenting: Today, Tomorrow

"Is it worth it?" The work, the worry, the undivided responsibility, the struggle with time and money. Those who look in on single parenting from the outside—from the security of two-parent situations, with the comparative freedom of living childless or from the detachment of trained counseling—often ask this question. We ask it of ourselves, too; the answers given here come from us.

What Do We Give Our Children?

"Love and guidance. Caring for a child's needs, from food to fun. Spiritual and emotional comforting. I'm so happy I was blessed with being the parent of my son and daughter. It's wonderful." (From a mother whose 8-year-old son spends summers with her and lives with his father and stepmother winters. She receives $30 per week child support for her 6-year-old daughter, who lives with her full-time.)

"Raising these little creatures from dependent infancy to intelligent, compassionate and understanding people. They have become more independent and loving, less quick to anger and tantrums through my love and patience, and it suddenly hits that those bad times finally paid off and I can say 'Hey, I'm a good mother.'" (From a parent who's been divorced three years and is raising a daughter 5 and a son 4.)

"Teaching my children things I've recently learned so they can better understand others and adjust to life more easily. I know I'm making up for my mother's mistakes with me. I'm passing on my love so they can pass it down to their children." (A mother whose ex-husband has custody of their three children, aged 13, 15 and 18.)

"Raising my children to be themselves, independent, thoughtful, worthwhile individuals and doing it alone. (But not really alone as many people help.)" (A widow whose 20-year-old son is now married and whose 21-year-old son is still at home.)

"They are turning out to be normal, well-rounded individuals with many interests—also well adjusted. They are learning to *cope* with whatever life has in store for them." (A mother with two teenage daughters and a 12-year-old son.)

"This was a career and I did a fairly good job of it. Now my children are friends, good friends—and I'm looking for another career." (From a Minnesota mother, divorced for four years, whose children are all old enough to live away from home.)

"I'm making up for *my* mother's mistakes with me."

What Do We Get from Our Children?

"A big fat hug and the words 'I love you, Daddy!' " (From John, the California father who had custody of his daughter up until a few months ago.)

"The little 'thanks' and 'I love you's.' " (From the father of an 8-year-old son.)

"The biggest reward is when one of them comes and gives me an unexpected hug, kiss, compliment. As we were checking off the things my 8-year-old needed for a slumber party and I said 'There, everything you need,' she replied, 'Except you!' and hugged me." (This mother has two daughters 8 and 10.)

"I'm loved and needed. There's the hope that some day my boys will be worthwhile men." (This mother's boys are 14 and 17 and she's been divorced three years.)

"My children confide in me about growing up and share their feelings with me." (That's Kevin, the solo father whom you met in Chapter 9.)

"The chance to watch the kids develop and grow and learn, little by little. Seeing the expressions on their faces when they learn something new or discover something for themselves." (The Canadian father who has grown children from his first marriage, a 9-year-old son from his second marriage and a 4-year-old daughter from his third.)

"What's the biggest reward I get from being a parent? When one of my children says 'I love you' for no reason at all. When I see how just a hug is enough reassurance to soothe a bump or a fear before they are off again to play. When someone comments on how happy my children look." (A mother with two sons 6 and 3 who's been divorced three years.)

These are the rewards enjoyed by all parents who accept the role willingly. That we share them comes as no surprise to us, although it may to others. But are there any special rewards we gain from single parenting, strengths or joys we might not have experienced otherwise? Once again, listen to those who, like yourselves, have lived the experience.

"My biggest reward is knowing that I can be so strong and dependable, knowing that I'm capable of loving someone so much . . . knowing that I can put me second when it's necessary . . . knowing that I am a very important person to someone and that I don't let them down." (This mother has a 9-year-old daughter and has been divorced for five years.)

"To be, gradually, more accepted as an adult friend by my children. To no longer be needed and not need them, either. To be OK plus HAPPY." (This busy mother combines a full-time job on a child study team with part-time waitressing to raise her four kids, who range in age from 14 through 21.) "The feeling I get when my children are both asleep after a day at school and play—and we've made it through another day together and are safe. Knowing I'm doing a *damn* good job and I'm proud of *me!*" (This is the mother from Chapter 1 who looks herself in the mirror, says "Go get 'em" and does. She has a 12-year-old adopted son and a daughter 10.)

"Assisting young people to learn about themselves, the world around them and encouraging their self-respect and self-confidence to grow. Sharing in their discoveries is a joy!" (This father's three children—a son 9 and two daughters 8 and 5— live with him six weeks of the year.)

"In daily coping with single parent problems *by myself,* I have discovered that I am more capable, more intelligent than I thought before. When I solve a problem or face a new situation *alone,* I know *I* deserve the credit. I am thrilled to know I'm not an extension of my husband. For the first time in my life *I like me!*" (This woman faced one of the most difficult of all marital situations. Several years ago her husband became an overt homosexual and asked for a divorce. At that time, her three children ranged in age from 6 to 10.)

"I get great pleasure from seeing my children's pleasure and happiness. They prove the point that a close, sharing family with one parent is better than a traditional two-parent family where's nobody's happy." (Who could phrase it better than this mother, divorced five years, with a 7-year-old son and a 10-year-old daughter.)

> "When I solve a problem alone, I know that I alone deserve the credit."

What Does the Future Look Like?

Times are changing. And we and our children are part of the reason—or perhaps we're the result of it. At any rate we're here, we're surviving and, increasingly, we're insisting that our needs be considered within the structure of our social institutions. That is, we're asking for and helping to create modifications in our legal, financial, educational, child-care and therapy setups. Here are some of the changes that are being discussed or have actually taken place.

Child Custody Arrangements

As I've already indicated, courts are now much more willing to consider awarding custody to fathers. This doesn't mean it's easy. As Robert K. Moffett and Jack F. Scherer point out in their book *Dealing with Divorce*: "Some fathers have always received custody and what we may be seeing at present is no more than a statistical 'blip' with no real significance." Mothers who want custody "still have all the odds in their favor when it comes to a custody fight." However, "the best interests of the child" is becoming the increasingly accepted norm by which custody cases are decided. Moffett and Scherer point out that the most comprehensive act to be passed into law is the Michigan Child Custody Act of 1970 which declares that in awarding custody, the court should consider:

(a) The love, affection, and other emotional ties existing between the competing parties and the child.

(b) The capacities and dispositions of the competing parties to give the child love, affection, and guidance and continuation of the educating and raising of the child in its religion or creed, if any.

(c) The capacities and dispositions of the competing parties to provide the child with food, clothing, medical care, or other remedial care recognized and permitted under the laws of this state in lieu of medical care, and other material needs.

(d) The length of time the child has lived in a stable, satisfactory environment and the desirability of maintaining continuity.

(e) The permanence, as a family unit, of the existing or proposed custodial home.

(f) The moral fitness of the competing parties.

(g) The mental and physical health of the competing parties.

(h) The home, school, and community record of the child.

(i) The reasonable preference of the child, if the court deems the child to be of sufficient age to express preference.

(j) Any other factor considered by the court to be relevant to a particular child custody dispute.

The law specifically states that a judge "*must* take these factors into consideration in determining which parent gets custody." And with Michigan's "no fault" divorce law, the sole ground for divorce is "irretrievable breakdown" of the marriage. With fathers generally taking a more active interest in their roles as fathers, it seems fair to assume that more flexible custody laws eventually will be adopted by other states.

The June 3, 1979, issue of *Suffolk Life*, a weekly newspaper, carried an article entitled "Parent Custody Groups Speak Out" that began: "In what has been labelled the International Year of the Child, about 150 groups throughout the United States have become increasingly vocal about the laws which they feel are a violation of a fundamental human right—the right of a divorced parent to share the custody of his or her children."

Joint custody. I interviewed Dr. Radh Achuthan, an activist in the joint-custody movement and President of the League for Human Rights in Divorce, at his home in Southhampton, New York. Dr. Achuthan, who is a physics professor at Southhampton College, made the point that individuals should divorce as "spouses not as parents. The present setup creates divorce between parent and child." He also believes that in 99% of divorce situations, both parents are fit custodians. What he would like to see is a custody situation in which joint custody was awarded as the norm and it would take a special legal process to prove that single custody was in the best interests of the child. He sees the only exception to joint legal and alternating physical custody occurring "where one or both parents can be proven to be grossly unfit.... The physical residence of the children should be left to pragmatic decisions based upon the individual situations."

> **The most successful custody arrangements are those that are worked out between the parents.**

I sympathize deeply with fathers who are cut off from their children due to custody battles. It does seem that in theory, joint custody is fairest. And certainly flexible visiting arrangements that allow children stress-free time with both parents are desirable. However, I *can* see that joint custody which is legally mandated could create problems. What happens if one parent moves to a distant location and still insists on a 50-50 division of children's time? Or does joint custody merely imply that both parents have an equal say in the training and schooling of the children?

The most successful arrangements seem to be those that are worked out between the parents, as the situation grows and develops, regardless of what's down on that legal agreement. In fact, in an article for *Journal of Clinical Child Psychology* (Summer 1977) called "Children of Divorce: Legal and Psychological Crises," James S. Henning, Ph.D., and J. Thomas Oldham, J.D., state: "As the children grow and develop and as parents create new lives apart, the visiting needs of everyone involved will change. For this reason it may be opportune to institute a procedure for a periodic review of custody determinations." And they make the further point that:

> Most custody orders simply provide that the non-custodial parent will have "reasonable visitation rights." Such an order is flexible and provides desirable latitude to former spouses who are on amiable terms. It invites dispute, however, in those instances where there is significant hostility between the former spouses ... Visitation rights should therefore be set forth in much greater detail [when this hostility exists] and a quick, inexpensive procedure should be established for the enforcement of child support and alimony obligations.

In terms of the suggestion about child support and/or alimony enforcement, most experts agree that enactment of the proposed Uniform Child Custody Act would be a great help in enforcing these payments and in preventing childnapping incidents. Thirty-three states already have reciprocal agreements that prevent a delinquent parent from taking shelter in those states. But the problem is still acute.

In an interview, three school specialists—a teacher, a school nurse and a school social worker (all of whom are single parents themselves)—stated that they were in favor of joint custody. They also listed these objectives:

- Attain universal understanding that not every child has two parents, and if he doesn't, that does not necessarily mean that he is a troubled child.
- Establish more support systems: "In light of my professional experience [as a social worker], more community support systems are needed to assist single parents—men and women—make the transition. Also, older single parents need a vehicle to meet one another."
- Pass no-fault divorce legislation in every state, with divorce counseling by accredited professional required, in order that children will not be so hurt.
- Make child-support laws tougher by stiffening up penalties for evading them and providing more personnel for tracing the evaders.
- Provide more day-care centers for working single parents (both male and female).
- Give homemakers social security credit.

The Social Security Issue

The issue of extending our social security system to include full-time homemakers is one that particularly affects women who become single parents after years of marriage and homemaking. They face the problem of earning a living with almost no job skills and with no accrued social security benefits. And the whole issue of social security benefits is linked to another women's single-parent issue.

A College/Career Training Program

Women who become heads of families particularly need a subsidized program for college and for career training. When I interviewed Joan Russell, who founded the Single Parents on Campus (SPOC) group for the University of Colorado and the Boulder area, we discussed the problems facing single parents—particularly women—who want to undertake or complete a college education. She mentioned that in addition to the usual types of financial help available (the federally funded Basic Education Opportunity Grant; National Student Defense loans; student loans available through banks; and work/study opportunities offered by colleges), the University of Colorado offers minority students a Student Fee Grant. SPOC's goal: to have single parents classified as a minority group, and hence be eligible for this help. This is a pattern that other universities might follow. The University of Colorado also offers a mini-college arrangement for people over 25. This provides classes for credit to students who aren't necessarily fully matriculated. She also mentioned the need for more, and better, vocational training schools.

On-Campus Services. We discussed the special needs of single parents/students at colleges and universities. Joan's group, SPOC, has already put together an Emergency Locator Service that will find single parents in the event of a traumatic incident involving their child; a kind of big brother/big sister program to help give additional support to the children of single parents; a 9:00 a.m. to 5:00 p.m. drop-in center where single parents can obtain information and discuss their specific needs; and a weekly rap session where parents can exchange ideas and problems. At present, SPOC is trying to work out a plan to provide more activities for single parents living in University Family Housing, and they've started a Students of Single Parents (SOSP) group on campus for university students who grew up in single-parent homes.

SPOC's main goal is to help single parents develop a lifestyle of positive and rewarding experience. For more information on this group, write: *Single Parents on Campus; University of Colorado; UMC 331-G; Boulder, Colorado 80309.*

Another major problem for single parents/students is Christmas and spring holidays. Many live too far from family to share holidays with them, so this is a lonely and depressed time for such parents and their children. They need some way of getting in touch with each other and with community sources that can help them through these difficult times. Joan would like to see the development of a network of on-campus organizations like hers—resource centers that provide contacts and information to single-parent students.

> **We need expanded and more flexible grade-school arrangements.**

Child-Care Facilities

Much has been said about the need for expanded day-care facilities in our society. They are badly needed, as are publicly funded nursery schools. But the prospects for both are slim. What we also need, as several parents who answered my questionnaire pointed out, are expanded and more flexible grade-school arrangements. Since schools already have buildings and play areas that have met state requirements for safety, it should be possible for groups of single parents within each community to work out arrangements with local school boards for before-school and after-school programs. They could be staffed by volunteers or community service groups, and would provide much-needed supervision for children of working parents.

Another ongoing issue is the question of parent/teacher responsibilities: who's responsible for what. With more and more mothers working, it is the school and the teacher who must provide daytime "mothering," particularly for young children. In a *New York Times* article (May 3, 1979) headlined "When the School Is the Second Parent," Joseph Featherstone, a professor at the Harvard Graduate School of Education is quoted as saying:

> I think the boundaries between parents and teachers are nowhere near as clear as they used to be. But I don't see this as narcissistic parents dumping their kids on institutions and the teachers being left to raise our society's children. Rather, in response to big changes in society, both parents and teachers are reworking the old roles.

The article continues: ". . . single and working parents need the support of the school because today the child's grandparent or aunt is rarely living in the same house, and with parents having fewer children, older siblings are less often available for baby-sitting . . ." Professor Featherstone goes on to say that he is concerned that this new sharing of responsibility between parents and teachers will be useless if it means a greater burden for schools without increased financial support: "Any new tasks schools take on now are in a climate where people are shredding school budgets and cutting the services." Austerity school budgets and cuts in extracurricular activities deprive all kids of valuable educational experiences. They can also be particularly hard on single-parent homes, where they can mean that extra sitter hours are required. It pays us single parents to monitor our local school budget issues carefully and express our opinions through the vote.

Arbitration Instead of Litigation

Arbitration over litigation is another growing trend in deciding both financial and custody arrangements. When I interviewed Bob Meade, New York Regional Director of the Family Dispute division of the American Arbitration Society, he pointed out that their aim is to provide quick and peaceful mediation of these issues. They charge a minimal fee for private meeting rooms (about $100, adjusted upward according to the total sum involved in arbitration). In addition, they'll provide a qualified neutral party to act as mediator, usually at a charge of $35 to $70 per hour (if necessary the American Arbitration Society will mediate this cost).

Arbitration is usually much less costly and less time-consuming than a court case. It takes about one to two weeks from the time of application to schedule the first meeting. For more information about how to use this service, write any one of these regional offices:

Atlanta, GA: *India Johnson* / 100 Peachtree Street / 30303

Boston, MA: *Richard M. Reilly, William F. Lincoln* / 294 Washington Street / 02108

Charlotte, NC: *John A. Ramsey* / 3235 Eastway Drive, P.O. Box 18591 / 28218

Chicago, IL: *Charles H. Bridge, Jr.* / 180 N. LaSalle Street / 60601

Cincinnati, OH: *Philip S. Thompson* / 2308 Carew Tower / 45202

Cleveland, OH: *Earle C. Brown* / 215 Euclid Avenue / 44114

Dallas, TX: *Helmut O. Wolff* / 1607 Main Street / 75201

Detroit, MI: *Mary A. Bedikian* / 1234 City National Bank Building / 48226

Garden City, NY: *Mark A. Resnick* / 585 Stewart Avenue / 11530

Hartfort, CT: *J. Robert Haskell* / 37 Lewis Street / 06130

Los Angeles, CA: *Jerrold L. Murase* / 443 Shatto Place / 90020

Miami, FL: *Joseph A. Fiorillo* / 2250 S.W. 3rd Avenue / 33129

Minneapolis, MN: *James R. Deye* / Foshay Tower / 55402

New Brunswick, NJ: *Richard Naimark* / 96 Bayard Street / 08901

New York, NY: *Robert E. Meade* / 140 West 51st Street / 10020

Philadelphia, PA: *Arthur R. Mehr* / 1520 Locust Street / 19102

Phoenix, AZ: *Paul A. Newnham* / 222 North Central Avenue / 85004

Pittsburgh, PA: *John F. Schano* / 221 Gateway Four / 15222

San Diego, CA: *John E. Scrivner* / 530 Broadway / 92101

San Francisco, CA: *Charles A. Cooper* / 690 Market Street / 94104

Seattle, WA: *Neal M. Blacker* / 810 Third Avenue / 98104

Syracuse, NY: *Deborah A. Brown* / 731 James Street / 13203

Washington, DC: *Garylee Cox* / 1730 Rhode Island Avenue, N.W. / 20036

White Plains, NY: *Marion J. Zinman* / 34 South Broadway / 10601

> "I felt better once I'd met her and realized she was interested in my daughter."

Whole-Family Therapy

This newly developing trend brings ex-husbands and wives together with their children in discussion sessions that thrash out where the family stands at that point. Some therapists even include the ex's steady date or lover. One mother who had just completed some whole-family therapy sessions which had included her ex-husband's lover told me: "I thought I'd feel funny, or angry, but I was willing to try. Actually, it went well. She and I had a lot to talk about, because my daughter visits her father every weekend, which meant she'd be spending a lot of time *with* her father's girlfriend. I felt better about the whole thing once I'd met her and realized she was a nice person, and interested in my daughter."

Therapist Sally Finger persuaded two clients of hers (a former husband and wife who were still battling bitterly over almost every item in their divorce agreement) to move in with each other while they hassled out a new agreement. This was not an attempt to reconcile them but rather to make the point that they *were* already separated, free to leave at any time—so why not get an arrangement together and each get on with their own life! It worked. The couple got the arrangement together in record time and have managed to hold to it without further court battles.

Arriving at the Place of Peace: The Good Divorce

A close friend of mine and her ex-husband (I'll call them Vicky and Pete) agreed to do a joint interview with me in which they analyzed their present relationship with each other, and how it gradually got that way. They have a good situation. And each has a good relationship with the children. Here's what they had to say.

The Background

It started out a stormy marriage and stayed that way. Both are strong personalities and both had full-fledged careers when they married. Vicky was a successful publicist in New York City when she married at the age of 29. Peter, 34 when he married, was head of a medical research team at a prominent New York City hospital. They have a son Michael, now 14, and a younger boy Matt, 8 years old, whose twin brother died shortly after Vicky and Peter divorced. Actually, they were separated twice. The first separation lasted for two years, then came a reconciliation. The final divorce took place six years ago.

At the present time, Vicky is living in Westhampton, New York, where she was born and raised. Peter is still living in New York City. He visits the boys each weekend, staying in Vicky's house if she is going to be away for the weekend, or taking them to a nearby motel for the night if she plans to be home. "The boys love the night at the motel, they really do," Vicky explained. The boys also spend their three-week winter vacation and three weeks of their summer vacation with their father. "They go on marvelous trips with their father. During mid-winter, I tend to send them into the city for the weekend visits. It makes it easier on both Peter and the boys. They're not as cooped up as they would be here if the weather's bad."

The Interview

I interviewed Peter and Vicky one Saturday afternoon. Peter had arrived from the city for the weekend about three hours before. Michael, the older boy, was off mini-biking with a friend in a nearby town, and Matt was playing in the yard with a friend from next door. As we sat around the table in the high-ceilinged dining area of Vicky's converted farmhouse, there was an air of peace and acceptance between these two people, a sense of grass grown over battle-scarred ground, a feeling of arrival. Peter opened our talk by saying that a young doctor on his research team had just separated from his wife.

PETER: I told him, "You're going to feel guilty and angry and frustrated as hell." But I found that either you die from all that anger and frustration or you say to yourself, "I can't walk around feeling this way any longer." There was nothing dramatic that happened to me. No particular day that it all fell away. Vicky was right when she told you before that we just couldn't live together, as we were then. We were just two totally different people.

"We both want
what's best for
everyone in the
family."

VICKY: Neither of us could have changed within the marriage, become the people we are today. We were just . . . counter-productive to each other.

PETER: We were really expending our energies fighting rather than growing. Now, we both love each other. We both love the children. We both want what's best for everyone in the family. When you develop that attitude, "what's best for everyone," things tend to work out the way they have for us. We don't have the knockdown arguments anymore. We've stopped hurting each other. We don't have that lack of productivity.

VICKY: We were both immature when we married. Both frightened of life. Each expected the other to be a parent—that was the hidden wish. And we got angry when we were both disappointed. We ended up working at cross-purposes all the time. The first two years of our final divorce were very bad. So bad we really both suffered minor breakdowns. Michael, our oldest son, suffered a lot of damage from the marriage and from the breakup. I was alone with the children. Peter didn't come to see the children that first year. The legal battles were awful. They cost a fortune. The lawyers definitely made it worse. No question about it.

PETER: The things you get in written form. The things the lawyers insist on—that say cruel and inhumane punishment—or that you're a stingy, miserly beast who's letting your children walk around without shoes. You have no idea of the fury that involves. It *wasn't* just language to me. That was a sworn-to statement!

VICKY: One thing I'll never forget. One of the children died during this time—a crib death. And Peter's lawyer sent a request for a reduction in child support because now there was one less child to support. So, after two years of tremendous suffering and rage and lawyers and confusion—I got a woman lawyer, who knew Peter. She was a conciliator by nature, not a litigator.

PETER: At that point we stopped hitting each other over past sins. We all sat down and said, "What do we want for our children? What can we do from here on out for the benefit of the children and ourselves?"

VICKY: We've both allowed the other respect as far as the children are concerned. I don't get into Peter's relationship with the children. If I did, I'd probably find things to object to. I believe that's what his role *is*. He's their father and they must know their father as he is. And I'm sure it's the same way with you, Peter—I'm sure there are things about me that you object to.

PETER: Denigrating either parent for previous crimes is one of the most horrible things you can do to children. Both of us feel that way. And we've come together. We arrive at good conclusions through working things out for our children.

VICKY: It was very painful at first. Three children, no money, no place to live. "Who turned out the lights?" I was thrown back on myself in a way I'd never been before and I *had* to grow up. And Peter, you did the same thing. With no wife taking care of you and no mother . . .

PETER: While we were married, we weren't working toward the common good of the marriage. So we were frustrated all the time. Now we're working for the good of the children. When we see something good happening, one of the children growing in a way that's acceptable to us, there's a feeling of accomplishment.

VICKY: But we had to grow up alone. We couldn't grow up together. When we were married, he so enraged me that it kept me from living my own life. And the *drama* of this rage—I thrived on it in a negative way. It made me feel that I was really living—that I was really struggling. When we split, I continued to live on that drama for at least two years. It was so difficult for me to let go of that anger. It's been hard on Michael. He's OK now. But he didn't learn to read until he was 10. There was too much other terrible stuff going on.

PETER: Matt, who's grown up knowing nothing but the divorce, is much more solidly based, much more secure. For instance, he'll run up and hug me. He's willing to open himself up to life with the possibility of being hurt. I hope Michael will be able to do that. I'm sure he will.

VICKY: I think the kids are in good shape now. Michael's a freshman in high school and he's getting 100's in English. Things like that. Actually, I don't feel they are *that* affected by the fact that we don't live together. But they certainly would be if we did!

> **Let's not kid ourselves. Separation hurts, especially at first.**

Success or Failure: How Do Our Children See It?

This is the payoff for every parent—the ability to share childrens' reactions to the homes and parenting they've experienced. As single parents, we're particularly sensitive to the effects our life situations may have upon our children. I was fortunate to be able to interview a number of young adults who grew up in single-parent homes. Their situations differed widely. For some, the separation had occurred when they were very young. Others had faced divorce or death in their teens or early twenties. Sometimes the separation was unexpected. And sometimes it was the culmination of a long and trying period of illness or unhappiness. I am especially grateful to Joan Russell for arranging a taped interview with several members of Students of Single Parents (SOSP) at the University of Colorado. Like all those I interviewed, these young people were thoughtful and painfully honest in sharing their experiences. What have they learned, living in single-parent homes? What can we learn from them?

Separation Hurts

Let's hear from David first. He's one of the students from the University of Colorado, now age 22. When David was 11, his mother told him that she and his father were getting a divorce. She broke the news on the afternoon before a school concert he was singing in. He remembers "crying for hours." Even though he carried through with the concert, the experience was so traumatic that David finds "even today I still can't sing except in my own room." When his father greeted him after the concert and complimented him on his performance, "I just couldn't face him. Not at all. I had to get out of there. I remember getting out and walking around the outside of the gym building." The oldest of four children, David hadn't realized that his parents' marriage was going badly. So the shock of separation was very severe. David's mother had also hidden the first three weeks of physical separation by telling him his father was away on a business trip. How many of us have made that mistake?

Even when the marriage is painful, so is separation. In an interview with 19-year-old Carla, I found out that she and her two brothers had gone through life with an alcoholic and violent father. There was fear, abuse and finally, the need to call in the police to protect themselves and their mother. "It's hard to love him, but I feel sorry for him because I know he's very sick. Things are better now. More relaxed." Even so, Carla went through a period of crying spells for a year and a half after the separation. With the help of therapy, she came to realize that "It wasn't my fault. I had nothing to do with it." Her oldest brother, who had the closest relationship with their father, also reacted to the separation. "He got into drinking and drugs, wrecked a car. And he's basically not a bad kid." Right now, Carla feels that her brother is beginning to pull out of the reaction.

Andrea, a 19-year-old at the University of Colorado, was only 2½ when her mother left her father and returned to her parents' home. Andrea has never seen her father. "He never wanted me to be born." And even though Andrea feels hostility, she thinks about what it would be like to meet him and "see how he would treat me now."

Honesty and Openness Make It Easier

That came through with ringing clarity. Over and over, these young people I listened to made the point that children can deal with almost anything when parents are up-front with them. As difficult as Andrea's situation is, she makes it clear that she appreciated her mother's and grandparents' frankness. They told her the reason for the separation and where her father had gone to live. Right now, Andrea feels that her family situation is very good. Her mother has remarried, and Andrea and her stepfather have a good relationship. Also, she feels closer to her mother now that they have left her grandparents' home and have their own household.

Mark, whom I also met through the Colorado tapes, is living proof that parents can create a rotten marriage but a good divorce. Mark's mother was an alcoholic. Often, Mark would wake up at night to hear his parents fighting, and sometimes, the sounds of his father hitting his mother. "I'd scream 'stop, stop!'" Mark recalls. Yet today, eight years after the divorce, Mark feels that his relationship with both of his parents "couldn't be better." He and his younger brother and sister are all very close to their mother and father—a result of the fact that they can talk openly and honestly. This communication started when his father told him about the impending divorce. "He was honest about the situation, which really cleared it up for us. We kind of understood." And even though all three children cried a lot when he left, they "understood that that's the way it was and there was nothing we could do to change it." Their father's frankness and his trust that the children *could* understand and cope with reality built a foundation for a growing relationship. "Right now I truly love him," Mark says.

David, however, feels that neither of his parents were really honest with their children about the reasons for their separation. He realizes that there was a wide personal and lifestyle gulf between his parents, which probably made any kind of life together impossible. In fact, the first thing his father did after the separation was to move to a community that better suited his conservative nature. The important point is that David and his brothers and sister thought the marriage was all right; for

The most positive effect of single parenthood? That children can recognize the difference between love and compatibility.

them, it was working. The result? When his mother first lived with and then married another man, the family split in half. They all lived in the same house, but David and the other children formed one close unit. "We lived in one half of the house and they lived in the other half." It was years before David could explain to his mother just what was happening—how her children were separating from her.

Carla also feels that her parents aren't dealing openly and honestly with their children. She feels that her father "is mean to us as a way of getting back at my mother. And my mother gets even by refusing him a divorce." (He's currently living with another woman.) So Carla sounds both impatient and angry when she mentions that "they haven't really done much about the situation in two years."

Positives of Single-Parent Living

One strong impression I received while listening to these single-parent children was tremendous tolerance for individuality, their own and other people's. They expressed it in a number of ways. David, for instance, is able to recognize the kind of person his father is: "Conservative, an introvert, a workhorse, a person with whom there's not much interaction." When he last saw his father three years ago, "I felt like he was my uncle." David also recognizes that he himself is much more like his mother and so he has never "wanted his father around as a person. There would have been too much conflict." He's also been able to pass beyond anger, turning that emotion around into positive decisions.

Both Mark and David seem very secure in their own sense of masculinity, and they're amused by macho attitudes about "man's work and woman's work." Both are perfectly comfortable with household tasks and feel that this freedom within the masculine role is a direct result of their experience in women-headed single-parent homes. In fact, both seem proud of the independence these everyday living abilities give them. As Mark said, "I can cook better than most women. I iron my own shirts. When I was living with a girl this summer that was the problem. I was very independent." And along with household skills, both these young men feel they have a special level of sensitivity that amazes the women they meet—and that results from the fact they were raised in single-parent homes.

Perhaps the most positive effect of single parenthood is these children's ability to recognize the difference between love and compatability. They are very much aware that you may love someone but not be able to live with her/him. Mark described the breakup of a love affair by explaining that he really loves the girl and believes that she loves him, "but we're not friends. We're just not part of each other's lives." However, all those involved in the Colorado taping session agreed that they don't understand how love can turn to hate. But since they are so well aware of the importance of compatability, it probably never will for them.

Final Message

"Remember—all children suffer some emotional loss during their lives. So a parents' breakup isn't the end of the world." I was asked to pass this final message along to you. It comes from two very bright, very joyful, very successful young women, both of whom are lawyers and children of single-parent families. Holly's mother is divorced. Laura's mother is a widow whose husband spent 10 years in a nursing home before he died. Both are proud of the adjustments their mothers have made. They themselves are busy building satisfying careers protecting the rights of poverty-level Hispanic-American women in New York's inner city. But they're keenly aware of the worries single parents have about fulfilling the needs of their children. Thinking back over their experiences in single-parent homes, they've decided that "It's important to have something self-satisfying in your life. It relieves your kids of guilt and pressure. After all, you weren't born a parent. You're a person before, during and afterwards. So you damn well better make yourself as *good* a person as you can. Then you can really enjoy your children and allow them to grow into personalities." And, finally, this upbeat pair conclude: "There can't be so much wrong with single parenting. After all, it produced us."

**Do the successes balance out the failures? Yes.**

In Conclusion

What incredible creatures we humans are. With great holes torn open in us, we can still struggle forward, carrying our children toward a safer place.

Writing this book has been a deeply felt experience for me. I've had a chance to meet and talk with hundreds of other single parents, to share your troubles and your triumphs. Tonight I'm feeling fractured because I feel a parting from you. I've learned so much from what you've said and written. So many of you are parenting so well. You've told your kids, for instance, about the arrangements you've made in case anything happens to you. That's important. I didn't think to do it with CH, and I realize now it was a worry for him. He's still overly concerned about the driving trips I make to New York. Also, many of you have been very open and sharing with your children. And they've benefited from that.

Certainly my child is different than I was at his age. He's faced things I never had to, some of them I'm learning about only now. Like standing alone in that first apartment, with kids climbing over the backyard wall. Afraid. But he took a ceremonial sword off the wall as a weapon in case they broke in. He didn't call me at work.

He also has a sense of self I still don't have. You can't rip him off. He finds ways of dealing with it, quietly and without anger. When we were both working the same shift, pumping gas a couple of winters ago, I was raging inwardly at the shift manager—a complete flake-out whose favorite occupation was standing in the station house watching the customers wait. When CH joined the shift, he simply said, "I tell you how I see it, Ed. We do it one on one. You, me and her. Or we walk off the shift."

Have I reached Vicky and Peter's place of peace? I think so. And although the faint echoes of war drums still pound in his ears, I believe my son, our son, is arriving there too.

Do the successes balance out the failures? Would I do it again? Yes. You warm yourself in front of a lot of lonely fires. But each night ends and the next day rises and there's room to start again.

One mother with a son who was adopted before her husband died, and a daughter born of a later, unmarried relationship that broke up shortly after the child's birth, sums it up for all of us. The biggest reward she gets from being a single parent is "Knowing that I *chose* to have both my children—to know I'm giving them life and love. When I feel really lonely, I look over old photos, think of past joys we shared, hold my kids, tell them of the past and, finally, realize I was lucky— I *am* lucky—and I've got a lifetime of memories yet to make for me and the kids."

Bibliography

Books

Abeel, Erica, *Only When I Laugh*. New York: Balantine Books, 1978.

Adams, Jane, *Sex and the Single Parent*. New York: Coward, McCann and Geoghegan, 1978.

Ashdown-Sharp, Patricia, *A Guide to Pregnancy & Parenthood for Women On Their Own*. New York: Vintage Books, 1977.

Atkin, Edith, and Estelle Rubin, *Part-Time Father*. New York: New American Library, 1976.

Babcock, Dorothy E., and Terry D. Keepers, *Raising Kids O.K.: Transactional Analysis in Human Growth & Development*. New York: Avon, 1976.

Berman, Eleanore, *The Cooperating Family: How Your Children Can Help Manage the Household*. Englewood Cliffs, N.J.: Prentice-Hall, 1977.

Blos, Peter, *On Adolescence: A Psychoanalytic Interpretation*. New York: The Free Press, 1962.

Callahan, Betsy N., "Separation and Divorce," in *Workshop Models for Family Life Education*. New York: Family Service Association of America, 1979.

———, and Vivian Freeman, "Career Planning for Women," in *Workshop Models for Family Life Education*. New York: Family Service Association of America, 1978.

Crocker, Betty, *Starting Out*. New York: Western Publishing, 1975.

Gettleman, Susan, and Janet Markowitz, *The Courage to Divorce*. New York: Ballantine Books, 1974.

Gilbreth, Lillian M., Orpha Mae Thomas and Eleanor Clyner, *Management in the Home*. New York: Dodd, Mead, 1959.

Goldberg, Herb, and Robert T. Lewis, *Money Madness: The Psychology of Saving, Spending, Loving and Hating Money*. New York: Signet, 1978.

Goode, William J., *After Divorce*. New York: The Free Press, 1956.

Heffner, Elaine, *Mothering: The Emotional Experience of Motherhood After Freud and Feminism*. Garden City, N.Y.: Doubleday, 1978.

Hope, Karol, and Nancy Young, eds., *MOMMA: The Sourcebook for Single Mothers*. New York: New American Library, 1976.

Hunt, Morton, *The World of the Formerly Married*. New York: McGraw-Hill, 1965.

———, and Bernice Hunt, *The Divorce Experience*. New York: McGraw-Hill, 1977.

Ilg, Frances L., and Louise Bates Ames, *Child Behavior*. New York: Dell Publishing, 1955.

Information Please Almanac, 1979. New York: Information Please Publishing, 1979.

Josselyn, Irene M., *Psychosocial Development of Children*. New York: Family Service Association of America, 1978.

Kohen, Janet A., Carol A. Brown and Roslyn Feldberg, "Divorced Mothers: Female Family Control," in *Divorce and Separation*, George Levinger and Oliver C. Moles, eds. New York: Basic Books, 1979.

Krantzler, Mel, *Creative Divorce*. New York: New American Library, 1973.

Lakein, Alan, *How to Get Control of Your Time and Your Life*. New York: New American Library, 1973.

Levinger, George, and Oliver C. Moles, eds., *Divorce and Separation*. New York: Basic Books, 1979.

Moffett, Robert K., and Jack F. Scherer, *Dealing with Divorce*. Boston: Little, Brown and Co., 1976.

Montague, Louise, *A New Life Plan: A Guide for the Divorced Woman*. Garden City, N.Y.: Doubleday, 1978.

Norris, Gloria, and Jo Ann Miller, *The Working Mother's Complete Handbook*. New York: E.P. Dutton, 1979.

Parents Without Partners, *The First Twenty Years, 1957–1977.*

Pogrebin, Letty Cottin, *Getting Yours: How to Make the System Work for the Working Woman*. New York: Avon, 1975.

Royal Canadian Air Force Exercise Plans for Physical Fitness. New York: Pocket Books, 1975.

Schlesinger, Benjamin, ed., *One in Ten: The Single Parent in Canada*. Toronto: University of Toronto, 1979.

Stafford, Linley M., *One Man's Family*. New York: Random House 1979.

Tessman, Lora H., *Children of Parting Parents*. New York: Jason Aronson, 1979.

U.S. Bureau of the Census, *Current Population Reports*, Series P-23, No. 28.

U.S. Government Report, *Your Child from 1 to 12*. Foreword by Lee Salik, Ph. D. New York: New American Library, 1970.

Walker, Kathryn E., and Margaret E. Woods, *Time Use: A Measure of Household Production of Family Goods and Services*. Washington, D.C.: Center for the Family of the American Home Economics Association, 1976.

Weiss, Robert S., *Marital Separation*. New York: Basic Books, 1975.

Woolley, Persia, *Creative Survival for Single Mothers*. California: Celestial Arts, 1975.

Booklets

Children of Working Mothers. Washington, D.C.: U.S. Department of Labor, Bureau of Labor Statistics, 1976.

Establishing Good Credit; Consumer Credit; Measuring and Using Our Credit Capacity; The Forms of Credit We Use; Credit and the Consumer; The Emergency Problem: What to Do About It. Washington, D.C.: National Foundation for Consumer Credit.

Family Dispute Services. American Arbitration Association, AAA-96-5M-10-78.

Guide to the Food Stamp Project. Washington, D.C.: Food Research and Action Center.

How to Establish Credit, Consumer Information Report #3. San Francisco: Bank of America.

The Legal Status of Homemakers series. Iowa, New York, Missouri: Homemaker's Committee, National Commission on the Observance of International Women's Year, 1977–1978.

Money Matters, Leaflet #487. Virginia State University, Va: Cooperative Extension Service.

Publication #504, *Tax Information for Divorced or Separated Individuals*. Washington, D.C.: Department of the Treasury, Internal Revenue Service, 1978.

The Single Parent. Parents Without Partners, 1967.

Single Parents Project. New York: Community Service Society.

Your Automobile Dollar. Chicago: Money Management Institute, Household Finance Corporation, 1975.

Articles

Adams, Jane, "A New Man in the House." *Working Mother*, July, 1979.

Catlin, Nancy, "Some Do's and Don'ts for Single Parents." *The Single Parent*, July/August, 1974.

Chiancola, Samuel P., "The Process of Separation and Divorce: A New Approach." *Social Casework*, October, 1978.

"Dealing the Tax Man Out of a Divorce." *Money* magazine, June, 1977.

"Divorce: Make Sense, Not War." *Money* magazine, February, 1973.

"The Divorcee's Dilemma, or Making Do with Less." *Money* magazine, December, 1974.

Dlugokinski, Eric, "A Developmental Approach to Coping with Divorce." *Journal of Clinical Child Psychology*, Summer, 1977.

Dyer, Wayne W., "Questions Women Ask Me." *Family Circle*, April 3, 1979.

Everly, Kathleen, "New Directions in Divorce Research." *Journal of Clinical Child Psychology*, Summer, 1977.

"From a Woman's Point of View." *McCall's*, March, 1977.

Gardner, Richard A., "Children of Divorce—Some Legal and Psychological Considerations." *Journal of Clinical Child Psychology*, Summer, 1977.

Gasser, Rita D., and Claribel M. Taylor, "Role Adjustment of Single Parent Fathers with Dependent Children." *The Family Coordinator*, October, 1976.

Grollman, Earl A., and Sharon H. Grollman, "How to Tell Children About Divorce." *Journal of Clinical Child Psychology*, Summer, 1977.

Henning, James S., and J. Thomas Oldham, "Children of Divorce: Legal and Psychological Crises." *Journal of Clinical Child Psychology*, Summer, 1977.

Hetherington, E. Mavis, Martha Cox and Roger Cox, "Divorced Fathers." *The Family Coordinator*, October, 1976.

Hodges, William F., Ralph C. Wechsler and Constance Ballantine, "Divorce and the Preschool Child: Cumulative Stress." 1978.

Hoffman, Shirley, "Researcher Finds Proof That Exercise Gives You Brighter Mental Outlook." *The Star*, February 27, 1979.

Hormann, Elizabeth, "Family-Making for Single Parents." *Our Family*, November-December, 1978.

Kelly, Joan B., and Judith S. Wallerstein, "Part-Time Parent, Part-Time Child: Visiting After Divorce." *Journal of Clinical Child Psychology*, Summer, 1977.

Lynch, Mary, "Role Stereotypes: Household Work of Children." *Human Ecology Forum*, Winter, 1975.

Lynn, David B., "Fathers and Sex-Role Development." *The Family Coordinator*, October, 1976.

Lyerly, Bonnie Kay, "Time Used for Work in Female-Headed, Single-Parent Families as Compared with Two-Parent Families." M.S. Thesis, Cornell University, Ithaca, N.Y., 1979.

McGrady, Mike, "The Day-Care Mothers." *Woman's Day*, August 7, 1979.

Mendes, Helen A., "Single Fathers." *The Family Coordinator*, October, 1976.

"The Money Side of Divorce." *Changing Times*, The Kiplinger Magazine, September, 1973.

Moore, Shirley G., ed., "Working Mothers and Their Children." *Young Children*, November, 1978.

Nickols, Sharon Y., "Resource Management for Single Parents." *Journal of Home Economics*, Summer, 1979.

O'Neill, Barbara Mary, "Time-Use Patterns of School-Age Children in Household Tasks: A Comparison of 1967-68 and 1977 Date." M.S. Thesis, Cornell University, Ithaca, New York, 1978.

Orthner, Dennis K., Terry Brown and Dennis Ferguson, "Single-Parent Fatherhood: An Emerging Family Lifestyle." *The Family Coordinator*, October, 1976.

"Parent Custody Groups Speak Out." *Suffolk Life*, June 3, 1979.

Parents Without Partners, Peconic Bay Chapter #308 Newsletter.

Parks, Ann, "Children and Youth of Divorce in Parents Without Partners." *Journal of Clinical Child Psychology*, Summer, 1977.

_____, "The Relationship Between Perceived Adjustment and the Self-Esteem and Social Interest of Adolescents Following Parental Separation or Divorce." Seminar paper, Bowie State College, Md., 1977.

Pedersen, Frank A., "Does Research on Children Reared in Father-Absent Families Yield Information on Father Influences?" *The Family Coordinator*, October, 1976.

Pickhardt, Irene, "Rock-a-Bye Baby." *The Single Parent*, July/August 1978.

Quinn, Jane Bryant, "Money Facts." *Woman's Day*, July, 1979.